ANGER

# ANGER

## THE CONFLICTED HISTORY OF AN EMOTION

BARBARA H. ROSENWEIN

YALE UNIVERSITY PRESS
NEW HAVEN AND LONDON

**VICES AND VIRTUES**
Series editors Richard G. Newhauser and John Jeffries Martin

For information about this and other Yale University Press publications, please contact:
U.S. Office:     sales.press@yale.edu    yalebooks.com
Europe Office:   sales@yaleup.co.uk    yalebooks.co.uk

Set in Adobe Garamond Pro by IDSUK (DataConnection) Ltd
Printed in Great Britain by TJ International Ltd, Padstow, Cornwall

Library of Congress Control Number: 2019951719

ISBN 978-0-300-22142-8

A catalogue record for this book is available from the British Library.

10 9 8 7 6 5 4 3 2 1

*For Riccardo*

# CONTENTS

# CONTENTS

# ILLUSTRATIONS

# ACKNOWLEDGMENTS

I wish first of all to thank Richard Newhauser and John Jeffries Martin, editors of the series in which this appears, for their unflagging encouragement, useful suggestions, and practical help with this book at every stage of its development. When it was in its near-final draft, it received many thoughtful and welcome comments from an anonymous outside reader chosen by the Press. I owe much to Andrew Beatty, Julia Bray, Douglas Cairns, Jessica Callicoat, Erez DeGolan, Robert Dentan, Jan Dumolyn, Luke Fernandez, Zouhair Ghazzal, Alex Golub, Jamie Graves, Lynn Hunt, Michael Lieb, Susan Matt, Damien Patrick Nelis, Jan Plamper, Rose Spijkerman, Dionysios Stathakopoulos, Faith Wallis, and Graham Williams for their generous advice and assistance. I dedicate the work to Riccardo Cristiani, who participated in its every phase. I thank my sister, Naomi Honeth, for her unfailingly encouraging emails, and I thank my wonderful husband, Tom, for his comments on a draft of this book and, above all, for his unwavering love and support.

# NOTE TO THE READER

When citing primary sources I have, when necessary, used English translations, whether by myself or others. I have tended to favor online source materials—as long as the translations are acceptable—because they will be fairly easy for readers to access. All dates are CE/AD unless otherwise noted. When quoting from early modern sources in English, I have silently modernized spelling, capitalization, and punctuation. Primary sources have been omitted from the bibliography.

# FOREWORD

## RICHARD G. NEWHAUSER AND JOHN JEFFRIES MARTIN

What made you angry today? There had to be something, because lately anger has become our default vice—and sometimes our virtue. Was it abortion? Brexit? Climate change? Democracy's demise? Environmental degradation? Fascists on the march? There are more causes of anger than the alphabet can contain in this season of our wrath, in this time when outrage lurks around every corner, ready to stoke and celebrate our quick resentment or valorize our deepest convictions. Though other periods of history might be thought of as characterized by wrath, it is particularly important in the present moment to step back and look deeply at what anger has meant to our lives, and continues to mean.

The study of vices and virtues (and anger can be both of them) lies adjacent to many fields: from ethics, law, philosophy, and theology to anthropology, behavioral sociology, and psychology, but also, as Barbara Rosenwein's volume demonstrates, the study of emotions. One of her key insights is that we have simplified a very complicated matter by labelling so many different feelings and behaviors "anger." Moreover, different groups will respond with what they call anger to very different stimuli. These "emotional communities" value or devalue certain emotions and adhere to the same norms of emotional expression.

Anger is most often thought of as an excess or deficiency of some emotional substratum. The Basic Emotion analysts thought of anger as a natural element of human beings that could be detected and measured in facial expressions. Psychological Constructionists think of anger as part of a process of feelings. Enactivists speak of hard-wired circuits that can be called "anger" depending on the society in which they are expressed. For social constructionists, anger is created mutually by individuals acting in society and the tools (language, social settings, etc.) that society offers.

Different emotional communities will evaluate the moral valences of anger differently. Is anger morally negative? Buddhists seek to avoid anger altogether as a step towards avoiding suffering and stress; Stoics (like Seneca) counseled that anger should be actively resisted when it arises; some Neostoics, such as Descartes, thought it best to acknowledge anger, subject it to reasoned analysis, and turn it into the basis for a moral attitude that scorns anger. And all of these reflections on harmful anger have attracted therapies designed to alleviate the effects of this dangerous emotion, from a Buddhist therapist like C. Peter Bankart to the Neostoic echoes in anger-management therapy. But what, then, not only of the righteous wrath of God, but of humans who claim their wrath is a virtue? Christian communities justify anger when it serves to correct morals; Saint Augustine said anger should be directed at the sin, not the sinner. For Autonomists, like Hume, anger can be a source of morality when it is exercised as the disapproval of someone else's vice. Rousseau turned anger at social injustice into a virtue.

Is it still possible in our lifetime to avoid, control, redirect, or manage anger? Have we entered a new phase of anger's history in which the threatened loss of our identity—political, national, ethnic, religious—demands universal resentment? And must the expression of resentment always be outbursts of anger, unreflective, self-justifying? Perhaps. But Barbara Rosenwein's book holds out the promise that knowing more about our emotional and ethical past will make it possible for us to navigate our emotional, ethical, and political lives in the present with greater insight and—we can hope—with better outcomes.

# INTRODUCTION

Homer's *Iliad* begins with an order to the muse: "Anger, O goddess; sing the anger of Achilles!" In a way, then, anger is the first word in the written literature of the West. Is the *Iliad* the place to start a book on the topic? Many modern commentators think so. Indeed, Emily Katz Anhalt asserts that we need to read Greek myths like the *Iliad* precisely to overcome our own angry predilections: Homer's depiction of the horrors that flowed from the anger of Achilles will teach us to resist the violent times in which we live.[1]

But Achilles' anger, however useful to study, was not the same as ours. It was not even the same as all ancient Greek anger, for which there were at least two words, two meanings, and thus, presumably, two sensations. Our own anger is a product of history. Potentially, it does include the sort of anger Homer sang about, but it embraces as well numerous other traditions of feeling, some of the most important of which are covered in this book.

That is why I prefer not to start with the *Iliad*. I'd rather begin with my own story and then look back.

When I was about three years old, I had a beloved rubber baby doll. It could swallow water, then dribble and pee—endlessly fascinating. I loved that doll fiercely. But I would also hide behind the living room sofa and beat it soundly, pummeling it with my fists. I clearly remember the turning point: I heard my mother say to a visitor, "That girl has a lot of anger in her." I knew she was talking about me. I stopped; I was ashamed. What was this anger that I had a lot of?

I had plenty of models of anger in my childhood, though not for what I was doing to that poor doll. No one but she was beaten up in my house. But my parents fought a lot—making for many other times when I (and my sister) hid behind the sofa. Apart from arguing, my father fumed about his job and his boss. My mother, meanwhile, a budding artist, listened to her mother and my father, who told her she should not have a profession; she should stay at home and take care of the kids. She bickered every day with her mother (not just about that) over the telephone. She was angry when she did housework, which she detested. And since nevertheless she spent every day dusting the furniture, she was almost always angry.

It would be easy to say that I "had a lot of anger in me" because I saw and experienced it everywhere around me. I could even explain away the times when I get angry today by blaming my childhood experiences. Most of us do that, at least occasionally, holding our parents largely responsible for who we are. Then again, I might not want to reproach my parents but rather argue that I "had lots of anger" because people are born with lots of anger—it's a hard-wired, universal emotion, present in primates, useful for survival, separate from reason, and passed along to human beings in their DNA.

These are insights into my anger—and probably yours as well. But they are inadequate. Let's tackle the DNA argument first because, if it's true, if we are "programmed" to feel anger, then we need know nothing more, least of all the topics covered in this book. But "anger" does not come pre-loaded in the human psyche. When we begin life, we have no such word and no such well-defined feeling. The fact that some cultures have no exact equivalent notion should alert us to the problems inherent in this pseudo-evolutionary approach—pseudo-evolutionary because nowadays scientists have discovered that DNA is subject to change and that evolution may take place very quickly, even within one generation. Nothing is so hard-wired that it is immune to change.

Neuropsychologist Lisa Feldman Barrett points out that insofar as we humans are programmed, we are programmed to *learn*. Our brain is a mediator and a thermostat: it constantly monitors sensations from both within and outside of us, tries to make sense of them, and works to create the bodily states that are conducive to our survival. When we are babies, we don't know what to make of various sensations. But when the people around us talk and behave in certain ways that they call "angry," we start to lump together a variety of feelings and practices under that rubric. Our real "hard-wiring" comes from this sort of knowledge: we lay down the wires as we negotiate life in a particular household, school, and neighborhood, picking up cues. When people in our environment call certain feelings anger and when they label punching a rubber doll or fuming at a boss "anger," then we start to have a name for our feelings and those of others. But in societies where words are different, where feelings and behaviors are evaluated otherwise and cut at alternative joints, people may have names for very different sets of observations by that monitor that is our brain. The feelings that *we* call anger may be combined with others that *we* call shame or sorrow or shame *and* sorrow, and they may be given a name that doesn't quite correspond to any English emotion word. Anger is the Anglo-American term, but it is not universal.

That takes care of the DNA argument for the moment. The one about our upbringing is more complicated. Certainly, our childhood environment helps explain our later emotional life. But our parents were themselves shaped by *their* parents, by *their* upbringing. Nor do we or they live in a vacuum. We all live in what I call emotional communities. Let me sketch here what I mean by the term; in the course of this book, its meaning should gradually become clearer.

Emotional communities are groups that share the same or very similar norms and values about emotional behavior and even about feelings themselves. Think of a Venn diagram (Figure 1), in which the circles represent different emotional communities existing at the same

1 A Venn diagram of emotional communities

time. Each community favors some emotions and shuns others; each expresses its emotions in certain characteristic ways. At certain points, however, they may intersect.

Now please stop thinking of the Venn diagram, for it has at least four drawbacks. First, it makes all the circles equal. Second, it suggests that each circle is closed even though, to the contrary, emotional communities are open and porous, able to adapt and change and even at times to merge. Third, alternatively, they may be entirely separate, or as separate as they can make themselves. Fourth, the Venn diagram doesn't envision a larger circle engulfing all—or at least most—of the others. Consider my own family. When I was growing up, we belonged to a striving lower middle-class, urban, Jewish emotional community. We were a definite minority, even within the Jewish community, because we rejected organized, synagogue-based religion. At the same time, my family intersected at certain points with larger emotional communities, especially the one represented as an ideal of familial togetherness on television. And yet, again simultaneously, both my parents were part of an overarching intellectual community, represented above all by the University of Chicago, which both had attended and which at that time was seen as a bastion of high-minded thought.

When my mother called me "angry," she was being both rational and emotional. She was making an "objective" observation, true; but behind it was a feeling—in this case one of disapproval. There is no hard line between reason and emotion. We speak and think and participate in things because of some motive—because we want to or hate to or are forced to or need to do so. Our emotions in such cases may be pretty tepid; they may be hidden, but they are working away—they must be, because they are a product of our constantly monitoring and mediating brain.

And not just our brains. The brain is in vogue these days, but its relevance to our emotions has been recognized only quite recently. According to many earlier thinkers, emotions were in the "mind," which was the equivalent of the soul, and often the soul and its emotions were in the liver, the gut, or (most often) the heart. Some modern scientists are rediscovering the validity of those ancient views, as we ourselves recall in our day-to-day encounters, when we talk casually about our heart as the abode of our feelings: My heart is heavy; My heart is full of love; My heart skipped a beat. Our whole bodies are involved in our emotions and the ways we think about them. For anger: I blew my top; She is getting on my nerves; He was ready to have a cow. No one sends a brain image on Valentine's day, and there is good reason why the emojis for love are 🖤 and 😍 rather than brain scans.

We are bodies and minds. And just as our bodies are trained—to bow in silent prayer, to run marathons, to sit quietly at our desks in school—so too our minds are trained to know and respond to certain kinds of emotions, to approve of some, and to censure others. I learned from my mother what she thought anger was. I understood that pummeling a doll was not the right—the approved—way to express it, and I figured out how it should be expressed in my family's emotional community, namely volubly and dramatically, with an admixture of grief.

I learned otherwise when I got married and discovered a very different notion of anger in my husband's emotional community. It was political, not personal; it was righteous, not self-pitying. Did learning that anger ought to be directed against a "system" rather than at a person really change the way I felt? Yes. But this isn't just my story. We are all guided by ideas, and I mean not just what philosophers propound (indeed, perhaps that least of all) but what all sorts of people who matter to us say. Many of us care about whether our anger is justified, whether it can and should be expressed against those whom we love, whether it is okay to rage against the driver who is honking his horn behind us, and so on. These are questions about the sorts of anger that are "acceptable," and, as Peter and Carol Stearns showed more than thirty years ago, the answers to those questions have changed over time. The Stearnses called their study of changing standards "emotionology." Even if anger were universal (which it isn't), the ways in which it is supposed to be expressed, suppressed, eliminated, sublimated, or directed have been subject to constant transformation. Yes, there is a delay between the time that people are interested enough in a new standard to read about it (or hear about it in sermons or learn about it from a therapist or on radio or in a blog), and its implementation in "real life." But eventually there is an effect, and it can be profound. We shall see throughout this book the interplay between *thoughts* and *theories* about anger and angry *behaviors* in daily life.

The emotionology informing my mother's "she's got a lot of anger in her" came not from her DNA but her own emotional community, a mixture of the notions, standards, and practices of Jewish immigrants from East European shtetls; the tide of Freudian psychoanalytic assumptions that hit the United States after World War II and to which my family adhered with the fervor of converts; the domestic settings of sit-coms on TV, and more. The "more" is what this book is about. If I am to understand my own anger—and you yours—we need to explore its many possibilities, including the probability that "it" exists only as a convenient word that covers a great variety of feelings. That is why I offer here no handy definition of anger.

We need to know about how anger functions and has functioned in emotional communities other than our own; how some of these communities rose and fell and even so are still around us—in writings, in attitudes, in the practices and teachings of some groups.

Anger seems easy enough to understand. All of us think we know when we are angry, and we are pretty sure we can recognize anger in others as well. But these assumptions are far from true. Within our (and their) anger lurk whole realms of meaning. In the course of this book, we shall see various sorts of angers and many diverse attitudes about them. All are potentially available to us. Indeed, divergent notions of anger—and various feelings of rage, irritation, resentment, frustration—jostle together within us, our families, our neighborhoods, and beyond. Some of us worry that our many angers—so profoundly delightful, horrible, frightening, and powerful—will tear apart our delicate social fabric. But in part that is because we have simplified a very complicated matter by labeling so many different feelings and behaviors "angry." This book teases out the particulars and, in so doing, aims to give us a new perspective on ourselves and our era.

# PART 1

## ANGER REJECTED (ALMOST) ABSOLUTELY

# 1

## BUDDHISM

I knew I was doing something wrong behind the couch; the tone of my mother's voice told me so. Some 2,500 years ago, the Buddha would have agreed that my anger was wrong—indeed, wrong-headed and self-destructive. It was also, he would have noted, ruinous for another, my doll, ultimately making it doubly self-damaging, for I was attached to that doll as we are all (opines the Buddha) attached to one another, even to those whom we hate.

From the *Tipitaka* (Three Baskets), the collection of Buddhist canonical texts in the Pali language, we know that however much the Buddha would have concurred in censuring my anger, he would not have approved of my singling it out, as if it were separate from all the other afflictions—poisons, really—that prevented me from "awakening" and thereby freeing myself from the endless cycle of rebirths (or, more correctly, repeated deaths) that condemned me to perpetual suffering. For life, all life, everyone's life, means suffering. Not that there are no pleasures; there are plenty of those. Even anger has its pleasures. But anger's joys, like all the rest, are fleeting, uncertain, and therefore unsatisfying.

Anger (*kodha* in Pali; *krodha* in Sanskrit) belongs to one set of mental afflictions, the one compassed by the larger mental category "hatred." In our own society we carefully separate hatred from anger. A "hate crime" in our legal system is worse than one committed for almost every other motive. By contrast, a crime committed in sudden rage is in fact *less* culpable than others, as if its perpetrator were "beside" herself, helpless in the face of her passion.

But the Buddha was not interested in such fine distinctions. He was intent on detaching people from the world and its fleeting pleasures and enduring pains. And so he made anger a form of hatred, and he identified just two other troublesome mental tendencies apart from hatred: desire and delusion. Even those categories were too many, for all have the same effect. They attach us to the world. We are chained to the things that we desire, even though they will inevitably decay and fall to dust. We are enslaved by our ideas, which are in fact delusions and misguided assumptions about what is right and wrong, partial yet dearly held notions of reality. Finally, we are fettered by our hatreds, which arise from our egoistical notions of ourselves: we are proud, we nurse our wounds, and we fail to recognize that we are part of a larger whole that includes all sentient beings. Anger is the bitter fruit of our self-regard.

These things imprison us, but they need not do so. We are responsible for our own chains. We cling to our desires, delusions, and hostilities toward others as if they were precious possessions. In truth, they are the sources of all our unhappiness. And because they belong to us, we can reject them. "Abandon anger" commands the Buddha. Anger is our desire to assert ourselves; it is a distress that grows out of our relationship with the world. "Abandon anger": the admonition is an absolute. There is no occasion on which anger is right or even appropriate. It can never be right because anger is as self-destructive as it is destructive of others. The angry person suffers; they are full of painful afflictions that torment their mind. If we enter into that mind-set, meeting that anger with our own, we suffer as well. When we get angry, we have missed our opportunity to care about the suffering of another. We have lost our hard-fought battle against our own ego and our dearly won prize of compassion for others:

Whoever doesn't flare up
at someone who's angry wins a battle
hard to win.[1]

The battle is won by patience. On the surface, this seems parallel to Christian patience: did not Christ say, "Turn the other cheek"? But the meaning of patience is rather different in the two traditions. Christ accepted his torments patiently in order to redeem mankind from the original sin of Adam and Eve. For the Christian believer, turning the other cheek means following in the footsteps of Christ and reaping the rewards of eternal and beatific life with God. The Buddha had a somewhat different purpose in mind: patiently bearing pain meant relieving both one's own suffering and that of the tormentor. In the Vepacitti Sutta (a *sutta*, or in Sanskrit *sutra*, is a discourse attributed to the Buddha), the Buddha tells a story about an ancient war between the demons and the gods. When Vepacitti, the chief demon, is captured and brought before the ruler of the gods, he spews forth a string of curses. The ruler is unmoved. One of his servants, frustrated with the ruler's seeming passivity, accuses him of weakness. In reply, the god praises patience as the virtue of the strong. Patience is curative, he says, healing both the offender and the offended at the same time.

Is anger not justified when someone threatens your life? Not even then, says one of the Buddha's parables: if "bandits were to carve you up savagely, limb by limb, with a two-handled saw," should you get angry? By no means. Having trained yourself to put aside greed and distress, you will say nothing in anger. Rather you will feel compassion toward the bandits; your mind will be full of good will. Aware of your connectedness to the bandits, you will "keep pervading" them with your benevolence, which you will extend even further, toward the entire world.[2] The first of the "five faultless gifts" of the Buddha is not to kill. This is considered an inviolable precept, but there are ways around it, as we shall see.

In the context of fifth- and fourth-century BCE India, where he lived and taught, the Buddha's doctrines were quite moderate. Indeed, they were a "middle way" compared to the extreme discipline advocated by many of the other religious wanderers who, like the Buddha, were rebelling against an increasingly powerful and entrenched political and religious elite. The dissatisfaction of these religious seekers implicitly critiqued the Brahman priestly class, specialists in ritual rather than ethical lives. The dissident strivers broke away, becoming renunciants who left home and ordinary attachments, lived on alms, and debated with one another. They elaborated a great variety of approaches to life and the afterlife. Siddhartha Gautama, who became the Buddha, tried extreme asceticism—no food, no sleep—but found the results unenlightening. Only after he rejected that path did he become the Buddha (deriving from *budh-*, to awaken from delusions, to understand; and related to *bodhi-*, perfect knowledge). His new, middle way of life stressed a healthy body and a calm and joyful mind. After attaining this understanding, he returned to the monks who had followed him in his earlier phase, outlining a series of precepts that emphasized asceticism tempered by moderation.

In general, the practices cultivated by Buddhists—both laypeople and monks—involve forms of meditation. Chanting is one. It involves repeating key Buddhist teachings over and over, in a low voice with tiny variations of pitch and rhythm. Another, normally guided by a teacher, begins with mental exercises. The method commences simply with breathing in and out, focusing on just that act, aware of the length of our breath, long or short. Then it moves to breathing in and out "sensitive to the entire body," as the Buddha put it. "Sensitive" here means that we widen our focus, still concentrating intensely on our breath but adding equal attention to our body "in and of itself." This last phrase is crucial: it means focusing on how our body moves and feels, but not on how it appears to the world. If we keep that focus, we are mindful. From sensitivity to the body, still breathing in and out, the meditator turns (perhaps after weeks, perhaps after months) to the other foci: feelings, mind, mental qualities. In all of these, the focus is "ardent, alert, and mindful—putting aside greed and distress with reference to the world."[3]

Such practices were available to lay Buddhists. There were more detailed and specific rules for monks and nuns. Nuns were especially hedged about by rules, many involving ways for them to show deference to the male monks—by bowing and so on. In some places, nuns and monks lived together in one compound, while in others they lived (and live) in separate communities. When monks or nuns got angry, they were expected to make full acknowledgment of the fault, either privately—in the presence of the Buddha or his image—or at a bimonthly ceremony. Thus, "should any monk, angered and displeased, give a blow to [another] monk, it is to be confessed."[4] Speaking helped exorcize the demon.

Let us return to the command to abandon anger. It was but the first line of a much longer versified sutta. The first verse goes as follows:

Abandon anger
be done with conceit
get beyond every fetter.
When for name and form you have no attachment
—having nothing at all—
no sufferings, no stresses, invade.[5]

Unpacking these lines allows us in effect to sum up the Buddhist philosophy and program. *Abandon anger* is not so much a command or a wish as it is one half of a promise: *If* you abandon anger, *then* suffering and stress will no longer invade you. The next line, *be done with conceit*, elaborates on what it means to be angry. Conceit is pride, the vanity of our ego, which imprisons us within our preconceptions, our received categories. We don't see or think about things as they are but rather as we have learned to think about them—not only during this life but also in the course of our nearly endless cycles of deaths and births. We are, as the next line says, "fettered" by the tangled web of our notions. They are part of us, part of our (false) sense of identity.

We can escape our chains. But that will happen only when we observe the things that we sense and think about them in a new way, seeing how things appear and how they pass away, recognizing their allures and their drawbacks, refusing to be ensnared by them.⁶ Through meditative practices, we achieve *no attachment*. Not all of us can manage that in this life; perhaps we will be reborn many times, perhaps just once more to become fully "awake." That is the ultimate achievement, when *no sufferings, no stresses, invade*: it is nirvana.

The essential insight of Buddhism is the recognition that life is suffering—endless misery through countless deaths and rebirths—unless the cycle is broken by means of a new way of perceiving, a new approach to thoughts and feelings, and a new practice of living. Anger is rejected absolutely. Even if bandits are ready to cut you up, you will not get angry but will "remain sympathetic, with a mind of good will, and with no inner hate."⁷ The first of the Buddha's faultless gifts is not to kill—not any sentient being, not even insects.

And yet these very precepts have led many Buddhist schools to embrace war and murder, often as forms of "compassionate violence." From the start, the Buddha was supported by various kings, and ever since that time, Buddhist rulers have generally been exempted from its strictures on violence. For example, an early Sinhalese chronicle recorded the bloody—and successful—battle of a sixth-century Buddhist king against an invading army. The king was penitent, but eight enlightened monks told him that the deed was "no hindrance" to his progress toward nirvana. The men he had killed were "of evil life [. . .] not more to be esteemed than beasts."⁸ The moral was two-pronged: the enemies were non-Buddhists and therefore of little virtue; and the king was acting out of "pure intentions" in his bid to save the Buddhists under his rule.

Nor was killing with "the right intentions" the prerogative of the ruler alone. Buddhists were allowed to murder if their motives were virtuous. According to the Mahayana Scriptures—followed by many in East and South Asia—Buddhists may kill people if their minds are empty of bad thoughts and feelings. Even better is to kill out of compassion. The concept of "skillful means" excuses an otherwise evil deed. In the Upayakausalya (Skill in Means) sutra, the Buddha is said to have been a ship's captain in an earlier life. In a dream, he learns from the ocean gods that an evil robber on board his boat plans to rob and kill all the five hundred other passengers. The deities tell him that "these five hundred merchants are all progressing toward supreme, right and full awakening; [. . .] If [the robber] should kill [them], the fault—the obstacle caused by the deed—would cause [the robber] to burn in the great hells for as long as it takes each one of these [merchants] to achieve supreme, right and full awakening, consecutively." After a week "plunged deep into thought," the captain/Buddha realizes that if he were to report his dream to the merchants, "they would kill and slay him with angry thoughts and all go to the great hells themselves." But if he himself did the killing, he alone would endure the pains of hell. He stabbed the robber "with great compassion and skill in means." As a result, the robber "died to be reborn in a world of paradise," the five hundred merchants went on to become enlightened, and the captain suffered not eons in the great hells but rather a painful thorn in his foot.[9]

The idea that killing a bad person may be a form of compassion was further developed in Vajrayana Scriptures, which sometimes saw killing as "liberating" the unvirtuous from the consequences of their bad actions (karma). When Tibetan king Lang Darma was assassinated by Buddhists in 841, the act was justified as a liberation not only for the Buddhists suffering under Darma's rule, but also for him, since it prevented him from doing further evil. Such ideas were supplemented by myths about wicked demons defeated and killed and then reborn as Buddhism's protectors.

Tantric Buddhism was particularly forgiving of violence once poisonous emotions were conquered. It created an elaborate pantheon of deities, both male and female, to help people learn mental control and achieve Buddhahood in one lifetime—a very fast track, indeed. For tantric Buddhists distressed by anger, there were "wrathful" deities (the males were called *Herukas*, the females *Dakinis*). Sporting hideous, seemingly rage-filled faces, they were nevertheless said to be anger-free. (See Plate 1.) Releasing tantric practitioners of their uncertainties, incomprehension, and mental turmoil, they displayed anger's grisly effects. Yet, as they trampled corpses beneath their feet, they evoked the glory of victory. The tantra known as Kalacakra celebrates a cosmic war between a bodhisattva king and a Muslim army: the king's forces annihilate the barbarians, destroy Islam, and re-establish Buddhism. Composed in the eleventh century, the story represents a Buddhist fantasy of retaliation against the contemporary Muslim invaders of northern India. Many of these violent traditions continue today, sometimes reinforced by nationalist fervor and Western myths of racial purity. We know that today Myanmar villagers join the military in killing, raping, and expelling Rohingya Muslims from their homes. We shall explore the contemporary situation in Myanmar in greater detail in the final chapter of this book.

In the West today, Buddhism has been imported with suitable adaptations. Vietnamese, now French, monk Thich Nhat Hanh, for example, writes books to inspire readers in the West with the sort of Buddhism that can be incorporated into the ordinary work week. He begins a book on anger with the story of a Catholic woman who, within a very short time, learned mindful meditation and compassion and healed her marriage, which had been roiled by anger and recrimination.[10]

Nhat Hanh gives laypeople counsel—from "eat healthy foods" to "do not spread fake news"—and offers a procedure for abandoning anger: make an appointment to confess your rage to the one who has apparently caused it. In the meantime, meditate so that you come to recognize that both you and your "enemy" are suffering. In the end, you should want to apologize. This is "caring for anger."

In most Western emotional communities today, certain forms of anger are accepted, even lauded, while others are shunned. For much of history, as we shall see, the wrong forms have been considered problems to be solved by self-control rather than, as the Buddha would have it, by revising our interpretation of reality. But recently some psychologists have recognized "inappropriate"—that is, socially unacceptable—or chronic anger as a psychological problem that requires outside intervention and treatment.

A Buddhist therapist like C. Peter Bankart adapts the Buddhist idea of suffering to help people today overcome their anger. In a chapter of a book edited by Eva Feindler that offers various therapeutic approaches to anger management, Bankart considers how he would treat the anger of "Anthony M."[11] A summary of Anthony's case history is offered here, as it will come up several times again in the course of this book as we compare treatment methods.

---

ANTHONY M.'S CASE HISTORY

"A 48-year-old white male of Italian descent and a non-practicing Roman Catholic," Anthony sought treatment when his increasingly intense moments of fury seemed likely to estrange him from his wife and daughters. While recognizing that his anger was directed particularly at those whom he loved, he also became enraged when people or events frustrated his hopes and expectations. He had had an "embarrassing incident" just before seeking treatment: while coaching his daughter's softball team, he became furious at the girls' "lack of competitive drive," yelled at them, drove some to tears, and threw a

---

bat at the backstop. Parents witnessing his behavior called for his resignation as coach, and he himself felt "ashamed."

When he was young, Anthony's mother often hit him and was generally unsupportive and distant. When he was seven years old, an uncle began to abuse him sexually, a practice that continued over the course of five or six years. As a teenager, he was (in his words) "hyper masculine," a champion swimmer and talented football player. However, he lost an athletic scholarship to college because he got into a fight with a teenager at a bar, and, although he attended college, he never finished his degree. Chronically out of work, Anthony resented the fact that his wife was the main wage-earner in the family.

A Western Buddhist, Bankart has seen a number of men like Anthony and has considered ways to adjust Buddhist ideas to their problems. No longer stressing the cycle of deaths and rebirths, Bankart focuses not on the suffering inherent in life itself but rather on the pains caused by mental disease. Like all the other contributors to Feindler's book, Bankart has not met Anthony; his discussion is purely theoretical. Nevertheless, it provides a good idea of how Buddhism may be a therapeutic tool.

Bankart begins by observing that Anthony's suffering is tied to his desires and attachments. At first Anthony will be convinced that his anger is justified: he will say that he raged at the girls at the softball game because they were acting as if they didn't care about it; their nonchalance was "profoundly wrong." But Bankart will point out to Anthony that "he was mindlessly and selfishly attached to his desire to have the world the way he wanted it to be." This, according to Bankart, is part of a more general issue: Anthony's "desire to be right, respected, and obeyed." Anthony, in Bankart's view, is fettered by his greed for recognition and unaware that he is connected to others and therefore bound to feel compassion for both them and himself.

Bankart's role is above all to "model" this compassion, to suffer and rejoice along with Anthony. He will insist that Anthony neither despair nor find excuses for himself but rather realize that his anger is a poison, a "corrosive outer layer," around his heart. Within, Anthony has a "Buddha nature" (one of love and compassion); he has only to break through the hard shell of his egotism. But how? Bankart incorporates Buddhist practices into a meditative exercise program. It begins with several short sessions during the day. These focus at first simply on breathing, then they add the body—concentrating on its movements, balance, ability to stretch, sensations of touch, sight, taste, and so on. The meditation gradually embraces thoughts: as Anthony becomes aware of them, especially as he becomes fully conscious of his erroneous belief that he is morally in the right, Bankart will tell him to keep a journal and be in constant touch with Bankart himself by phone and email. This is how Anthony will slowly shed his former attachments. Bankart is sensitive to the cultural values that keep Anthony in fetters; angry men in the American subcommunity of which Anthony is a part, cling to "absolutist rules about 'right' and 'wrong'" and invoke numerous abstract principles to justify them. They are convinced they must live up to manly standards, which, in accord with American culture, tend to privilege violence. Men in Anthony's emotional community distrust all authorities apart from themselves, putting a premium on rugged individualism, heroic righteousness, and on supermen who "stand up for what is right." They feel victimized and enraged when others disagree with them. All too often, they need to control what in fact does not need to be controlled. Their anger, Bankart concludes, is a mixture of the three poisons: they are greedy for mastery and obedience, hostile to those unwilling or unable to follow them, and delusional about reality.

Within the "sanctuary" offered by the therapeutic space, Bankart will ask Anthony to add to his practices of mindfulness a ten-step program. It begins with asking Anthony to reflect on the authoritarian rhetoric that he has hitherto made his own. "The entire gender-package of masculine anger must be uncovered and processed in therapy." Then Anthony should move on to see the habitual patterns he has practiced: stridently disagreeing with others, challenging them, experiencing disappointment, and then becoming enraged. He must accept, at least intellectually, that (as the Buddha says) anger not only hurts others but is self-destructive. The rest of the therapy works to create new habits, having Anthony practice acts of kindness rather than confrontation, and asking him to enjoy the resultant pleasure of others. Eventually, Anthony should circle back to his childhood, transforming its pain into the protection of those he loves; he should heal himself by forgiving his abusers.

For Bankart, anger has no good use, no ethical justification. He echoes the Buddha's "Abandon anger." To the objection that anger is part of human nature, he would reply that human nature—true human nature—is "Buddha nature." What we ordinarily consider natural must be transformed and *may* be transformed through the insight that life is suffering and by practicing mindful meditation.

What is anger? A definition for all time makes no sense. Like all emotions, anger cannot be seen under a microscope or manipulated with an instrument. It is known only by observing how people define it and what they imagine are its causes and effects—perhaps insults, raised voices, elevated blood pressure, oxygenation in certain areas of the brain. What "counts" as anger varies with the emotional community, as does the way in which it is judged. My mother concluded that I was "angry" because I punched my doll. I was sure that my parents were angry when they argued with each other. My mother disapproved of my behavior, and I was very scared and uncomfortable with theirs. But no one in my emotional community suggested that we should "abandon anger." Indeed, there was a sense in which arguments "cleared the air," and even hitting my doll was thought to do some good in that it "got the anger out," as if anger were a gas or a noxious food that I had to expel. Expressing anger was much better than "repression," a term popularized by Freud, who postulated that repression was responsible for mental disorders.

For the Buddha, however, discomfort, disapproval, approval, getting things off your chest—these were not the issues at all. Anger meant suffering. It was not to be "expelled" or "repressed" but rather transcended. It was a matter of ego. Since we are all interconnected, we must give up this "ego." In the story of Vepacitti, the Buddha's model was a "teflon" god who refused to be harmed or to harm in return; in the parable of the two-handled saw, the exemplar meets his own dismemberment with sympathy and good will.

When dealing with anger today in the United States, a therapist like Bankart finds it necessary to adapt Buddhist philosophy to a certain sub group in American culture that valorizes anger, seeing it as "masculine" and righteous. But he does not veer from the Buddhist position that anger in *any* form is bound to make both the enraged and his object suffer.

The Buddhists who killed King Lang Darma in the ninth century did not think that they were angry. Instead, they were part of a long tradition of non-angry violence. But there are many Buddhist schools, many Buddhist emotional communities. Not all are convinced that murder may be justified. Today in Myanmar, even as the persecutions of the Rohingya continue, some villages cultivate Buddhist-Rohingya cooperation. In 2014 a Buddhist abbot, U Witthuda, opened the gate of his monastery to hundreds of Muslims fleeing violent clashes in central Myanmar. Soon a hostile crowd gathered outside, demanding the refugees be handed over. The abbot replied, "I am helping those people who are in trouble. [. . .] If you want to get them you have to kill me first. I can't bring them out."[12] The group retreated.

✳

There are many Buddhisms. One version says that all killing comes from anger and is bad. Another justifies anger and violence in the name of Buddhism's survival. Still others teach that killing is sometimes, if committed without anger, a form of compassion. In Myanmar, as the incident with abbot U Witthuda shows, people may hesitate as they confront the discordant convictions and clashing emotional norms that uneasily co-exist within Buddhism. "Abandon anger" is a Buddhist absolute, but what it means in any given circumstance is open to interpretation.

# 2

## STOICISM

Numerous commentators have seen parallels between Stoicism and Buddhism. But had the ancient Roman statesman, courtier, and Stoic philosopher Seneca (d.65 CE) known about the Buddha, he would have found him exceedingly strange and optimistic. In his view, very few people (mainly men and perhaps a woman or two), if brought up properly and with the right philosophy, could become anger-free. That was the goal, and all should aspire to it; but it was unlikely to be met. Seneca's assumptions about human nature, life, and the natural order were very different from those of the Buddha.

Above all, Seneca never claimed to have accomplished the abandonment of anger himself. In fact, in a letter to his friend Lucilius written toward the end of his life, Seneca described a moment in which he had recently flared up. He had returned to one of his country estates and found his house in dilapidated condition. "I got angry," Seneca admitted, "and I seized on the nearest excuse to vent my anger." That "nearest excuse" was his estate manager. But the poor servant explained: the house was too ancient to be repaired. Now Seneca saw the humor: he himself had built the house; they were getting old together. Seneca, likewise, was too old to fix.[1] A bit of good humor was part of the Senecan recipe for avoiding anger.

That was a close call for Seneca. A decade or so before he confronted his hapless dependent, he had written three books on anger. A treatise in the form of a discourse, it argued that everything about anger was wrong and miserable and that it ought to be avoided altogether. Pulling out every rhetorical stop, Seneca described anger as ugly, indecent, forgetful of personal ties, keen only to inflict pain. Even as it crushed others, it turned the angry man or woman into rubble.

Writing in Latin, Seneca used the word *ira* for anger. It is the root of many other Latin terms (*iratus, iracundus, iracundia,* and so on) and the distant ancestor of English ire, irascible, and irate. Latin had two other words with much the same meaning: *indignatio,* from which English gets "indignation," and *bilis,* whence "bile," the bitter brownish yellow fluid secreted by the liver and stored in the gallbladder. When Seneca talked about anger, he did not—perhaps could not—imagine mild forms. His *ira* was a very strong feeling. That fact helps give anger a history: it did and does not "feel" the same in every culture and every period of time, even if, in many cases, the same or similar words are used.

We must wonder why Seneca easily admitted to being angry in his letter even though he scorned the emotion utterly. He was, in fact, a man of many contradictions: wealthy yet railing against wealth; an imperial adviser yet wary of power; irate, yet an uncompromising critic of anger. He said that he wrote his treatise on anger because his brother Novatus had asked him to "prescribe a way of soothing anger."[2] In fact, however, he hardly touched on the question of "soothing." Instead, he wrote about why anger should be avoided altogether and the ways in which one might do so. His "all or nothing" attitude about anger was one of Stoicism's underlying assumptions, and Seneca was a convinced Stoic. As a young man, he had studied with Stoic teachers. He said that he followed one of them in a nightly practice of self-reflection: "I examine my entire day." After each review, he vowed not to make the same mistakes again.[3]

Initially, Stoicism was a Greek creation, born in the aftermath of Alexander the Great's conquests (that is, after 323 BCE). It flew in the face of the classical Greek philosophical traditions that had dominated until then—those of Plato and Aristotle. Plato's dialogues, always slightly ambiguous and open-ended, nevertheless were clear enough in envisioning the human soul to be tripartite and hierarchically arranged. The immortal part is highest—literally in the head. Beneath it, the heart and liver house the emotions. The better passions—manliness and anger—are in the heart, while the liver, located further down, is filled with appetites and desires. Later, Platonists spoke of the head as the site of reason, the heart as the container for the spirited, irascible passions, and the liver as the locus of desirous, concupiscible feelings. For Plato, anger was good—energizing and emboldening—as long as it (like all the other emotions) obeyed the commands of reason. But he warned that the irascible passions tended to be wild; they were hard to tame and not always under reason's sway.

Aristotle, who was once Plato's pupil, did not entirely agree. He located emotions in the "intellective" part of the soul—the part that embraced reason—and, although emotions themselves were in the alogical half, that half and its logical counterpart could and should work together. If emotions were felt in the right way for the right reasons at the right time, they were useful and conducive to virtue.

Unlike Plato and Aristotle, the Stoics did not divide the soul into parts. The soul (which was also the mind) was for them a unified "command center" in the body.[4] Strategically located near the stomach, heart, and lungs, the mind was a spirit and yet had physicality. In adult human beings, it was rational. The little girl behind the couch had no capacity to choose, make decisions, nor to put one goal ahead of another. But adults had that ability—if they kept their reason uncontaminated. Emotions were diseases of reason, reason run amok, reason deranged. Anger could never be under reason's control in the ways that Plato and Aristotle had envisioned because, once contaminated by anger, reason itself became wrong, bent out of shape. Seneca likened the mind infected with anger to the body of a man who falls off a cliff: "It's not allowed to check its onrush: its own weight and the downward-tending nature of vices must—must—carry it along and drive it down to the depths."[5] Notice here the word vice (*vitium*); it would have a long afterlife. Seneca, like other Stoics, used it to refer to people's commitments to "externals"— money, food, even health and life. Externals are beyond our control. By contrast, virtues—generosity, using externals appropriately, loving friends—are up to us.

Giving in to anger means losing our reason and, because human beings are by nature reasonable, becoming angry really means losing ourselves. We are never uglier than when angry; never more of a slave to something foreign to our nature; never more wicked, treacherous, and criminal. Anger causes our blood vessels to burst, our bodies to suffer illness, our minds to go insane. In short, anger hurts the angered as fully as it tries to harm someone else. The Senecan insight is not that life is suffering and that we must give up our attachments to transcend the pain, as is the case in Buddhism; it is, rather, that we should use what life offers, accept what it does not, and strive to control what is within our control, namely ourselves.

We are by nature rational: we judge, we make decisions. For example, when we need food, it is reasonable for us to go to the store and buy something to eat. But reason is not infallible, and sometimes—often— we reason falsely. Emotions are the results of bad judgments. Anger, said Seneca, is our mistaken idea that someone has intentionally and unjustly harmed us, and we must do something—punish, take vengeance, retaliate—to get back at that person.

Aristotle had had a superficially similar definition of anger. Like Seneca, he said that anger was the desire to take vengeance when a person thought he had been slighted by someone who had no right to do so. Unlike Seneca, however, he thought that such a desire might be very reasonable. Of course, if you were slighted by a person who did have the right to do so—as a master has the right to injure his slave, for example—then it would be absurd and wicked to get angry. But if you were hurt by someone with no right to harm you, then you would be justified, indeed morally obligated, to be enraged. Aristotle assumed that anger was a natural function of both the body and the soul and that there were clear social and political circumstances in which it was appropriate. By contrast, Seneca and the Stoics in general thought that anger was unnatural: "What is milder [than human nature], when its mental condition is not warped?"[6] While Seneca knew that there were nearly limitless occasions that might evoke anger, none could do so justifiably.

Certainly, some people needed to be reproved. But Seneca differentiated between "reasoned punishment" and unleashed anger. We might pretend to be angry at a wrong-doer, but our real goal should be to "heal under the guise of harming."[7] Judges should reprimand first with gentle words; if that proves ineffective, they should impose mild penalties. Death sentences should be rare and as much a favor to the criminal as to society at large.

Seneca scoffed, as well, at Plato's idea that anger might have a useful, energizing effect. To the contrary, said Seneca: Rome's soberly planned victories against enemies who were fueled by anger proved that anger hindered the soldier. If it was useless in war, what proper function could it have in peace? But let us say that the wise man "sees his father being murdered, his mother raped?" He should not feel anger, replied Seneca, but rather "a proper sense of devotion." He continued: "If my father is being killed, I will defend him; if he has been killed, I will see the matter to a proper conclusion—because I know that's right, not because I feel a grievance."[8]

In this, Seneca was deviating a bit from the Stoic "hard line." A Stoic in its formative period, before the Greek world had been conquered by the Romans, would never have consented to vengeance as a "proper conclusion." Seneca was not cut from that cloth. He lived in a milieu in which power—in the family, the army, the imperial court—depended on the whims of a small, wealthy, and privileged elite accustomed to getting its way. Had Seneca dismissed vengeance itself as fundamentally immoral, he would have had no audience, and he might have been unfaithful to his own convictions. He was part of the very elite to whom he was writing. At the time he composed his treatise on anger, he had resumed his place as an imperial courtier after returning from an exile ordered by Emperor Claudius. He was now (or would soon be) the tutor of the boy who was to become Emperor Nero. When Nero took power, Seneca became one of his advisers and an occasional apologist: he wrote, for example, the letter that Nero sent to the Senate to defend his murder of his mother. Seneca lived in an atmosphere of vengeance.

All the more reason for him to write about the times when revenge was wrong and to worry about anger's role in it. He argued, as did the Stoics generally, that anger is not just an occasional misapplication of reason. It is a *habitual* misjudgment, its way prepared for by upbringing, education, social standing, and cultural expectations. These experiences helped explain why most people got angry and why some people's very disposition was irascible. Seneca admitted that people might have some inborn tendencies to anger. He subscribed to the ancient version of DNA, which hypothesized that people were composed of four elements—fire, water, air, and earth—and their matching properties— hot, cold, dry, and moist. Human variation arose from different combinations. A person with a moist, watery makeup was slow to anger, for example; someone with a hot, fiery temperament was prone to it.

Even so, people were not simply the products of their initial endowment. Life experiences molded people; setbacks such as illness, working too hard, sleeplessness, and falling desperately in love made the mind weak and prone to false judgments. Upbringing was equally important. The little girl behind the couch might have been born with an irascible nature, but her mother was not about to let her sink into that pit. Rearing a child meant compensating for her weaknesses and developing her strengths. Seneca thought that children should be rebuked when they expressed anger yet encouraged when they displayed strong spirits. This was tricky: praise might lead to a good self-image, but it could also encourage arrogance.

Worst of all was spoiling a child, bringing her up coddled, granting every wish. When no impulse is thwarted, when the word "no" is never spoken, anger becomes habitual. Seneca could see the truth of this when he observed the politicians of his day. He was one himself, and he had to be careful, for, as the incident with his estate manager showed, even he was liable to get angry. Worse than spoiling, however, was allowing children such free rein that their anger hardened into cruelty. Cruel people are not angry; they are so warped that they delight in thrashing, harming, and killing others. "This is not anger, it's bestiality."[9]

Habit and upbringing were therefore key to both vice and virtue. Together they could turn a person into a monster. More often they produced a mind that was weak, inconsistent, and hasty in judgment. Very rarely, they shaped a mind that was strong, constant, and deliberate. It is unclear whether Seneca considered the sociopaths of the ancient world to be culpable for their bloodlust. But in every other case, he insisted that each person was responsible for his or her judgments and opinions. All were personally to blame for their emotions and their consequences. Since people are often not very coherent—since their minds support a variety of conflicting judgments—they fall into the clutches of emotions. Swayed this way and that, they seem out of control. Yet, they are not, for they themselves agree to be swayed. Only the hypothetical wise person has a fully coordinated set of beliefs that allows him or her to assent to a set of "good emotions" that are in accord with virtue: joy in doing a generous act, for example, or aversion to seeing something shameful.

If ordinary people's emotions are mistaken judgments, then how did Seneca make sense of physiological changes? Many today consider a palpitating heart, sweaty palms, and the like to be important aspects of emotions. Seneca disagreed. Shivering, flushing, feeling a headache coming on: these are beyond our control. Seneca called them "first motions" and, more colorfully, "shocks" or "bites." They occurred before any assessment. They were not emotions, but they spelled danger because people had to judge their significance.

In the instance of anger, consider a pounding heart to be the first motion. At once a "second motion" begins as our mind considers whether to concur in that initial shock. We imagine we have been slighted, and that brings the thought of revenge to mind. Yet, like the physical reaction, this thought is not yet an emotion, for it may be stopped by another judgment.

Here is a likely scenario: we are driving along at a reasonable speed when suddenly someone behind us honks. Immediately, we have an initial shock, the first motion. Then comes the second: we think we are the object of the honking and that we've been wronged. We have the provisional wish to do something hostile in response. Is this second motion "anger"? No: "I don't call this anger," Seneca wrote, "anger's something that leaps clear of reason, that snatches reason up and carries it along."[10] That "snatching up" is the third motion: we want to retaliate, come what may. Thus, the third motion is a more deliberate judgment to wreak vengeance. In our car-horn scenario, if we judge that the honking was truly malicious, we slow down to a crawl—even against our best interests—to taunt the driver behind us. In many instances, though, the third motion never happens, as when we realize that the honking was simply meant to signal our trailing muffler. Then we change our mind and calm down.

Of the three motions, only the second is amenable to control. We can't stop the initial bite, nor can we check the grip of passion at the third stage.

Some cognitive psychologists today agree with the general contours of Seneca's sequence. Nancy Stein and her colleagues, for example, note: "Both infants and adults respond automatically and affectively to certain types of stimuli. Automatic physical responses are generated in a fixed action pattern, without evaluating information."[11] In Seneca's terminology, these responses constitute the first motion. As for Seneca, so for Stein: they are not emotions. But they do produce physiological changes that focus our attention on them. We then evaluate those changes to assess their impact on our wellbeing. That's akin to Seneca's second motion. Finally, says Stein, our beliefs about the actions we should take in response to the stimulus are activated. This is comparable to the third motion. While for Seneca this phase is out of control, in Stein's formulation, to the contrary, it is still part of the appraisal process. In the case of anger, Stein's steps are these: 1) a precipitating event, such as the honk that makes us look in our rear-view mirror, leading to 2) "the failure of an important goal or the inability to avoid an aversive state" (when we judge that someone has intentionally harmed us), which is followed by 3) the belief "that the focal goal can somehow be reinstated, that an aversive state can be removed, or that the source of goal failure can be removed." This final step in what Stein calls the "emotion episode" seems on the surface to be more general and more "rational" than Seneca's final step, which is vengeance. But Seneca, too, had in mind a whole set of possible forms of retribution, including simply the *wish* to harm. For both theorists, there is no emotion without this sort of sequence.

Moreover, both Seneca and today's cognitivists (appraisal theorists) engage with values and goals. Both maintain that emotions involve beliefs long in the making through upbringing, education, habits of mind, and the like. But Seneca argues that it is *never* right to be angry, while Stein's team endorses no particular value system. Indeed, it speaks simply of "personally significant goals." Then, too, Seneca says that anger—that is, recognizing that someone has done something injurious—will *always* lead to one desire, the desire for revenge, while Stein's group, at least abstractly, entertains other possibilities.

Let us imagine that we thought we had been harmed but realize that we were wrong. That is the ethical moment. We see that the "harm" was inadvertent. Or we realize that the so-called offender had her reasons. If children offend, we should blame their age; if a woman, we need to blame her normal tendency to make mistakes (this was very typical of the ancient view of women); if someone is acting under orders or in fear of his life (Seneca had experienced both), we need to see the matter from their point of view. None of us is perfect. We are all human and thus should understand what it is like to be in another's shoes.

Unlike all the other emotions, a whole collectivity may be infected by the "pestilence" of anger. With this argument, Seneca proved how far he was from our own day. We never see an entire people burning with love, he declared, nor a whole society devoted to gain, nor everyone in competition to get ahead. Seneca could not imagine the adulation conveyed by the "Heil Hitler" of German Nazis or the collective weeping of North Koreans. For him, it was only anger, not any other emotion, that was uniquely capable of infecting a crowd: "a whole people has often become angry *en masse*," he observed. To their fury he attributed even the violence of war, with its "butchery and poisoning, [. . .] cities destroyed, entire nations wiped out, [. . .] dwellings put to the torch."[12]

"Abandon anger," said the Buddha. "Destroy it entirely," said Seneca. There is a difference. In the first case, we leave anger behind as we "awaken" to a new reality. In the second, we are still mired in the world and its temptations to get angry. We are in a battle that we must fight continually.

Yet, in his plays, Seneca at times seemed to favor not resistance to wrath's seductions but rather the sweetness of revenge. His Medea, for example, positively courts fury's feverish energy: "Arm yourself with wrath!" she commands herself.[13] Jason, hero of the Argonauts and formerly her husband and the father of her two sons, has repudiated her and wedded another, the daughter of King Creon. But, as he explains, he had good reasons, for otherwise he and his family would have died at the hands of a vengeful King Acastus. Now he and the children have a defender in his new father-in-law, King Creon. Medea is unmoved. With her magical arts, she causes the death of Jason's new wife, and, because she knows his sons are supremely precious to him, she kills them, leaving Jason to bitter sorrow. (See Plate 2.) By murdering her own children, she has certainly brought ruin upon herself, as Seneca says in his treatise. But the play ends in her triumph, as she rides off to heaven in her "winged chariot on the winds."

Seneca's *Medea* thus seems to contradict his treatise on anger. But A.J. Boyle, a recent editor and translator of the play, shows how the two may be reconciled. Unlike Seneca's treatise, which talks about the consequences of anger for each individual, Seneca's drama illustrates the long-term destruction wrought by ongoing cycles of anger and vengeance. We learn about these other angers as the characters in the play justify themselves. Creon, for example, says that he is protecting Jason from the wrath of Acastus, whose father had been murdered by Medea's trickery. The gods, meanwhile, have their own reasons for vengeance. Jason's Argo was the first ship ever to ply the seas. Before his journey, water and land had had their separate spheres. Because Jason "wrote new laws for the winds" by harnessing their power in the sails of his boat, he betrayed the original harmony of nature. The gods were not wrong to punish Jason: Stoics prized the laws of nature, and those laws had indeed been injured by Jason's hubris. Medea's vengeance was a tool of the gods. Seneca did not condemn all vengeance—not when it was the "proper conclusion."

✳

Seneca was not particularly popular or influential in his own day. His greatest impact came in the Renaissance and afterward, when he was invoked as part of a Neostoic philosophical movement that took European elites by storm. But Seneca's views are important for understanding the place of anger in the Roman Empire. Not that he was "typical." Rather, in Roman society, as in our own, a variety of emotional communities experienced, expressed, valued, and devalued feelings in their own ways. Seneca was typical of one rather small—but influential—such community. It was not so much a social group as a literary one: the audience for Stoic teachings on anger. It included, among others, Cicero and Caesar.

Classicist William Harris has shown that Romans associated the very foundation of their city with anger.[14] Like the story of Cain and Abel, that of Rome involved brother killing brother; the Roman historian Livy said that Romulus killed Remus out of anger. During most of the republican period of Roman history—that time (ending in 14 CE) when Rome was ruled by elites but not by an emperor—few Romans blamed anger for the problems in their political life; rather they railed against corruption and ambition. We might see anger, but the Romans saw avidity and depravity.

This was to change. As they engaged with Greek thought—increasingly the case after Greece was incorporated into their Empire in 146 BCE—some Roman Senators began slowly but surely to see anger as a vital ethical issue. When the orator, politician, and philosopher Cicero wrote a letter of advice to his brother Quintus, who was serving as the provincial governor of Greece, he isolated Quintus' one fault as irascibility.[15] Quintus couldn't hold his temper. "Because your mind is surprised by anger before cool calculation has been able to prevent it," wrote Cicero, the remedy is to "deliberately prepare yourself beforehand [. . .] being most careful to restrain your tongue." Holding one's tongue was a far cry from Seneca's admonition to destroy anger. But it demonstrated Cicero's sensitivity to the issue.

There is no evidence that Quintus took heed of his brother's advice, but, around the same time, the historian Sallust attributed to Caesar a strongly worded statement about the deleterious effects of anger. The occasion was the aftermath of the revolt of Catiline, a disgruntled candidate for the consulship at Rome. When the senators were deciding the fate of some of the conspirators, Caesar argued against execution. Roman policy—its very laws—prohibited killing citizens. Execution, said Caesar, was an emotional—an irrational—response. He warned against passion. "It becomes all men," he asserted, "to be free of hatred, friendship, anger, and pity." Such feelings displaced reason; no one could make proper judgments under their sway. It didn't matter much if unimportant people acted out of anger. But those who deliberated and made decisions on the public stage had less freedom. They had to appear dispassionate, "and least of all does it befit them to get angry. For what in others is called irascibility is, in the powerful, termed pride and cruelty."[16] The speech persuaded some, but only momentarily. Cicero had the final say, which was for execution. He did not, however, argue that he was inspired by anger. To the contrary, he said that he was inspired "by a singular humanity and mercifulness." He was not raging but saving Rome. Confronted by men who conspired to "murder us, and our wives, and our children," he was counseling a rigorous response that was in fact truly merciful. That was his position; it was adopted, and the conspirators were put to death.[17]

In short, around mid-first century BCE a few members of the Roman elite recognized that it was politically expedient not to seem angry and indeed to present themselves as merciful. In this early phase of Roman anger denunciation, the emphasis was on performance—making a "show" of non-anger while possibly feeling otherwise. But even when performed, freedom from anger was not generally admired. It was still widely accepted that when powerful men were injured, they would and should act. In defending Marcus Caelius of a crime, even Cicero acknowledged the common view: "When [vigorous men] are hurt, they suffer, when angry, they get carried away, when attacked they fight." But he brought up such men only to vilify their role as witnesses for the prosecution: "Exclude their excesses, O judges, from your consideration."[18]

The minority position that Cicero and Seneca represented remained minor for many centuries thereafter. At the end of the fourth century, Christianity became the official religion of the Roman Empire. The barbarian conquests, which took place during the fifth and sixth centuries, did not change that fact, since the barbarians, too, professed— or would soon profess—one or another form of Christianity. Christians generally stood Roman values on their head: the "soldiers of God" were martyrs, not battlefield warriors. Family, the body, wealth—all those old foundations of the Roman good life—were scrutinized and largely rejected. But the Roman ambivalence about anger remained.

This was in part because Christianity itself had a number of contradictory models of anger to reconcile. The Old Testament presents a God that is often—and righteously—angry. In the New Testament, by contrast,

Jesus rarely gets angry. In Mark 3:5, he looks around, in anger and distress, at the Jews in the synagogue who are doing nothing to help a man with a shriveled hand on the Sabbath. In his Sermon on the Mount (Matthew 5:22) he condemns "everyone who is angry with his brother." In all four Gospels, Jesus drives out the buyers and sellers in the Temple, and in some versions he overturns the tables of the money changers. But none of these accounts of the Temple incident says that Jesus was angry. Nor did patristic authors writing about this episode consider how Jesus felt.

Because of the importance of the Old Testament God, few Christian thinkers or practitioners condemned anger entirely. Nevertheless, a small number did keep the Senecan tradition alive, in the process adapting it to a Christian context. An early and wholesale enthusiast of Seneca's treatise was the sixth-century Bishop Martin of Braga. While Seneca wrote for his brother and other members of the Roman elite, Martin wrote for a fellow bishop in the Iberian Peninsula who was worried, as was Martin, about the salvation of the Christian community.

The concerns of these priests were pastoral, not philosophical. Therefore, while Martin borrowed most of his words from Seneca, nevertheless he radically reorganized and shortened his source. After summarizing the horrible effects of anger—its ugliness, lunacy, recalcitrance—he turned to three practical remedies, offering a handy self-help guide. There are three ways to "oppose anger," he said. First, just say no. Refuse to give in to anger. Second, if you have allowed anger to "burst through" then "hold off for a while. [. . .] If you wait, it will stop." Third, cure the anger of others. Find ways to delay their anger, pretend to be angry yourself in order to play the "sympathetic fellow sufferer," or contrive to make them ashamed or afraid.[19]

Martin's advice had an impact. Our picture of barbarian Europe—with its livid kings, raging civil wars, fierce vendettas—is largely based on the account of the Franks written by the sixth-century Bishop Gregory of Tours.[20] But Gregory's history was not objective; it was colored by his conviction that the evils of his age were the result above all of anger in its most virulent form. In the preface to his *Ten Books of History*, he blamed the savagery of peoples and the fury of kings for the woes of his day. Nor did he let his fellow bishops off the hook: he identified anger as their chief vice. As for himself, he resisted anger by wielding sarcasm, humor, and irony. Gregory was familiar with Martin of Braga. In a sense, he took Martin's advice for curing the anger of others: his *History* was meant to make his contemporary kings, bishops, and literate laypeople both ashamed and afraid of their fury.

But after the sixth century, Seneca's thinking on anger suffered a long eclipse, as did Stoic philosophy generally. From the eleventh until the thirteenth century, Seneca's treatise on anger was read and copied only in southern Italy—and there only by monks. In the thirteenth century, however, it was "rediscovered" in Paris by Franciscan friars who used it, as had Martin of Braga, for pastoral purposes. The great difference was that the audience of the friars was far wider than Martin's, consisting of the men and women—lay and religious—in the urban centers of Europe. But soon the monopoly of the Church would be shattered; war justified by religious differences would usher in new reasons to detest anger and new adherents to that cause.

Unlike the popular view of Stoicism, the point of the ancient form of this philosophy was neither shrugging indifference nor patient endurance. Its aim was to be reasonable and in control of the only thing that we might ever hope to master fully: ourselves. Anger was not natural or necessary. In fact, it was perverse and hurtful. No doubt most people experienced bites of anger and fleeting thoughts of revenge. But they also had the tools to bring themselves to their senses: right judgment on the spot, observation of their feelings, reviews of their daily actions, laughter at their follies, learning from their mistakes.

# 3

# VIOLENCE AND NEOSTOICISM

When I pummeled my doll, my mother pronounced me angry. How did she know how I felt? If I said anything while I was punching, it was probably, "Bad baby, bad baby," not "I'm angry." The violence that I was inflicting on my doll could just possibly have been a proper judgment on my part, a punishment of the sort that Seneca called "reasoned." (Perhaps, in my mind, my doll had done something bad.) But my mother disapproved of what I was doing and interpreted my hitting as "angry." We often equate anger with the instances of violence that we censure. The corollary is that when we approve of violence—when we lock people up in jail, support capital punishment, or proudly march off to war—we rarely deem these acts to be galvanized by anger.

Does anger always imply violence? Not invariably, as we shall see. But many emotional communities make the link. In the sixteenth and seventeenth centuries, virulent religious wars sparked by the Protestant Reformation engulfed the Netherlands, Germany, France, and England. To many people living at the time, such violence seemed absurd and unfathomable. Some turned to the Stoics, and to Seneca in particular, for guidance; historians call them Neostoics. But here we need to separate out those Neostoics who blamed anger for their troubled times from those who looked to Stoicism to teach them how to remain calm even as they were being robbed, forced into exile, and buffeted by marauding armies and warring states. Quite the opposite were some emotional communities in the Early Modern period that praised anger.

"Buffeted" well describes the life of Justus Lipsius (d.1606), usually considered the first Neostoic. Lipsius had to flee his home in Belgium and then again in Germany. When he produced a critical edition of the works of Seneca, including Seneca's treatise on anger, he could well have drawn upon its equation between anger and violence. But he didn't: rather, he reconciled Stoic tranquility with Christian patience. He advocated "constancy," which he defined as "a right and immovable strength of the mind"; that strength came from his presumption that worldly woes had godly purposes.[1] For a truly Senecan approach to anger and violence, we must look beyond Lipsius.

We find it in the work of Johann Weyer (d.1588), one of the court physicians serving William the Rich, duke of Jülich, Cleves, and Berg. As ruler of a conglomeration of regions straddling northern Germany and the Netherlands and thus right in the crosshairs of war, William had constantly to negotiate between a largely Protestant populace and Catholic Spanish Emperor Charles V, whose troops sometimes occupied William's territories. Living in the midst of conflict, Weyer saw echoes of Seneca's "butchery and poisoning." Indeed, he quoted those very words as if they referred to his own day.[2]

Weyer agreed with Seneca: violence was the offspring of human anger. However, unlike Seneca, who considered anger a lapse of reason, Weyer thought of it as an epidemic disease. Its cure was a multifaceted therapy, which he outlined in detail. The humors—the four elements that determined bodily health according to prevailing Galenic medical theory—had to be kept in balance through diet, exercise, and music. At the same time, anger had to be held in check through new daily tasks. Seneca had found it salutary to review at night all the moments when he had felt angry during the day. To this Weyer added a morning audit. Both morning and evening, Weyer said, you should ask yourself: "Which bad deed did you correct?"; "What vices did you resist?"; "Did you restrain your anger?" The key point was "to conquer yourself."[3] Then too, during the course of the day, Weyer's hypothetical "patient" (always a man; wives were to keep quiet while their husbands were engaged in anger therapy) was obliged to perform numerous tasks. He had to repeat to himself various handy aphorisms about anger's horrible effects. He had also to meditate on edifying historical examples, scold himself when he saw signs of ire, and bring in a personal trainer—a good friend—to monitor his behavior.

Even with all this, Weyer did not imagine that the wise man could resist assenting to anger. Unlike Seneca, Weyer had a long Christian tradition of original sin to contend with. That taught him that human nature was corrupt and liable to vice. Weyer considered it inevitable that even the wisest among us will become angry. When that happens, we should immediately run to a mirror and look at ourselves; nothing will be more "loathsome, ugly, or disgusting" than our angry faces.[4] The Stoics, as we saw, had also recommended looking in a mirror. But their purpose was to convince us to reject anger, whereas Weyer's was for us to handle the anger we had already assented to. Nor was Weyer necessarily thinking of a real mirror (surely a scarce commodity in the sixteenth century). We can see ourselves in our mind's eye, observing not only our external appearance but also the agitations going on inside us: our irregular pulse, pounding heart, frayed nerves. Facing our anger, we conquer it by repenting.

Weyer drew on Seneca, then, but his notion of the human condition was not the same. The Stoics considered human beings to be rational and self-sufficient. Christians of Weyer's stamp believed that people had control over their lives only insofar as God's grace allowed; human reason by itself was feeble. While Seneca thought it possible for some few to fully eradicate anger, Weyer thought that anger could at best be stopped in its tracks, and only by men engaged in constant, life-long therapy. Anger was not, for Weyer, the terrible misjudgment of reason gone amuck; it was a disease, a pestilence that affected the body as well as the mind and was liable to infect others, bringing all the pain and desolation of war and violence in its wake.

Did Weyer really expect his "medicine" to be swallowed? It involved nine exercises, many of them open-ended and potentially very time-consuming, all to be practiced every day of one's entire life. Probably he did: punctuating the day with moral exercises was a commonplace by his time. Catholic aristocrats used Books of Hours to intersperse their daily activities with prayers. Monks divided their day into hours: seven times a day they filed into church to chant psalms, lessons, and prayers. At around the same time that Weyer elaborated his program, Ignatius of Loyola was working out his regimen of *Spiritual Exercises*, with self-examination three times a day and various additional activities.

The foremost philosopher of the emotions of his day, René Descartes (d.1650), also had a Stoic-inspired anger management program. His treatise *On the Passions of the Soul* presented a general theory of all the passions. But because intense anger was the worst of them, the one to be most studiously avoided, it was a sort of "poster child" for Descartes' position.

Let us summarize his theory briefly. We may start with the famous words, "I think, therefore I am." For Descartes, the only thing that is undoubtedly true is the self, the soul, as a thinking reality. But this did not separate the soul from the body, as some interpreters would have it. For the soul thinks about what it "learns" via the body, which is constantly sensing and monitoring the internal and external world. (There is one exception—doubt is the one thought that the soul may have without relying on the body.)

The soul is utterly "joined" (Descartes' word) to every part of the body. The pineal gland in the brain is the privileged place in which it operates, the site where the interactions between body and soul occur. Representations about the outside world (colors, sounds, shapes) as well as the interior states of the body (thirst, heat, cold, pain) come to the soul from the nerves. These are the raw materials of thought.

Some thoughts are "active": when we hear a honking car behind us, the sound, which we hear through our ears, is communicated by our nerves to our soul. Then our reason and judgment (among the active functions of our soul) assess that perception. If the assessment is that the honking doesn't matter, our free will (another active function) may well direct our attention to something else, so that we hardly take note of the sound. But if the assessment is that the honking matters, that it is an "evil done by others" in reference to us and that we wish to take revenge, then we feel anger.[5] Anger is a "passive" sort of thought. We are agitated by such thoughts, such "passions," far more than by other kinds of thoughts. Unlike hearing a honk and knowing what it is and how it is produced and whether it is loud or soft and what its results might be and how it might be connected to other things—all active sorts of thoughts—the sensation of anger is "confused and obscure."[6] But passive thought is just as powerful as active thought, and it, too, may lead to bodily reactions. In the case of anger, our faces will take on a characteristic grimace, our cheeks will turn pale or red, our blood will boil, we may raise our hand to make an obscene gesture at the driver behind us, and so on.

There is another possibility: when we feel anger, our free will/reason can help us reassess the situation, and that has the potential to change both our feeling and our response. In the simplest revision, reason can reformulate the honk as a kindly signal that something is amiss with our car or our driving. More profoundly and importantly, reason can incorporate our various experiences of anger into its judgments, recognizing that, even if the honking is unjustified and terribly annoying, retaliation has bad consequences, both for others and ourselves. Such appraisals will help us overcome anger. The more we feel anger and can oppose it with convincing reasons, the more ethical we become. Thus, in a roundabout way, anger itself helps us overcome it, allowing us to take a larger view of our social lives and surroundings.[7] Through repeatedly experiencing the violence, regret, and hurt that are caused by anger, we learn to feel not anger but "magnanimity" (*générosité*). Thus armed, we have "absolute dominion over ourselves," for we "esteem very little any goods that can be taken away"[8]—including our pride, our social position, our power over others. What remains of anger once magnanimity supersedes it? A new moral sensibility: "scorn or at most indignation for the wrongs at which others usually take offense."[9] Descartes' magnanimity was a kind of tranquility that ironically arose from experiencing the most disturbing of all the emotions.

Descartes lived through the Thirty Years' War (1618–1648), and his treatise on the passions appeared the year after it ended. Although he cultivated the fiction that he was above the fray, in fact he was deeply involved in political issues.[10] He did not have a nine-point program for eliminating anger, but in the long run Descartes was saying much the same thing as Weyer: we cannot eradicate anger, but by exercising it, we build up our resistance to it. Feel it, think of all the ways in which it makes no sense and is, in fact, harmful to ourselves and others, and overcome it so habitually that we almost cease to feel it.

Did the thoughts of Weyer, Lipsius, and Descartes matter to how people "felt" and lived with their anger on the ground? Certainly, scholars of their day all across Europe were eager to give lip service to the Neostoic view that emotions must be suppressed or overcome. Yet there was no "Neostoic emotional community" that agreed on which emotions to value and which to suppress. Indeed, there were several "Neostoicisms." Lipsius thought anger could be tamed. Weyer wanted it to be treated like a disease, and he offered a cure. Descartes justified it as a way for men to strengthen their moral fiber, much as muscles need weights and gravity if they are not to atrophy.

Some historians have argued that Neostoicism was incorporated into the justifications that rulers of the early modern state used in order to control social behavior, including emotions of every sort. Others have seen it at work within Protestant churches, where (they claim) medieval "emotion-oriented piety" came to an end, and reformers like Luther tried "to reduce the intensity of some forms of [emotional] expression, to suppress others entirely, and to shape appropriately still other approved types of feeling."[11] According to such theories, talk of anger, as of other emotions, should have seen a falling off in the sixteenth and seventeenth centuries, especially in Protestant areas.

We see some evidence in favor of this hypothesis from a group of religious testimonials made by men and women who wanted to join a Puritan church in Cambridge, Massachusetts, when it was an English colony. Led by Thomas Shepard (d.1649), it required (as did many other such churches) a public personal confession before a worshiper could join the congregation. The idea was for each believer to offer a spiritual autobiography ending with evidence of his or her suitability for church membership. From 1648 to 1649, Shepard recorded sixteen such oral accounts (nine from men, seven from women) in a notebook.

In these testimonials, God's anger—manifested in pestilence, pain, and scourges of every type—was understood as a punishment for sins. As Goodwife Stevenson said, "When the Lord was pleased to convince me of sin, it was by affliction [. . .] I [was] in the midst of [the] wrath of God." For her part, Mistress Gookin worried that the Lord "was turned away [from her] in anger." Human anger, however, was never mentioned. Shepard's would-be congregants repeatedly mentioned their feelings of love, hope, and fear; they mourned their stony, desolate hearts. But they never talked about being angry. Here, it seems, we see how "Neostoic emotionology" made a difference in people's self-perceptions.

Yet, if we consider England and its English-speaking colonies as a whole, this conclusion is not fully warranted. A large sample of the books published in English between 1430 and 1700 reveals a significant *increase* in the use of the words "anger" and "wrath" during the seventeenth century, with a recognizable peak between 1640 and 1680. The age of

Neostoicism did not, then, spell the end of anger. And this fact poses a newly pressing question: did the heightened interest in anger correlate with greater violence? The essentially coterminous rise in the use of the word "violence" during the same period suggests that this was so.[12]

Thus, it would seem that anger and violence went hand-in-hand—at least with regard to the written language. Did they also go together in historical fact? Was the period of the crest more violent? The answer seems to be yes. The 1640s saw a religious and political rift widen between Anglicans (who favored hierarchy and ritual, and who were represented by King Charles I) and "Puritans" (a catch-all term for those who resented the state-supported form of Protestantism, and wanted to purify the church of its formal elements in order to focus on individual godliness). A largely Puritan Parliament was convened in 1640. It revolted against the monarchy shortly thereafter, created its own army, and fought a civil war. In 1649, the Puritans executed the king and created a Commonwealth under Oliver Cromwell. In 1660, the monarchy was restored under Charles II.

May we therefore conclude that people blamed the violence of their day on anger? Some evidence points in this direction. For example, in a sermon before Parliament, John Warren (d.1696), a Puritan minister in Essex, preached at length about a passage in Psalm 76:10: "Surely the wrath of man shall praise thee, the remainder of wrath shalt thou restrain." The wrath of man was anger, which he called "a soul-enflaming passion." Its causes were, first, "the *malignity* of man's nature," which served as combustible fuel, and second, "the *Malice* of *Satan* first against God, and then against his people" which kindled and fanned the coals "in the hearts of wicked men." Warren used the Gunpowder Plot, a purported Catholic attempt to bring down the monarchy earlier in the century, as a good example of the wrath of men against the godly. In that way he explicitly linked anger to violence. On the other hand, he saw some salutary uses for it: "Anger is good in respect [to] the object when it is excited by sin. Sin is the proper, formal object of *anger*. Gods *anger* is only at *sin*."[13]

A sermon like this, so far from the rarified heights of a Weyer, Lipsius, or Descartes, may for that very reason have been closer to the ways in which people actually thought about anger in their lives. But if Warren generally condemned anger, other emotional communities at the same time were far less Senecan. Recall that Weyer advised his readers to tell their wives to be quiet while they devoted themselves to contemplating their angry moments. How did the wives feel about that? Did they get angry? Some men thought it likely. Helkiah Crooke (d.1648), King James I's personal doctor, wrote that "the passion of Anger, we many of us know by woeful experience to be quicker and more vigorous in women than in men, for they are easily heated and upon very slight causes."[14] If anger was gendered female and women were supposed to be subordinate to men, then who indeed would not wish to avoid anger at all costs? Who would not want to be a Neostoic?

As it happens, however, some voices were raised in opposition to this view. Thus, *Jane Anger her Protection for Women*, written by an anonymous author, defended women's anger. This broadside was part of what the author called an ongoing "trial"—a sort of phantom court case pitting the sexes—during which women needed a defender. Not only did the author assume the surname Anger but also claimed that Anger itself was writing the defense, responding to an unnamed man's attack on women. "Fie on the falsehood of men, whose minds go oft a madding [on a rant]. [. . .] Was there ever any so abused, so slandered, so railed upon or so wickedly handled undeservedly, as are we women?" Men take advantage of women's weakness and their kind natures, and they mistake women's virtues for vices. When men accuse women of wrath, they are really objecting to good counsel; when calling them "wrathful," they mean that women will not "bear with their knavish behaviors." In short, "if our frowns be so terrible, and our anger so deadly, men are too foolish in offering occasions of hatred." Men are lecherous, gluttonous, deceitful, and out of control. The drunkard who mistook his wife for a cross was "an Ass," but when his wife, "keeping him from his drunken vain [habit], put his nose out of his socket, he thereby was brought into a mad mood."[15] In Jane Anger's diatribe, female anger is judicious; male anger is wild. But no one is without anger, nor is expected to be. As Gwynne Kennedy says, "Anger claims for angry women a right to invective without being labeled a shrew or scold."[16] Kennedy identifies a number of authors around the same time who took Anger's position. In the age of the Neostoics, the anti-anger stance dominated, but it did not overwhelm.

✳

Today, Neostoicism is hardly the prevailing norm. Yet it has echoes in some anger-management therapies. Almost all clinicians agree that *some* anger is normal and salutary. So, too, did all the Neostoics. While not thinking in terms of "normalcy," which is a modern notion, they granted that anger had some good uses.

Lipsius thought anger fortified courage; Weyer praised ire against crime and sin; Descartes agreed on both counts. All wanted to eliminate "excessive" anger. That's precisely what many anger management therapies today hope to do as well. For example, anger management therapists Howard Kassinove and Raymond Chip Tafrate say that they rely on an "objective judgment" to determine whether someone's anger is "*excessive in frequency and duration, and is disproportionate to the event or person* who triggered it."[17] In practice, the decision is made by the client him- or herself, or by a family member or colleague, a school or criminal justice institution or, indeed, the therapist, who is likely to use a variety of standardized tests to assess the full parameters of the disorder.

Kassinove and Tafrate's "cognitive-behavioral approach" has some points in common with Stoic and Neostoic models. The two therapists postulate a dual "pathway" to anger that corresponds with Seneca's two movements: the first is "automatic and inflexible," the second "relies on higher-level cognitive processes." But there the correspondence ends, for while Seneca thought that there was no way to change the response to an initial "shock," which wasn't really anger anyway, Kassinove and Tafrate say that such "reflex" reactions may be modified by conditioning. Like Descartes, they see value in repeated exposure. They ask their clients to rehearse non-angry reactions to "typical anger triggers." For example, patient and therapist might together act out or imagine the horn-honking episode. Then, proceeding to the "second movement," the therapist will suggest new and more adaptive ways to think about the event, such as putting traffic conditions into a larger perspective.[18]

While stressing that different people require different intervention programs, Kassinove and Tafrate's discussion of Anthony M.'s case (see Chapter 1, pp. 18–19) affords a good example of their general strategy. Like Lipsius, Weyer, and Descartes, Kassinove and Tafrate see themselves as offering a way to greater life-long tranquility. They want their techniques to become habits. First, they will ask Anthony to review in detail his anger episodes to see what triggers them and to recognize their negative consequences. Much in the tradition of Seneca's and Weyer's daily reviews, they will ask Anthony to keep a record of his anger episodes.

Their therapy continues with "change strategies." Like Weyer, they offer ways to escape inducements to anger; like Descartes, they rely on exposure. They will, for example, teach Anthony how to cope with his anger by practicing PMR (Progressive Muscle Relaxation) every day, and they will confront him with anger-inducing verbal barbs to teach him to "maintain nonreactivity."[19] They will create "cognitive coping statements," much like the aphorisms Weyer favored.

The "Neostoic" anger management treatment of Kassinove and Tafrate does not hope to eliminate all anger from the human psyche but simply "to make anger less of a problem" for people who need help. The all-or-nothing "abandon anger" of Buddhism or "resist anger" of Seneca is not their brief, even though they, too, focus on defusing anger.

✳

Unlike seventeenth-century Neostoics and modern anger-management therapists, contemporary philosopher Martha C. Nussbaum wishes to revive the more absolute stance of Seneca, with whose work she is closely connected as both commentator and translator.[20] Like Weyer, Nussbaum is worried about the violence of her times. She invokes Martin Luther King Jr and Nelson Mandela as her models, and the last words of her book are "Give peace a chance." She positions herself as a powerful voice against the current valorization of anger in public life. Accepting the prevalent association of anger with violence, Nussbaum extends the Stoic critique by arguing that the idea of revenge is absurd. Hurting the perpetrator of an injury does not—never can—right the wrong. "Payback"—as she terms it—rests on magical thinking: it postulates a "cosmic balance" that does not exist and that leads to consequences worse than the original offense.

Nussbaum admits that anger may have some minor uses. But even in those few cases, she asks that we transform anger into a more productive emotion. She speaks of making an emotional Transition, with a capital T. The right Transition is never "forgiveness." In its unforgiving "score keeping," forgiveness debases the very person it purports to absolve and thus is itself a form of payback.

Dividing life's domains into three "realms of human interaction," Nussbaum looks at the contexts of our anger and the various Transitions that they require. Her first realm is intimate: relations among loved ones.[21] Let me try to apply her solution to my own family. Rather than falling into what Nussbaum calls the "trap of anger," my parents should have stopped their arguing, recognized their mutual failures, and taken "constructive forward-looking action."[22] My mother hated housework; my father earned a meager salary. Making a Transition, my mother's anger should have turned into the self-confidence she needed to get a job. My father's anger should have converted into compassion for my mother's predicament and a new notion of masculinity that allowed his wife to work. That their lives were trapped in the emotionology of the 1950s would mean little to Nussbaum. She does not think in terms of emotional communities, as I do, with values and practices that are of a piece with the larger way of life of a group. She considers us masters of our selves, wants us to see the uselessness of our own personal anger, and asks us to make the necessary Transition.

Nussbaum's so-called Middle Realm comes closest to Seneca's world. It involves the confrontations that we have with casual acquaintances and salespeople, with vengeful employers and unscrupulous doctors, with robbers, rapists, and murderers. Here she finds the Stoics to be largely correct: most of these encounters are not worth our spleen. But a few of them are, particularly those that involve our health and safety. If Seneca's wise woman were confronted by a honking driver, she would not assent even to the first shock. But Nussbaum's wise woman would concede to "carefully limited Transition-Anger." She would declare that such honking is "outrageous," and if it endangered her (perhaps by causing an accident) she would call the police.

Finally, Nussbaum turns to the Political Realm. The legal system is (at least ideally) Nussbaum's equivalent to Seneca's wise person. She admits that today the institutions of justice all too often act as if crimes were insults that must be avenged. She wants the law to make its own Transition, punishing crimes not out of retribution but, as Seneca would say, out of reason and compassion.[23] Under such conditions, the wise woman subjected to the annoying honk and ensuing traffic accident would call the police, check into a hospital, and get on with her life. Nussbaum argues that Medea's revenge was not only wicked but also foolish. It did nothing to help her "escape from the actual predicament of having no spouse, no love, no conversation, no money, and no children."[24] She should have mourned her losses and moved on.

In all of these realms, Nussbaum calls for a generosity of spirit that taps into "significant strands or counter-strands of Christianity, Hinduism, and traditional African religion, as well as the entirety of Buddhism"—in other words, she asks us to join the emotional communities that reject anger (almost) absolutely.

✳

The ancient theory of Stoicism made a significant comeback in the Early Modern period. As bitter warfare raged across Europe, men and women confronted the ravages of angry vengeance—or so they imagined. Their solution was not precisely Seneca's; rather than avoid anger, they hoped to tamp it down or even possibly turn it into an ally of moral thought and action. Did anger and violence have to go together? Perhaps not: mitigating anger's fury was the Neostoic objective. That charge spilled into Protestant religious thought and found its way, over centuries, into modern anger-management therapies and Nussbaum's many Transitions. At the same time, the gendering of anger and violence—making both the province of women—was countered by a new feminist literature that, like Seneca, separated the harshness animated by justice from the madness born of fury.

# 4

# PEACEABLE KINGDOMS

Nussbaum's Neostoicism unquestioningly connected violence with anger, for revenge occasioned by anger is precisely the impulse that she asks us to transcend. In her view, the antidote to anger is peace. The association of violence with anger, by now ingrained and habitual in the minds of many, does not, however, well represent reality on the ground. Even Nussbaum's "peace" involves the violence or potential violence of the state—the police force and the judicial apparatuses that will (humanely, she hopes) apply the law. Coming at the matter from another direction, legal anthropologists talk about the "peace in the feud": the very threat of violence, they argue, is what allows peace to be maintained. But that sort of peace is not necessarily anger-free.

Anger, violence, and peace are all constructed and contestable terms. We have been exploring anger for three chapters, yet we still hardly know what it is or has been. Violence is equally problematic. Normally we think of physical violence, but there are other sorts: the mental violence of the Facebook bully, the hurtful words of a friend turned enemy, the systemic violence of poverty, the threatened force of the state. Peace is the most ambiguous and relative of all these terms. If family members are not on speaking terms, are they nevertheless "at peace"? Is the United States at peace or at war in Afghanistan? Is the soul of the convicted murderer at peace while he waits for execution on death row? Are the "peacekeepers" in the Sudan keeping the peace, and what sort of peace is it?

We must look more closely at the chains that seem to bind together anger and violence and, as if their mirror image, lack of anger and peace. An obvious place to begin is heaven—the archetype of the Peaceable Kingdom. Indeed, as Saint Augustine put it, heaven is peace. Does that mean that there is no anger in heaven? No violence? Not necessarily. Almost inadvertently, some descriptions of paradise reveal the presence of anger. An example is the vision of the seventh-century monk Barontus, who saw an angry Saint Peter in heaven. As Barontus recounted it, he was lying on what he thought was his death-bed. Demons came for his soul, barely held off by the angel Raphael, who flew his soul up to heaven with the demons trailing behind. They presented their case to Peter, recounting Barontus' many sins. The saint countered with the monk's virtues. The demons persisted. At last, Peter grew furious and told them to leave. When they refused, he tried to hit them with his keys.[1] (For an eleventh-century illustration of a similar narrative, see Plate 3.) Dante's Paradise, too, featured an angry Saint Peter, red with fury at the popes who usurped his role. "Rapacious wolves, in shepherd's garb," he called them.[2]

So heavenly peace might involve both anger and violence. Those were not the barriers to peace on earth; human sinfulness was the barrier. That had been Augustine's point. What would the world look like with better people? Visions of heaven were one imaginative solution. Fantasies of utopias were as well. Yet their authors rarely mentioned any of the terms of this chapter.

The pursuit of peaceable kingdoms apart from heaven was, it seems, a product of the late nineteenth century. It came in the wake of the creation of the academic discipline of anthropology, which proposed to study the laws of Western society by looking first at cultures "simpler" and "more primitive," as if they presented the ideal conditions of a science lab. The search for the "secrets" of peaceful cultures began in the early twentieth century but became decidedly more popular after World War II, when the G.I. Bill in the United States made it possible for returning veterans to get a college education. For the first time, universities filled with students who were not part of the American elites. In the mid-fifties, with the launching of the Russian spacecraft Sputnik, there was another push to educate talent from all parts of the United States. Some of those students, a nouveau-elite, became anthropologists, looking for answers to their own identity and society by studying other cultures. By the 1970s, they thought they had found a key to war and peace: foraging societies were "egalitarian, generally peaceable," while hunter cultures were "patriarchal [and] generally warlike."[3]

These generalizations did not bring anger into the equation. That variable was first introduced in the work of Robert Knox Dentan who, in turn, attributed his observations about anger to the self-insight of the people whom he studied: the Semai of the Malayan Peninsula. The Semai told Dentan, "We do not get angry" and "We do not hit," and they connected those two assertions, as if anger were the only source of hitting, and lack of anger the reason for their own non-violence and peacefulness.[4] And indeed, this seems generally to have been the case.

The Semai knew all about violence. Brutalized, kidnapped, and enslaved by nonaboriginal Malays as abetted by the British colonial regime that gradually dominated the peninsula from the eighteenth century until the 1950s, the Semai learned to defend themselves with guerrilla tactics, and, above all, by slipping away. Fleeing to the hills, where the land was mostly worthless and pursuit by their enemies relatively fruitless, they elaborated a world view and way of life that made violence moot precisely because they avoided getting angry.

How does the Semai way of life stave off occasions for anger and violence? (I will discuss them here in the present tense, but currently the conditions of their lives are rapidly changing.) Semai try not to turn down requests for food, sex, and other desirable things. They do not make promises they cannot keep. They cooperate, yet avoid interfering with others, respecting their autonomy. They are egalitarian. They share. If a delicious food is only seasonally available, they wait for the season, then apportion it. People do not say "thank you" when they receive the fruit; it is their due.

Behind this extraordinary amiability, this extreme generosity, lies the certainty that if people's desires are not met, terrible harm, injury, and even death may result. In Semai tradition an injury is met not by anger but by the certainty that god will reinforce the harm. In the terms of our modern, Western example of an anger scenario: in Semai culture, when the driver behind us honks, we don't get angry. Rather, god makes us crash our car, and the driver who honked is responsible. He will have to pay a fine or make up the damage somehow, and he too will meet with some disaster. Of course, there are no cars in Semai culture, so the example is absurd. A more pertinent instance would be if a Semai were denied some of the seasonal fruit. She might die, and those who had not shared the fruit would be responsible, liable to a penalty, and subject to unforeseen calamity.

The Semai god is the opposite of loving; it is ugly, cruel, and willful, delighting in havoc. The Semai see god in the terrible thunderstorms that ravage their hills and valleys: lightning crashes, thunder roars, rain pours down in sheets. Mothers use the occasion to teach their children the right response: "Fear! Fear!"

Given the dangers that lurk in the cosmos and that may unleash calamity upon each frustrated desire and every dashed expectation, people try to curb their passions. They do not directly ask for anything; they are vague about anticipated obligations; they hide their desires. They rarely show any emotion at all. "Emotional outbursts virtually never occur: husbands and wives seldom quarrel, neighbors do not argue, children seldom fight [. . .] mourning is subdued, even laughter is restrained."[5]

It would seem, then, that the Semai link anger, violence, and peace. By showing no anger—indeed having no anger and no occasion for it—they signal their non-violence and peacefulness. But this is not the whole story. For Semai have a word for anger, *lesnees*, and on occasion they will get angry; this is especially true of children and rejected lovers. Moreover, they sometimes quarrel, and they have informal but well-known mechanisms for dispute resolution. A headman may act as a mediator, though the disputants are ultimately free to ignore his decision. Town meetings may be called; there the disputants and their supporting kin-folk present their sides—without, however, expressing "anger or other emotion"—and everyone present has his or her say. This may take days. Then the headman "gives voice to the group's consensus."[6] The "wrong" party pays a fine, but the fine is later returned to him or her fully or in part, as a gift. Thereafter, both sides are reintegrated into the community. This doesn't always happen, but generally it does. In addition, the Semai can also kill, but not out of anger: when they were recruited into the Malay army, they killed as if in a trance.[7] If we agree that killing is a form of violence, then Semai are on occasion violent *without* getting angry and also without losing their various social strategies to keep the peace. Thus, the Semai are usually peaceful, and usually not angry, but they are not invariably so. The fact that they can kill without accounting themselves angry should remind us of the Buddha/captain who kills the robber aboard his ship. Anger is not the only cause (or excuse) for violence.

What of other normally peaceful societies? (I leave aside the possible argument that even our own society is normally peaceful, though I think it is true, if by that we mean that we are more often sociable and cooperative than not.) Jean Briggs famously called her study of the Utkuhikhalik Eskimos (Utku for short) *Never in Anger*.[8] She chronicled a people that, like the Semai, seldom get angry. The Utku consider anger a childish emotion, one that is normally outgrown. Living in fear of it and avoiding situations that might give it rise, they consider anger a kind of unhappiness. Indeed, one of their words for anger, *urulu*, literally means "unsmiling." Children are taught to deny that they feel *urulu*, and people call others *urulujuq* to express their disapproval of their nasty temper. The corollary is that happiness is highly valued. People smile, laugh, joke, and giggle; their good humor signals that they are not angry. Laughter is often the way that the Utku deal with anger and moral censure, denying both by finding annoying things funny. Joking signals happiness rather than anger, and people who jest a lot are not frightening.

On the other hand, as with the Semai, the Utku censure undue laughter: feelings, they say, should be under the control of reason. As children grow up, they learn to restrain their emotional performances, becoming shy and subdued. Adults are boundlessly affectionate towards babies, but towards older children and one another they avoid "excessive" love, which, they say, is both painful to the lover (who feels lonely away from the beloved) and intrusive to the beloved.

The Utku, like the Semai, have informal social practices meant to make anger moot. If they want something, they generally hint at it obliquely rather than asking for it outright, so as not to risk a confrontation. Likewise, if they have something others want, they often offer it without being asked. They are ever vigilant not to refuse a request.

Again like the Semai, the Utku link anger with violence. They have a saying: "a man who *never* lost his temper could kill if he ever did become angry." It seemed to Briggs that people were especially careful not to annoy the one man in the village who seemed to be struggling to control his "inner intensity."[9] But "it was partly his very atypicality that made it possible for me to learn from him what the proper patterns are."[10] Those patterns include showing mildness and making the gentlest of demands on others. Nevertheless, that does not mean that the Utku are never violent. They beat their dogs, calling it a "disciplinary action." While they are genial with kin, with others they show their resentments, albeit "subtly expressed and often strongly denied." They engage in hostile gossip behind the backs of those they dislike.[11]

Anthropologists constantly cite the Semai and Utku as examples of anger-free communities, but these are not the only groups that practice "non-anger." Very similar practices have been chronicled for the Fore of New Guinea, for example. Much like the Semai and Utku, the Fore shared "food, affection, work, trust, and pleasure." When, in a famous experiment by Paul Ekman, they were shown photographs representing Western facial expressions of emotions, they frequently "misinterpreted" what they saw, identifying anger in faces that were supposed to show sadness and fear. Anthropologist E. Richard Sorenson, who observed and criticized Ekman's experiments, commented that "anger, even incipient anger, was a serious matter, something to be forestalled," for it threatened the group cooperation that was essential to the Fore way of life. Studying Fore children, Sorenson remarked on the way parents deferred to them and their needs, so that the children were never frustrated and did not have reason to nurture resentments. Thus "anger, squabbling, and fighting did not become natural to their lives." If they expressed anger, it was short-lived. If one Fore "bothered" another, it was laughed off as amusing. If a Fore family was troubled by a neighbor, it moved elsewhere.[12] And yet, even as Sorenson was writing, he noted that the Fore were engaging in raids and murderous retaliation and observed that the forces of the Australian state had to move in to preserve order.

"We don't get angry." Why not? Because the Semai, Utku, and Fore, among others, have social practices that mitigate anger's sway: giving when asked, not asking for much, laughing, not hitting. The Semai tell their children to be fearful. The Utku tell them to be cheerful. The Fore avoid frustrating them. These are generally peaceful societies. But even so, they have words for anger, know people who flare up on occasion, and sometimes behave violently even when they are not angry. The "take-away" from anthropological "peaceable kingdoms" (which, of course, are not kingdoms at all!) is that the Buddha's "abandon anger" and Seneca's "avoid anger" are on the whole possible, given certain community practices of trust and sharing. There is, therefore, no good reason why only non-Western societies can end anger's dominion. Indeed, the pioneering book on anger's emotionology by the Stearnses concludes that "the goal of restraining anger [. . .] forms an important part of the American character ideal."[13]

✳

But the absence of anger will not end violence. This point is perhaps most clearly made not by looking at various peaceable kingdoms but rather at real dystopias. Consider Auschwitz, the Nazi concentration camp to which the young Italian chemist Primo Levi was sent in 1944. The current interdisciplinary consensus is that anger is triggered by frustration, threats, insult, a sense of injustice and, in general, "goal blockage."[14] But at Auschwitz, where all of these triggers existed—and much worse—the prisoners evinced anger only very rarely. That, at least, is what emerges from the account that Levi wrote of his experiences. Clearly, he understood Auschwitz through the lenses provided by his own emotional community, that of the Italian Jewish intelligentsia. In that sense, Levi's Auschwitz is his individual "vision." Yet this sort of objection will be true of any account. Acknowledging that fact, let us nevertheless use Levi's report to explore the place of anger, emotions, and violence at Auschwitz.

While we may speak of Semai communities and Utku communities, we cannot speak of a community at Auschwitz. The inmates were ever-shifting, and outsiders determined residences and work patterns. Yet, like the Semai and Utku, people at Auschwitz apparently felt and expressed very little anger. In this desolate hell—where prisoners were from the start separated by languages; where every day some died and new ones arrived; where nearly forty separate camps housed different groups variously treated (Jewish men were in one set of barracks, political prisoners in others, women were housed at nearby Birkenau); where deprivations and hardships were unimaginably extreme—the very foundations of what makes a person human were lost. People were numb and in pain. "Everything is nothing down here, except the hunger within and the cold and the rain all around."[15]

That must help explain why, even though all the mechanisms of eliminating anger among the Semai and Utku were lacking, flashes of anger were rare at Auschwitz. Consider that nothing was more common than turning down requests. Each prisoner jealously hoarded his own bit of bread, his spoon, his bowl, his thin shirt and wooden shoes. Stealing was rampant, and each man had to be wary of his neighbor. There was some sharing, but only between one friend (usually a fellow countryman) and another; for the rest, Levi, like everyone else, would not—and could not—heed cries from others for food or warmth. When, at the end of the war, the Germans fled the camp and no more food was to be had from the kitchen, Levi and a few others in his small infirmary room (he had scarlet fever at the time) managed to scavenge supplies from the quarters of the SS. The dysentery patients in an adjoining room howled for some of the food, and Levi once brought over some soup, but they never stopped pleading thereafter. "I could bring them no relief. I felt close to tears, I could have cursed them."[16] Here we see a glint of anger—at his inability to live up to his ideal of generosity, and at their reminding him of the fact.

Precisely unlike an egalitarian society, Auschwitz thrived on hierarchy, with the SS at the top, guards next, and variously privileged prisoners lording it over the others. "All are our enemies or our rivals."[17] When Levi was a newcomer at the camp, he was put to work carrying heavy cargo from the railway to the warehouse. Two prisoners had the plum job of loading down the others, and, to keep that perquisite, they worked at breakneck pace. "This fills me with anger, although I already know that it is in the normal order of things for the privileged to oppress the unprivileged."[18] Here again is anger—fellow prisoners should identify with the imprisoned, not the masters. But note that this rare glimmer came only at the start of Levi's internment.

Even those in power did not often seem to feel or express anger. "How can one strike a man without anger?" Levi asked himself (and his readers) when he received his first blows from German guards.[19] When an officer from the SS entered his infirmary barrack to decide who would die and who would live that evening, neither the officers nor the condemned betrayed any feelings: "In this discreet and sedate manner, without display or anger, massacre moves through the wards of [the infirmary] every day, touching one man or another."[20] When the Kapos—the imprisoned criminals utilized to guard the others—beat their charges, some did so "from pure bestiality and violence, but others beat us almost lovingly [. . .] as cart drivers do with willing horses."[21]

At Auschwitz there were almost no emotions whatsoever. For the prisoners, there was sometimes fear, but more often they felt nothing at all, shuffling through the motions of their lives in a "dull torpor."[22] Laughter, which defused and countered anger in the peaceful societies studied by anthropologists, was impossible. Lack of feelings—or, at least, the inability or unwillingness to recognize and express feelings—is itself part of emotional life. It seems to have been yet another horrific aspect of the concentration camp.

Nevertheless, one emotion was expressed and felt everywhere, always, and by all at Auschwitz. It was hatred, however dulled at times by routine and sheer familiarity. The prisoners built a tower in the center of the complex: "Its bricks [. . .] were cemented by hate, hate and discord, like the Tower of Babel [. . .] and we hate it as our masters' insane dream of grandeur, their contempt for God and men, for us men."[23] And the masters, too, hated. The most hated and full of hate were the "Jewish Prominent." These Jews, given positions of power over the other Jews, were "monsters of asociality and insensitivity"; their "capacity for hatred, which remains unfulfilled toward the oppressors, will spill over, unreasonably, onto the oppressed."[24] As for the Germans: at first, they seemed not to hate per se but rather to say to themselves, "This something in front of me [in this instance, Levi himself] belongs to a species that it is obviously right to suppress," in much the same way as many of us squash a cockroach without feeling any rancor toward it.[25] But as the war came to an end, Levi observed, "the German civilians raged with the fury of the secure man who wakes from a long dream of domination, and sees his ruin and is unable to understand it." They had lived in a bubble of absolute power and could not make sense of their new and inglorious circumstances. In general, the Germans, "felt in the hour of danger the ties of blood and soil. This new fact reduced the tangle of hatreds and incomprehensions to their elementary terms."[26]

It is instructive to compare Levi's Auschwitz to the Gulag camps chronicled by Varlam Shalamov (d.1982) in his lightly fictionalized *Kolyma Stories*.[27] Here again we are dealing with but one man's experiences and observations, in this case the son of a priest hounded by the Communists for both his social origins and political beliefs. In 1937, Shalamov was sentenced to Kolyma, the largest and most grim of Stalin's forced-labor camps. After a brief respite he was sent back again until his final release in 1951. Set up in the Arctic to mine gold and other metals, Kolyma was not an extermination camp like Auschwitz. Nevertheless, hundreds of thousands of prisoners (and perhaps more) died there from malnutrition, cold, disease, and the effects of relentless hard labor.

In a fragmentary list of "What I Saw and Understood in the Camps" written in 1961, Shalamov reported that "I realized that the feeling a man preserves longest is anger. There is only enough flesh on a hungry man for anger: everything else leaves him indifferent." There followed two contradictory observations: "I realized that one can live on anger [. . .] I realized that one can live on indifference." There is an example of how the two worked together in Shalamov's tale of a prisoner named Andreyev. He was indifferent: after suffering eighteen months of forced labor in the gold mines, he had lost both all fear and, equally, all love of life. Anger alone remained: "there was nothing except anger in his soul."[28]

However, very little of the violence at Kolyma was driven by anger. It is true that a supervisor calling out the name of a prisoner who didn't reply "angrily chucked the thin yellow file of the prisoner's 'case' on the barrel and crushed it with his foot." But serious violence came from "the passion for power, to be able to kill at will." This was the prerogative of everyone at the top—"the [camp] chief and the supervisors subordinate to him; the chief guard with his detachment of fighting men serving as escort guards" and so on. Yet most of these officers, crude and rough though they were, did not kill. The people who routinely murdered were the gangsters: prisoners who hustled, bribed, intimidated, got ahead, and received privileges. These were Kolyma's equivalent of the "Jewish Prominent" at Auschwitz. In one of the camps for women, Shitsel, a doctor, "was hacked to death with an ax by her own nurse, the criminal convict Kroshka." At one of the men's camps an unlucky prisoner named Garkunov was stabbed to death by a gangster because he refused to give up his beloved woolen sweater. Shalamov summed it up: "The evil acts committed by the thieves in the camps are beyond counting."[29]

Indifference, the lack of all feeling altogether, was the norm. One felt absolutely nothing, a numbness, a "dulling of the spirit," a "cold lack of sympathy." Indeed, cold pervaded everything. Forced to labor all day outdoors wearing thin jackets and rubber shoes (no socks), the prisoners' toes became "lifeless and stiff," and during the night, their "hair froze to the pillow." The relentless artic winters made their brain cells "wither," wrote Shalamov, and caused their very souls to "shrink." The men could no longer taste food; eating now meant only a momentary obliviousness from a warm (but never full) stomach. Reality "was the minute, the hour, the day from reveille to the order to stop work." When a prisoner named Dugayev couldn't fulfill his work quota and was led off to be killed, his only thought was to regret that he had "wasted his time working and suffering all this day."[30]

Friendships were impossible: none "could arise between hungry, cold, and sleepless men." The only thing common to all the men in the camps was "mistrust, anger, and lies." Stealing from one another was "the main virtue in the north." When one man got supplies from home, the others in his barracks knocked him out and stole everything. When the poor fellow awoke, everyone looked at him with "spiteful pleasure."[31]

It is true that amid the indifference and cruelty were flashes of decency. A carpenter allowed two men who knew nothing about carpentry to pretend that his own hand-made ax handles were theirs so that they could warm themselves by the shop's fire for a couple of days. Some prisoners shared their cigarettes, or at least their cigarette stubs. A doctor said a kind word to a patient. Needless to say, none of this was normative, none the basis for a "peaceable kingdom."[32]

There was plenty of violence at Auschwitz and Kolyma, and certainly Shalamov reported plenty of anger. But anger was rarely the cause of violence in either place. This is important because in the modern Western mind, anger, violence, and aggression are persistently associated, almost a "knee-jerk reaction." That association helps to explain why a recent *New York Times* article on the aftermath of an attack on African immigrants in Italy was headlined "Italy's Populists Turn Up the Heat as Anti-Migrant Anger Boils."[33] Attributing anti-migrant violence to anger is the logical consequence of a largely unquestioned assumption. Why not attribute anti-migrant violence to fear or disgust or hatred, or to ideologies of purity and racism?

Certainly, much of the violence in the dystopias we have been looking at derived from causes other than anger. There was, first, the fact of unequal rank; the men "on top" were in positions of power that demanded (at least in their culture) a good deal of violence, whether due to notions of masculinity, mastery, or ideology. At Auschwitz there was, in addition, hatred of the Jews, a cultural artifact that lay quasi-dormant for years, only to spring to life again when encouraged by the emotional community in power. We see a similar phenomenon in the United States today, when Donald Trump and his allies stoke anti-black and anti-immigrant sentiments that long flourished within certain American emotional communities.

Both anger and violence are attractive to many people. So is peace. But the connections among these elements are problematic. Our definitions of all these terms are shifting and discordant, and different emotional communities put them together in a variety of ways. Visions of heavenly peace may involve an angry and violent Saint Peter, while earthly hells like Auschwitz and Kolyma may be utterly violent, yet rarely because of anger. Peace is not the opposite of anger, and violence is not necessarily anger's outcome. But why, then, is anger so often linked to violence? Perhaps it is because anger is regularly understood to be an irrational force, uncontrollable and destructive once it is unleashed. Behind angry gestures, postures, and words lies the threat of mayhem.

# 5

## ANGRY WORDS

One form of violence is verbal, and here too anger is often implicated. Words do things, and sometimes they hurt. The philosopher John L. Austin coined the word "performative" to describe words that do not simply describe but also transform. "I pronounce you man and wife (or, today, spouse and spouse)," said by an appropriate person in the right setting, transforms two separate people into something new: a married couple.

Emotion words are performative, and this is certainly true in the case of anger. When we say "I am angry" aloud, or when the tone of our voice is angry, we are performing our anger, as if in a play. And, as in a play, the other characters in the drama react. They change, becoming angry themselves or apologetic or hurt or puzzled. Moreover—and this is probably true only of emotion words—we ourselves change when we make an angry utterance. The officiant who pronounces that two people are married does not change with those words. But William M. Reddy argues that emotion words always transform both their object and the person saying them. He calls emotional utterances "emotives" to emphasize the two different directions of their effect: they perform not only on others but also on those who use them.[1] Perhaps saying "I am angry," or acting it out somehow, reinforces our feeling; perhaps it makes us think better of it; perhaps it changes or adds to our original feeling.

Angry words are particularly hurtful. In the Bible we read, "The stroke of the tongue breaketh bones" (Eccles. 28:17; Ps. 57:4). Ancient Egyptian advice literature, directed to courtiers and other men of affairs, was sensitive to the harm angry words might cause: "Don't start a quarrel with a hot mouthed man [. . .] Sleep on it before speaking," and beware the speech of "one who is angered"; beware the "heated man."[2] We have already seen that in ancient Rome, Cicero told his brother to bite his tongue.

Today many commentators declare that we live in a world uncommonly full of angry words. "What resonates most in Donald Trump's America is the way that empty, stupid boasting devolves into paranoid rage," says a *New Yorker* critic.[3] It is hard to know for sure if the age of the internet is unusual in this respect. Google's Ngram Viewer shows a marked increase in the use of the words "anger" and "angry" in printed books since about 1970. But a dip beginning around 1995 suggests that both words are now losing their cachet. In any event, trends like these are not very good measures of angry words, since angry utterances most often come in the shape of curses, gestures, accusations, and irate tones of voice.

Ancient Roman legal rules and practices provide one way to gauge attitudes toward angry words in the past. The Roman legal system depended on private accusations; there were no public prosecutors to bring cases. But if someone brought an accusation in anger, was he guilty of defamation, that is, of damaging the reputation of the other person because he was angry? In such cases, should the accuser be punished? The *Digest* of Justinian (published in 533) said no, for "unrestrained anger lacks the vice of calumny [i.e. defamation]" and may be pardoned.[4] But the *Theodosian Code* (issued in 438) included a law promulgated at Rome that abolished an accuser's right to bring a charge orally, for, as the law's interpreters explained, verbal accusations were often made in anger, and that was unacceptable. Instead, henceforth, "the accuser shall state in writing that he will prove what he said in anger." Even better, added the jurists, let the accuser "come to his senses" and drop the case entirely.[5] Clearly, these jurists belonged to an emotional community that distrusted anger and considered the angry person not fully responsible for what he said. From that same community came the opinion that when a man divorced his wife "in the heat of anger," the divorce was invalid.[6]

Yet at the same time, some legal interpreters argued that the anger of a *judge* was appropriate and justified; it was, indeed, an adjunct to his (there were no women judges in ancient Rome) authority. Perfectly legitimate, for example, was the anger that an accuser aroused in a judge by "the dishonesty of the words or the character of the matter" in court.[7] Indeed, accusers with malicious intent were to be punished immediately when they rightly stirred "the minds of the Emperors to anger by bringing false charges against some innocent person."[8]

In short, angry, malicious words could rightly rile up judges but nevertheless disqualify accusers. And it could also—paradoxically—excuse the accuser. There were, it seems, two contradictory but co-existing attitudes toward anger at Rome around the same time: one looked to anger to energize a judgment, the other considered it a form of temporary insanity.

In the Middle Ages, these two attitudes were joined by a third. An influential group of thinkers considered anger not a form of madness nor an adjunct to justice but rather a sin, and thus utterly condemnable. These thinkers, clerics all, dominate the sources available to us. Yet the very frequency of their censure suggests that cursing, swearing, and insulting were habitual among ordinary people.

Thus, in his popular manual from the early fourteenth century devoted to "handling sin," English cleric Robert Mannyng took the opportunity in one poem to warn parents not to curse their children for their little faults or beware the horrible consequences. Consider, he said, the instance of a mother who cursed her child. Having told her daughter to guard her clothes while she was bathing, she was incensed when, ready to get dressed, the little girl did not come immediately at her call. Mannyng warned: "the mother who sat in her bath / waxed full of ire and of wrath." She cursed the poor child bitterly and said, "the Devil come on thee, / for thou art not ready for me." The Devil heard and promptly possessed the child, never to be expelled.[9]

Mannyng was building on a tradition only about a century old. In the thirteenth century the theologian William Peraldus created a new category of sins: those of the tongue. He delineated twenty-four such sins, and cursing was one of them. Even people who avoided all the other vices fell victim to the oral sins, Peraldus said, as if the tongue were an independent and particularly willful creature. Certainly, the mouth was the gateway into and out of the body, letting in healthy (or poisonous) food, letting out (via the tongue) good (or noxious) words. The tongue's proper job was "to pray, to praise God, to receive Christ's body and blood, and to proffer holy words." But it often failed in its duties. Blasphemy—speech uttered to insult God—was the first and worst of its verbal sins. The typical example of the blasphemer was the "angry person who, wanting to take revenge against God, names some part of His body that should not be named."[10] Peraldus was referring to the practice of cursing or swearing by God's limbs—"by God's arms," "by Christ's foot." In the next few centuries, tales and paintings of the torments inflicted on Christ through such blasphemies multiplied, since swearing by Christ's foot was said to amputate it! Curses like these demanded an appropriately terrible punishment. As one late medieval poem put it: "By God's body I swore ever in ire, / Therefore I am scalded and burn in fire." Hell awaited the blasphemer.[11]

Insults and quarrels, too, were sins born of anger. Here Peraldus focused particularly on women, whom he accused of never-ending blather. They were forever arguing, like "the constant dripping of a leaky roof," an image found in Proverbs 19:13. The unhappy husband of a wife like that will "never have any peace." A life of poverty would be better. Peraldus was the medieval backdrop to the nagging wives of the later Neostoics.

Peraldus' treatise was immensely popular and inspired a small mountain of moral literature on verbal sins across Europe. In the Netherlands, one treatise outlined ten such sins; another named fourteen. While anger was not the cause of all the sins of speech, it was always to blame for cursing, swearing, raging, and arguing. (For anger's sharp tongue and fiendish progeny, see Plate 4.) These ideas became part of the catechism of the Church and normal pastoral care: the sins of the tongue were denounced by preachers and formed a large portion of the subject matter addressed by confessors. (Since the Fourth Lateran Council of 1215, the faithful were obliged to confess their sins at least once a year.) With the widespread rise of literacy in many parts of Europe, some pastoral works were composed in the vernacular, providing suitable reading materials for lay households and religious communities. Soon, spread orally and via popular dramas, sculpture, stained glass, wall paintings, and other media, even the unlettered knew about the sins of the tongue. The idea continued to be popular into the seventeenth century.

Having decided that insults, swearing, and quarreling were sinful and detrimental to the public peace, both Church and State claimed the right to prohibit or shape those practices. In England, ordinances were passed banning abusive speech. Local courts—both secular and ecclesiastical—heard defamation cases brought by plaintiffs who claimed that their reputations had been harmed. Nothing was more important than honor, nearly all agreed, and so defamation was a major source of contention and legal action.

But to pass muster before the courts, plaintiffs had to show that the person they were accusing of calumny had malicious intent. Thus, when John Greenhode called John Topcliff a parasite and a sluggard, Topcliff brought suit in a church court at York in 1381. He claimed that Greenhode had spoken "publicly, repeatedly, falsely, wickedly, and maliciously."[12] Malice is hard to prove, so courts had recourse to two basic strategies: they called witnesses to testify about intention, and they tried to ascertain whether the "calumnies" were in fact statements of truth.

An example is the suit brought by Thomas Robinson, again at York. Thomas declared that John Rayner had "falsely, evilly, maliciously, for the sake of hatred and gain" said in the presence of many others to Thomas, "You false side-glance [furtive] thief. Do you say that you have not beaten me?" The court asked in depositions whether witnesses knew of Thomas actually beating John and whether John had spoken in anger. Two witnesses testified to being present at the ruckus. They said that John had indeed spoken "violent words" with a "wrathful frown" on his face. And they claimed that Thomas had done nothing to provoke him.[13] Cases like this presumably were decided in favor of the plaintiff (Thomas, in this instance), though we cannot know for sure because the records do not tell us the verdict. In any event, it seems clear that there was a decided bias on the part of the judges at York against people who spoke in anger.

Nor did this bias change when, under Henry VIII, the English Church broke with Roman Catholicism to pursue its own course. Even with different personnel in charge and a somewhat different theology, the ecclesiastical court at York continued to probe whether there had been angry and malicious intent in cases of defamation. But now the records, which are much richer and more numerous, show that women constituted a majority of the plaintiffs and a near parity of defendants. While in other sorts of cases brought to court, women constituted only 28 per cent of the plaintiffs and 24 per cent of the defendants, in slander suits they made up 55 per cent and 41 per cent respectively.[14] Even the words in such cases were gendered: the word "scold"—a person of ribald or abusive speech—almost always referred to a woman.

According to some medical and moral theories of the time, women should not have been scolds at all. Women, said this school of thought, had less of the choleric humor than men. As Anglican churchman Richard Allestree (d.1681) wrote, "nature has befriended women with a more cool and temperate constitution, put less of fire, and consequently of choler, in their compositions." He considered women feeble by nature, unable to "assert their angers with any effective force." Clearly God did not intend them to get angry. And yet they did so, and they expressed their anger with their one "feminine weapon"—their "barking" tongues: however impotent it was in reality, their verbal rage terrified all who heard it. The remedy, said Allestree, was for women to turn their tongues against themselves and beware their "ill constitution of mind" and their propensity to say whatever came into their heads, both of which were stimulated by their native passions of envy, spleen, and revenge.[15] Yet, as we saw in Chapter 3, a different seventeenth-century physician, Helkiah Crooke, said that women's anger was exceptionally forceful. We can reconcile these two statements by noting that medical opinion was divided on the topic, but one way or the other, feminine anger was deplorable. Allestree simply emphasized women's wagging tongues more than Crooke did.

The words that were felt to harm and defame in the court cases were sexual innuendoes (which hurt women the most) and accusations of dishonesty (which damaged the reputation of men). Ever since the Council of Oxford, held in 1222, "all those who, for [. . .] whatever cause, maliciously impute a crime to any person who is not of ill fame among good and serious men," were to be excommunicated.[16] At York, anger was often proof of malice and the two were paired together.

The Oxford provision meant that if defamation harmed the plaintiffs, the imputation of anger and malice would wound those who made the insult in turn, since they would be excommunicated and often have to pay the fees of litigation as well. Sometimes the disgraced defamers had to march in public procession in penitential garb, shamed before the eyes of all. At Mass they were to beg pardon—in a loud voice so that everyone could hear them—of those whom they had slandered.

No wonder that many defendants denied speaking in anger. They insisted that their words were innocent, devoid of rancor. In 1704, when George Lotherington accused Robert Allen of adultery, he said it not out of malice but rather (he argued) to make a factual statement. Allen's servant had given birth to a child and had named Allen as the father. As Overseer of the Poor for the parish, Lotherington had to investigate bastardy; calling Allen an adulterer was simply doing his job. Witnesses in fact testified that Lotherington spoke to Allen "very civilly and without any anger or passion."[17] In other cases, defendants reframed their words as spoken in jest, not anger. And yet, as late as 1700, a learned treatise on Anglican Church law declared that even if the words spoken were not defamatory, still, if the plaintiff proved "that the words were reproachful, he shall obtain the victory. And then the Party uttering them is to be punished at the pleasure of the judge, [. . .] the reason [being] because these words were uttered out of a malicious and angry mind."[18]

Nevertheless, when it came to the courts, there was more than one emotional community in England at the same time. Not all judges considered anger an aggravating circumstance, evidence of guilty intent. To the contrary, for some anger was exculpatory, as if a person couldn't help himself. Royal courts considered homicide "in hot blood" less blameworthy than murder committed with malice aforethought.[19] Something similar seems to have been true even in certain church courts hearing cases of defamation. For example, at Chichester in 1507, John Fontans sued Sir John Clover for calling him "a proven thief," but Sir John declared that "in his rage, he called the party plaintiff a thief, and not otherwise." That is, he insulted John only because he was angry. And the reason that he was angry was that John had insulted him in turn.[20] The two men reached an agreement out of court. But it is clear that Sir John thought that unpremeditated anger was a good defense for his slander. Chichester is about as far south of York as one can go in England. There were regional differences, then, as well as differences in judicial training, that mattered in the conception, evaluation, and even the expression of anger. And some districts and judges recognized yet a third sort of anger, an appropriate kind, not only exculpatory but correct. We see it in 1442 at Hereford, where the defendant had to ask pardon publicly at the altar of the church at High Mass, when a crowd of faithful would surely be on hand, and where he had to profess "that he said the [slanderous] words out of ill will and not from virtuous zeal or anger." *Virtuous* anger would have helped to clear him.

The same assortment of attitudes was true in German-speaking lands as well. There, when people were hauled into court for uttering insults, they sometimes defended themselves by claiming that they had been drunk or had spoken "out of anger." At Augsburg, penalties were waived when insults were hurled out of "excessive drunkenness, sudden anger, or for other unintended reasons." In these cases, anger was assessed as an uncontrollable madness. But other municipal leaders disagreed; in their view anger was no defense at all, since it could voluntarily be kept in check. At Freiburg im Breisgau, the civic statute on defamation, with penalties for insult particularly in mind, concluded that "everyone will choose their words carefully and know how to keep their anger in check."[21] In still other instances, however, anger was considered proper— when, for example, it defended the honor of an individual or his or her family. Some civic codes even included the "right of retort." Historian Allyson Creasman has traced this dispensation back to the theories of medieval Italian glossators, who reasoned that, just as people were entitled to defend themselves against an assault on their person, so they might properly counter an insult to their honor with a verbal rejoinder.

✳

It may seem a great leap from early modern civic legislation to today. But some aspects of that period seem applicable even now. We tend to think that loose talk, internet shaming, the ubiquity of curse words in everyday speech, and increasing use of profanity in movies and on television, are peculiar to our own age. But Creasman points out that early modern German citizens thought the same to be the case for their own era. They lived cheek by jowl in crowded cities whose housing was insufficient for their burgeoning population. In such conditions, urbanites were acutely aware of the threats to public peace and amity posed by insults, "careless talk," and scabrous songs.[22] Today, city sprawl may be for some a greater threat to a sense of community than overcrowding, but our homes, connected electronically to the babble of the wider world, are in many ways like a crowded public forum, open to rumor, "fake news," shaming, and abusive talk.

The attitudes created and reinforced in earlier times remain with us today—not unchanged, to be sure, but rather as potential repertories of feeling that are drawn upon for a variety of purposes. While few now speak of anger as sinful, many do see angry words as a serious social and interpersonal issue, fraying the delicate fabric of common courtesy and fellowship. While anger and malice have dropped out of most cases of defamation (malice remains, but only in cases brought by public figures), nevertheless the two are still so commonly coupled that the *New York Times*, for example, calls Trump's insulting and self-aggrandizing tweets "angry": "Trump's Evolution from Relief to Fury over the Russia Indictment" is the headline characterizing Trump's tweets during February 17 and 18, 2018, with the reporter summing up the period as "a two-day Twitter tirade that was unusually angry and defiant by Mr. Trump's standards."[23] Our tendency to see anger behind insults and disparagements, and our implicit condemnation of angry motives, have, as we have seen, a long backstory.

Even Donald Trump generally avoids saying explicitly that he is angry, as if the very epithet were itself demeaning. The "Angry Black Woman" is an example of how the adjective has become a form of humiliation in the United States today. The phrase harks back to early modern prejudices about "scolding wives" as well as persistent stereotypes of women as emotional and men as rational. But now insult is added to injury by associating anger with women of color in particular. Vanessa E. Jones writes, "Stereotypes about black women have coursed through pop culture for centuries [. . .]. But the one getting a major workout these days is the angry black woman."[24] While some black women find the epithet funny or even empowering, Jones observes, others consider it hateful. Therapist Wendy Ashley argues that the Angry Black Woman image contributes to misdiagnoses and faulty treatments of black women in clinical settings. Affecting their self-esteem, the label is sometimes so overwhelming that the women "may suppress disclosures of anger and minimize its impact in their lives. [. . .] As a result, clients may feel unsafe in the treatment environment and [leave it] with feelings of helplessness, hopelessness, and self-hate."[25] They may actually become angry, though for Jones, *that* anger is a good sort, one stirred by social injustice, not the "overbearing" and "loud-mouthed" brand of anger portrayed by the stereotype.

The effect of such labels on the psyches of black women is the therapist's worry; some legal scholars have other concerns. The trope of the Angry Black Woman fuels aggressive behavior against black females, who are injured but have no "form of redress." Blame falls on the women, who find themselves cast in the role of "angry" simply because they are unwilling to compromise or back down on principles. While the complaints and protests of white women are sometimes considered virtuous, black women find themselves judged as "Angry. Out of control. Unreasonable. Temperamental. Threatening." Black professional women fear speaking up—indeed fear speaking at all—because they dread the rolling eyes of colleagues, who will view them as "troublemakers." In short (argue two law professors in the *Iowa Law Review*), "a black woman who pushes back against her marginalization gets transformed by society into the 'Angry Black Woman.'" And yet, if she does not push back, she feels "complicit in her own oppression." The stresses involved in being a black woman and contending with these contradictions lead to a modern version of hell: "emotional distress, depression, anxiety, nightmares, post-traumatic stress disorder, high blood pressure, diabetes, cancer, heart disease, and stroke."[26]

Black men, too, have not been spared the epithet "angry." Some turn it into a badge of courage.[27] But others find themselves coping with "the Angry Black Man image." That label has a very long pedigree. In 1747, for example, Benjamin Franklin, a "Founding Father" of the United States, argued that if Philadelphians did not arm themselves (which Franklin advocated) then, in case of a British attack, they would be better off surrendering to ships under royal command than into the hands of privateers, whom he characterized as "negroes, mulattoes, and others, the vilest and most abandoned of mankind," subject as they were to "unbridled rage." Today, however, the stereotype is applied to the "middle-class, educated African American male who, despite his economic and occupational successes, perceives racial discrimination everywhere [in his workplace] and consequently is always enraged."[28] Countering this stereotype calls for what sociologist Arlie Hochschild terms "emotional labor," in this case the labor involved in seeming unperturbed so as to counter the possible perception of resentment.[29]

In truth, most professionals today of whatever race are constrained not to show anger while on the job. The idea of emotional labor comes from Hochschild's observation that many jobs require people to display (and even to feel) certain emotions, whether cheerfulness (as in the case of airline stewardesses whose training she studied) or anger (as in the case of the debt collectors she also researched). At the Delta Airlines Stewardess Training Center women were given instructions on flight safety and service. In their very first class, they were admonished to smile—constantly and with real feeling. In a refresher course, they were confronted directly with the issue of anger and its deleterious effects: as their teacher explained, when you are angry, your heart beats faster, your breath gets shorter, your adrenaline spikes. Anger is bad for you. What, then, do you do with "irates"—airline company lingo for chronically hostile passengers? The Delta instructor told the women to reconsider their labels: is someone drunk? reframe her as a child; is someone cursing? imagine he is a trauma victim. By changing the descriptor—the word—the stewardess would change her response from anger to, say, sympathy.

As we have seen, when anger is decried, then calling someone angry is an insult. But sometimes the word serves as a "catch-all" term all too easily substituted for more subtle feelings—sorrow, hurt, amazement, pride. This was the insight of the flight-school instructor. It is telling that, although as a society we have become increasingly interested in "feelings"—our own and those of others—our emotional vocabulary has become progressively impoverished. Americans once used numerous anger words: passion, rage, indignation, fury, wrath, peevishness, and so on. Each term had a slightly different shade of meaning so that, for example, in 1758 people disputing with each other could be described as "warmly engaged in conversation."[30] Today, no matter how differently we may experience various forms of anger, we tend to fall back on one: "He's angry; I'm angry!"

As Lisa Feldman Barrett points out, naming emotions—whether as descriptors or as judgments—is crucial to how we understand our own feelings, for such words organize and chunk together a great variety of sensations. From my mother I learned that the feelings of pleasure and righteous indignation that assailed me as I hit my doll went together with shame, and all were embraced by the term anger. That understanding of the word is mine but probably not precisely yours. Further, over the years, other feelings have coalesced together with my initial, childish sense of anger, while other sensations have broken off, to be embraced by terms like fury, acrimony, and cruelty. Emotion words matter: they evoke whole scenarios of feeling, predict the responses of others, and take on new meanings as we experience their many resonances within and outside of our communities.

# PART 2

ANGER AS A VICE BUT ALSO (SOMETIMES) AS A VIRTUE

# 6

# ARISTOTLE AND HIS HEIRS

Part 1 looked at anger as a feeling on the whole to be avoided or, better yet, simply not felt. But there is a long contrary tradition: while seeing some forms of anger as vices, it asserts other kinds as positive virtues. Aristotle was the major pioneer of this tradition.

Aristotle said that anger is caused by a judgment—a belief. We get angry when we think that we have been slighted. The slight is felt as a type of pain that makes us angry. We are moved to act—to get back at the person who caused our pain. The pleasure we gain from revenge—indeed, just from contemplating it—undoes the pain of the original slight. This is a perfectly normal response, Aristotle said, and, in many cases, it is totally justifiable and even noble. Only foolish people never get angry; only irascible, self-indulgent people always get angry. The trick—the path to virtuous anger—is to get angry "at the right times, with reference to the right objects, towards the right people, with the right aim, and in the right way."[1]

But what are those "right times"? And don't they change as societies change? Well yes, circumstances are always slightly different, Aristotle would reply. But the general principles remain constant. If we are aiming at a goal and someone gets in the way—even if our goals are different today from any pursued in fourth-century BCE Greece, when Aristotle was alive—we will get angry at that person. In fact, we will get angry when someone simply belittles our ambitions, and we will become especially furious at a friend who is not supportive. We will always feel ire towards people who seem to feel contempt for us and be particularly indignant when those who are inferior to us slight us even so. We will feel angry when we are not treated as well as others in our position, as if we are less deserving. The particulars may change, but the situations— of status, of injustice—remain constant. It therefore matters rather little that Aristotle's formative years were spent in Athens, where men were keenly anxious to maintain their honor vis-à-vis one another. And only men. Women did not fit well into Aristotle's scheme because their emotions and their judgments (he thought) did not work together properly. We'll come back to this.

But first, I want to talk yet again about my family, for, although my parents were not consciously Aristotelians, they were pretty good ones all the same. Dolls were not appropriate objects of anger, in their view. But it was perfectly right and proper for my father to come home from work with his face flushed with anger at the outrages that his boss had inflicted on him. He was a social worker, and social service was then—as now—a profession dominated by women. He earned very little and saw others—women at his own agency—promoted ahead of him. His boss was a woman. Apart from the very real possibility that her gender added insult to injury in his mind, let us consider the greater slight: my father believed that she treated him less well than she did other, less qualified, employees. He found pleasure in his pain when he talked with my mother about what he might do to escape his situation. In that last endeavor—planning to get away—was he violating the Aristotelian model? Aristotle says explicitly that angry people want to hurt—not to avoid, nor (the other extreme) to eliminate—the person who has insulted them. "No one," he declares, "grows angry with a person on whom there is no prospect of taking vengeance."[2] But I do not think my father was violating this dictum. If he were to quit his job, his boss would know why, and she would be left with the unappetizing prospect of finding, interviewing, and hiring a replacement. It would make for a nasty little interruption in her complacent life. That was part of the escape fantasy.

Beliefs about unfair treatment, plans to get away (in fact my dad eventually did get a promotion), all of this seems quite "rational." Aristotle meant it to sound that way; it *was* rational. The very causes of emotions were judgments, perhaps incorrect judgments, but certainly reasonable ones. Before his time, most philosophers—insofar as they thought about emotions at all—said that feelings like anger were totally irrational, like diseases, curable only through magical incantations or drugs. After Aristotle's time, as we have seen with Seneca, many philosophers agreed with the Stoics, considering emotions to be caused by wrong judgments and thus to be rejected entirely. In between those two views was Aristotle and, to some extent, his teacher Plato. In some of his works, Plato suggested that reason and emotions went together. But he didn't say how. Aristotle explained how.

To do so, Aristotle theorized the nature of the soul in a new way. For Plato, the soul (or mind) had three parts—reason, spirit, appetite. If properly directed, reason aimed at discerning the true forms of reality, which were far different from the false appearances of ordinary things. These forms were Plato's obsession. Aristotle, however, had a different focus. He was interested in the things of this world—both natural and man-made—and the logical tools necessary to understand them. Plants have a simple, nutritive soul. Animals have a bipartite soul, both nutritive and sensitive. Human beings have a tripartite soul: nutritive, sensitive, and intellective. The intellective has two parts in turn—one logical and the other alogical. In full-grown men the alogical part listens to and obeys the logical. When the logical faculty thinks, "I have been slighted by someone who has no right to do so," the alogical part feels angry. Then, once the alogical part gets angry, it affects the judgments of the logical part. In this way, the two work together.

According to Aristotle, the logical faculty of children is not fully developed, so they must be guided by adults to feel properly, at the right times, and regarding the right objects. Those feelings become habitual. As children grow up, they reinforce the habits instilled in them by their teachers with their own reasoned judgments. Women, all of whom are defective males (in Aristotle's view), have both logical and alogical faculties, but their reason does not have the sway that it ought to have over their emotions, and so they must be guided by the superior rationality of a man.

Of course, rationality is not always noble or excellent. Anger may be virtuous, but it may also be vicious. Returning to my father, it seems fair to say that his anger satisfied all the criteria: he felt it at the right time, when he was passed over for a promotion in favor of someone less able. He chose the right object: a higher salary, a more prestigious position. He felt angry toward the right person: his boss. He felt it in the right way, by considering what he might do to get back at his boss. Even so, Aristotle might argue that my father felt anger less than virtuously because (at least as I recall it) he came home almost *every* night with the same complaints and the same feelings. Aristotle says that virtue is the state that is "intermediate" between too much and too little. The person who practices the *virtue* of anger is "good tempered." He "tends to be unperturbed." He does *not* always follow reason! Rather he errs "in the direction of deficiency." That is, he gets angry less often than might be justified by the situation, strictly speaking. "For the good-tempered man is not revengeful, but rather tends to forgive."[3]

The forgiving man was the one that Aristotle talked about in his books on ethics. But he was decidedly not the man Aristotle had in mind when he wrote his books on rhetoric. There Aristotle taught the orator—the "lawyer" of the ancient Greek world—how to make judges and juries feel anger. Evoking that feeling might get a client off the hook or soundly punished, depending on whether the orator was defending or prosecuting. Aristotle knew very well that "the arousing of prejudice, pity, anger, and similar emotions has nothing to do with the essential facts." He knew that "it is not right to pervert the judge by moving him to anger or envy or pity."[4] But, he said, he had to fight fire with fire: other orators persuaded through emotional appeals, so Aristotle's orator needed to know the tricks as well, both to spot them and to use them. As he said quite explicitly, emotions are "all those feelings that so change men as to affect their judgments."[5] Aristotle named fourteen emotions, each one paired, though he admitted that they were just representative examples: anger and mildness, love and hate, fear and confidence, shame and shamelessness, benevolence and lack of benevolence, pity and indignation, and (lastly) envy and the desire to emulate. Evoking emotions was precisely the way in which the orator could change the reasonable views of the judge and jury. That is how the alogical part of the soul could influence the logical.

All of this seems entirely mental, as if anger consisted only in thoughts rather than (as we all know to be true) in physical feelings as well. But Aristotle did not deny the important role of the body. It is true that the *cause* of anger—the incident that sets it off—is always a cognition on the order of "that person unjustly slighted me." But once anger is triggered, it affects the whole organism. Aristotle did not separate body and soul: to the contrary, we might say that for him the soul was embodied. Since all living things are body and soul together, the feelings of the soul are also somatic. The physician would define anger "as a boiling of the blood or warm substance surrounding the heart" because he is thinking about its matter.[6] The philosopher, however, would say that "anger causes the heat round the heart to boil up" because he is thinking about what initiates the bodily effects. A red chest, swelling neck veins, bulging temples: these are signs of anger. No wonder, said Aristotle, that people speak of "anger 'boiling up' and 'rising' and 'being stirred up.'"[7]

Anger is always directed against one particular person only. In this, it is different from hate. We can't get angry at a whole class of people, says Aristotle, but we can hate them. Everyone hates thieves and murderers, for example. Hatred is what fuels racial and religious violence. The sort of personal pain that produces anger is not the same pain that we have when we hate. Aristotle's point is well illustrated by Levi's experience at Auschwitz, filled with people who hated but only rarely became angry. When we hate, thought Aristotle, we wish to eliminate the person or persons whom we hate; we do not care if they feel the vengeance of our anger; it doesn't matter to us if they know how we feel about them. Aristotle had rather little to say about hatred; for him, it was not a complicated emotion. In a way, it was too "rational." It was also endless. Anger could dissipate once the offender had been dealt with or forgiven. Hatred never died.

✳

Aristotle's thoughts on the emotions were eclipsed by the Stoics and later by the rise of new monotheistic religions (Christianity, Islam) that had entirely different takes on the nature of man and God. Within that context, Aristotle did not become important again until the eleventh and twelfth centuries. And even then, at least at first, it was his writings on logic, not on the passions, that interested thinkers. Muslim scholars were the first to translate Aristotle's Greek into Arabic; but soon thereafter Europeans traveled to the places where Christian kingdoms bordered on the Islamic world—Sicily, Spain—to make or obtain Latin translations.

At the same time, there was a real need for theorizing the emotions, for people at every level of society were thinking, writing, and singing about them. In the West, great lords claimed to "love" their vassals and expected to be loved in turn. But if their expectations were not met, they threatened to wreak their "anger" by going to war in place of showing their love by showering their men with support, favors, and gifts. At princely courts, troubadours and other entertainers sang lustily and tenderly about their ladies; even more often, they sang about their broken hearts and their anger. To his lady Mais d'Amic ("More than a Friend"), the thirteenth-century poet Raimon de Miraval wrote:

Mais d'Amic, the best and the worst
one should share in common.
But you have the joy and the merit and the profit,
and I have nothing more than sorrowful anger and a melancholy
heart.[8]

In monasteries and cathedral schools, the very theology surrounding
the nature of Christ was changing. From the awesome lord of heaven,
Jesus was taking on new personas: the tiny infant tenderly held by his
doting virgin mother, the suffering man on the cross. One twelfth-
century abbot wrote a glowing treatise on how to contemplate every step,
every phase in the life of Jesus: "Accompany the Mother as she makes her
way to Bethlehem. Take shelter in the inn with her, be present and help
her as she gives birth. [. . .] Put your lips to those most sacred feet, kiss
them again and again." And when it came to the moment when Jesus was
arrested: "I know your heart now is filled with pity, you are set on fire
with indignation. Let him be, I beg, let him suffer, for it is on your behalf
he is suffering. Why do you long for a sword? Why are you angry?"[9]
Meditations like this, so dependent on feelings, virtually demanded
that scholars try to understand emotions: their causes and effects, their
purposes, virtues, and vices.

And so they did, at first drawing on Plato and Neoplatonic thinking,
but gradually turning ever more firmly to Aristotle, relying on the tools
of logic that they learned from him. This was the context in which the
thirteenth-century scholastic Thomas Aquinas wrote the most complete
treatise on the emotions produced in the medieval period—indeed, one
of the most thoroughgoing of all time. His theory was "Aristotelian,"
but it also went far beyond Aristotle: in systematizing the emotions, in
showing how they worked together, and in granting anger a far more
important place than Aristotle had given it in human feeling in general.

Aristotle had theorized a three-fold soul—nutritive, sensitive, and
rational. But we must complicate this picture now, because he also

added two other "powers" of the soul—locomotive and appetitive. These, like the parts, were "modes of living." Most animals not only grow (a consequence of their nutritive power) but also have the capacity to sense (reflecting the sensitive part of their souls), to desire (the result of their appetitive power), and to move about (the outcome of their locomotive power). All human beings, and only they, have rational powers. As we noted, the emotions are produced in the rational part of the human soul; non-human animals have no emotions.

Thomas modified this scheme somewhat by putting enormous emphasis on the appetitive faculty—the power of the soul that desires, reaches out, and longs for things. His purpose in doing this was to understand and explain the human quest for beatitude. For Thomas (unlike for Aristotle), God created man, and man's ultimate goal was to return to God. Emotions were essential to that return; they were the driving force, the motor. To be sure, emotions may also lead far from God and straight to sin. But they do so inadvertently: everyone wants pleasure and avoids pain, but some people mistake food, or money, or sex for true pleasure, and they avoid prayer, virtue, and godly meditation as pains. As those misguided people pursue their goals, their emotions are bent awry, as it were, reaching out for the wrong things. But that ability to reach out—that appetitive power—is also the way to God.

And so, unlike the Buddha, unlike Seneca, unlike the Neostoics and other visionaries who sought a world without anger, unlike those who called others "angry" as a shorthand for "hateful" or simply "out of control," Thomas welcomed anger and saw good uses for it, as he did for all the emotions. The trick was—and here he followed Aristotle—to feel anger at the right time, regarding the right object and the right person, and in the right way. But Thomas' notion of "right" was quite different from Aristotle's. Furthermore, rather than see anger and other emotions as caused by diverse and separate judgments (as had Aristotle), Thomas said that all the emotions—he named eleven: love and hate, desire and avoidance, joy and sorrow, hope and despair, fear and courage, and the sole singleton, anger—worked together, animated by one in particular: love. All the other emotions strove to help love gain its object; even hate assisted love by opposing the evil contrary to love's good.

Thomas was interested in how feelings function in this life, in this world, even though his main focus was to explain how that life leads to resting in and loving God. He put special emphasis on the "desiring" ("concupiscible") emotions—love and hate, desire and avoidance, joy and sorrow—because they are the movers and shakers. They latch onto goals and reach out towards them. What then is anger's role? It is one of the "irascible" emotions, whose job it is to help the desiring emotions get to their goal. The path to love's object is often beset by difficulties. A person may want something very badly, but she usually needs help getting it. She may hate something very fiercely, but avoidance per se may not accomplish much. At such points, it is the turn of the irascible emotions to go to work. The emotions that help us avoid evil are fear (prompting us to run away) or courage (causing us boldly to confront the object of our hatred). If we fail nevertheless—if we end up in sorrow—then we become angry. Similarly, in the case of love: if desire has to struggle, hope (which adds intensity to desire) and despair (which recoils from the goal as impossible to attain) come to its aid. If hope succeeds, then there is joy and no need for anger. But if despair ensues, then, again, we end up in sorrow and anger.

Thomas' theory connected anger to all the other emotions, adding layer upon layer of feeling. In his hands, anger was not the result of just one particular thought but of many judgments, desires, and feelings. In the first place, it was aroused by love, since no one gets angry without first loving something that proves difficult to attain. Then, too, anger itself is a complex emotion, involving its own pertinent hopes and desires. Rather than flaring up as soon as one makes a judgment (as Aristotle postulated), anger is, for Thomas, emotions' last resort. Nevertheless, for both Thomas and Aristotle, anger is (potentially) good and useful: it is right and just "to rise up against things contrary and hurtful."[10]

To consider the anger of my father in this light is to think first not of his conflict with his boss but rather of his many loves. His love for himself and his family led him to desire a certain kind of job. He looked to that to give him joy. It would not be his only joy; he had many other loves. But it would help make some of them possible (such as buying lots of books, relishing food and drink, listening to music, supporting his family) and it would introduce him to new ones—the practical joys of a position in which he might do some good for his social-work clientele. As I think about those dinner table conversations, I realize that he and my mother talked not just about their shared anger and frustration but also their loves, hopes and despair. These were not the pure sorts of feelings that Aristotle talked about. Rather, they were mingled with other emotions: my father's desire to leave the agency where he worked, his fear about what might happen if he did so, his enkindled courage to move on even so. Always the specter of sorrow loomed over these exchanges—the pain of hopes dashed, initiatives blocked.

The Aristotelian and Thomistic views of emotions had enormous impact on subsequent theories and practices. Indeed, in one way or another, every thinker dealing with the emotions since the thirteenth century has had to respond to them. Thomas' notions, institutionalized within the Catholic Church, held sway as the ultimate authority until the seventeenth century. At that point, even while one strand of intellectual history remained affiliated with the Church and its Thomistic persuasions, another group of thinkers, beginning with Descartes, strove consciously to break away. Descartes collapsed the distinction between desiring and irascible emotions, and he denied the objectivity of good and evil. He did not insist that God was the proper and ultimate love object. Instead, he emphasized the variety of people's subjective responses to things outside of them, depending on their own individual proclivities.

As we saw in Chapter 3, for Descartes, the character of our anger at any particular time depended on our life experiences and the repertory of judgments that we personally made.

Although Descartes gave the pineal gland in the brain the chief role in the production of emotions, his emphasis on subjectivity meant that he was chiefly interested in mental activity. That is why many scholars claim that Descartes separated the mind from the body. Whether or not this is true, it is indisputable that after Descartes' day theorists tended to emphasize one side (the mental) or the other (the corporal). Very generally, scientists, whose stature was just beginning to rise in the century of Descartes, tended to make the body the site of emotions and therefore to deny the primacy of subjective experience. They insisted that emotions were best understood via blood pressure, adrenaline secretion, and other bodily phenomena amenable to measurement. At the other extreme, theologians and "humanists" valorized the subjective side of feeling. In the twentieth century, Freudians, whose works were largely considered "unscientific," hardly talked about bodies except insofar as they considered corporal symptoms to be the by-products of disordered psyches. Behaviorists, by contrast with everyone, belittled the importance of emotions altogether.

In sum, theories of emotion after the time of Descartes rejected Aristotle's idea that emotions were evaluative judgments. It was quite a jolt when, in the 1960s, a few cognitive psychologists returned to the view that emotions are "thoughts." Magda Arnold was among the first of these. She did not simply revive Aristotle and Aquinas, but she also endeavored to meld the cognitive view of the emotions with findings from the neurological and physiological sciences.

Key to Arnold's theory was the idea that an emotion is the result of an appraisal. "To arouse an emotion, the object [whether a thing or an event or a situation] must be appraised as affecting me in some way, affecting me personally as an individual with my particular experience and my particular aims." Like Thomas, she identified emotion not with the appraisal itself, but with "a definite pull toward or away" from the object—an action of some sort.[11] Each emotion, she argued, has its own bodily "feel" and its own characteristic action.

Arnold changed the name of the irascible emotions to "contending emotions," but their role for Arnold was much as they were for Thomas, as were her names for the "basic emotions." She, too, began with love and hate, followed by desire and aversion, and, when the goal was attained, joy or (in the case of hate) sorrow. But since few easily attain their goal, the other emotions are enlisted: hope and despair, courage and fear. Compared with Thomas' scheme, anger has a lesser place in Arnold's theory, arising only when the goal is to evade something harmful and neither courage nor fear prevent the harm from happening. Blocked, we feel anger, which urges us to attack and remove the obstacle.

Unlike Aristotle and Aquinas, but much like the Neostoics and Freudians, Arnold had therapeutic goals. The prevailing Freudian view of the 1960s was that anger was an outcome of the human aggressive "drive." It had often to be repressed in the interest of peaceful relations with others. According to that view, my dad's anger at his boss was "repressed" at work. Freudian therapy would release the repressed anger and free him to express it (in suitable fashion) to his boss. For Arnold there was a neater explanation: the reason my father did not express his anger at work was that "we cannot attack the obstacle [like my dad's boss] as long as that attack threatens serious harm [such as losing a job]. Anger is not repressed, it is *replaced* by fear. [. . .] And once fear is aroused by anger, fear will increase with every similar frustration."[12] Arnold would say that my father's fear became a habitual substitute for his anger. The goal of her therapy would be to get my father to recognize his false appraisal of the situation as fearful and to reappraise it as properly anger-inducing.

Today most cognitive therapists deal not with anger-turned-to-fear so much as with people who get angry at the wrong times, with the wrong people, in the wrong ways. In that case, therapeutic interventions generally follow the sorts of procedures used in the anger management strategies discussed in Chapter 3. The idea is to get people to change their judgments about the many things that provoke their anger.

More recently, a new variant of cognitive theory has been proposed: the Psychological Construction of emotions. In claiming that both emotions and cognitions are "conceptualizations," it belongs fundamentally alongside Aristotle and his heirs. Indeed, its proponents call it "conceptual act theory."[13] They do not claim that anger is *necessarily* one of the concepts (though it certainly is one in our own culture), nor do they assume that the soul/mind is divided into faculties or power, such as the nutritive, sensitive, and intellective. Rather, they assert, the mind—which they identify with the brain—is all of those things as they are created by neural networks. The brain is constantly processing sensations (from both within the body and without), categorizing them and regulating them. Some of its categories are what we call emotions. Lisa Feldman Barrett, a major spokesperson for this view, agrees that emotions affect our judgments. Like Aristotle, she thinks about what this means for our system of justice. But Aristotle said that "the arousing of prejudice, pity, anger, and similar emotions has nothing to do with the essential facts."[14] Barrett disagrees. The essential facts cannot be separated from every other conceptualization that we associate with them, some of which will almost inevitably be varieties of prejudice, pity, anger, and so on. There is no clear line between a "rational" argument and an "emotional" one, between a "rational" judicial decision and one based on, say, anger. Barrett thinks that there is no unbiased judge, no "reasonable" jury.[15] But she also hopes that because emotions are concepts, as adults we may and will critique them and open ourselves to new ones. I will return to this theory in the context of modern scientific thought in Chapter 10.

The Aristotelian position says that emotions affect our judgments, and judgments may change. At bottom, that is a hopeful idea, even if the changes are sometimes not for the better. It means that we need not reject anger utterly nor imagine that there is nothing that we may do about our angry feelings. Aristotle would find it bizarre to imagine that anger might become part of our identity. For him, anger is fleeting. Human nature is such, he thought, that we cannot be locked into one angry stance for long, for we are all open to persuasion.

# 7

## FROM HELL TO HEAVEN

For Aristotle, anger was a virtue when it was felt under the right conditions; it was a vice when it was expressed in the wrong circumstances. For Barrett, in part critiquing our own society, it is a virtue only when so capacious as to include diverse perspectives, and it is a vice when held as an absolute truth. In between was and remains a tradition that nurtures at one and the same time two fundamentally opposite notions of anger: as a vice and as a virtue.

Of the two, the notion of anger as a virtue is not only furthest from the ancient world but also, perhaps, most prevalent today. It asserts that our virtuous anger is not just "appropriate," as Aristotle would have it, but righteous in an absolute sense. Recall that Anthony M. (see Chapter 1) felt not just annoyed or peeved when others frustrated his expectations but also outraged by their violation of a superior moral law known and enforced by him alone; he felt righteously enraged on behalf of this higher standard. Barrett wishes to lessen the grip of this feeling. She would tell Anthony that his notion of anger is too narrow: he should open himself to the many other ways to conceptualize his thoughts, sensations, and emotions. I have the same goal as Barrett, but I want to reach it from a historical point of view.

One of the things I would tell Anthony is that he need not and should not cling to the idea that his anger is incontestably righteous. People did without such a notion for a long time, and it entered our traditions only during the Patristic era (the second to sixth centuries). It was only then that the Church Fathers incorporated the notion of God's righteous anger into Christianity in such a way as to make us humans obliged to enforce it. Eventually, righteous anger became secularized, at least in part. We shall see how this happened in the course of this and the following chapter, but we have already seen one of its manifestations in Anthony's self-righteous rages.

Before the Patristic era, only the small but convinced emotional community of the ancient Hebrews had a notion of utterly righteous anger. But that anger belonged to God alone. It was grounded in His covenant, which promised the Jews that "if you will hearken, yes, hearken to my voice and keep my covenant, you shall be to me a special-treasure from among all peoples. Indeed, all the earth is mine, but you, you shall be to me a kingdom of priests, a holy nation" (Exod. 19:5–6).[1] In return for this promise, the Israelites were to obey God's Ten Commandments. But the Jews regularly failed to fulfill the covenant, and because of that, God's anger was repeatedly roused against them. His anger portended destruction and violence: "Lest the anger of YHWH your God flare up against you and he destroy you from off the face of the soil" (Deut. 6:15). This might also be a threat against enemies, for God often got angry at other nations when they harmed the Jews.

By contrast, human anger figures in Hebrew Scriptures mainly to censure it. Proverbs brings it up often: "Pressing anger produces strife"; "Wise men turn away wrath"; "A fool gives full vent to his anger, but a wise man quietly holds it back" (Prov. 30:33; 29:8; 29:11). From a moral point of view, human anger was clearly wrong.

The ancient Hebrews were a tiny minority, largely confined to a narrow strip along the Eastern Mediterranean coast. In the context of the Hellenistic world they barely counted, and in the Roman Empire that succeeded the Hellenistic, they were simply among the inhabitants of its rather marginal province of Palestine. Yet Christianity developed within this surprisingly creative backwater, and eventually (in the fourth century), it became the official religion of the Roman Empire.

Because Christ was seen as fulfilling the prophecies of the Hebrew Bible, its texts and their import had to be incorporated into the new religion. That meant that the role of anger, both divine and human, had to be assimilated into and adapted to Christianity. When it came to God's anger, that was by no means an easy task. Michael C. McCarthy speaks of the "embarrassment" of patristic authors, who had to find ways to reconcile a wrathful God with what they knew to be the "destructive consequences of human anger."[2] They experimented with various solutions. Some denied the testimony of Hebrew Scriptures; others argued that God's anger was a metaphor, nothing like the human emotion. These thinkers brought to Christianity the largely jaundiced views of anger in the classical world. For them anger was a vice. However, other patristic writers grappled more fully with the Hebrew legacy, maintaining that God could not love and reward the good without also having the capacity to get angry at and punish the bad.

These solutions were not simply arcane arguments among the intellectual elites. Both the Old and New Testaments were integral parts of Christian worship. The psalms of the Old Testament were important texts in the Christian liturgy, incorporated into the Mass in its very earliest form and remaining part of it today. Those who dedicated themselves to religion—monks, hermits, nuns—chanted all 150 psalms assiduously; even the most lenient monasteries punctuated each day with the singing of seven Offices made up mainly of psalms and designed to complete the entire psalter within each week. And so, with clockwork regularity, the monks repeated the terrifying questions, "O God, why have you rejected us forever? Why does your anger smolder against the sheep of your pasture?" and "Who can stand before you when you are angry?" and the nearly hopeless, "Will the Lord reject forever? [. . .] Has he in anger withheld his compassion?" The chants told the monks that when God learned that the Israelites sinned against him, "he was furious;

his fire broke out against Jacob, and his wrath rose against Israel." (Ps. 74:1; 76:7; 77:7,9; 78:21.) At first, words such as these were heard and thought about exclusively by specialists in the Christian religious life or by philosophers, theologians, and intellectuals working out the full implication of biblical texts—not just monks and nuns, but also bishops, priests, friars, and canons. But eventually, much of their thinking about anger found its way into the lay world through the central devotional practices of the faithful: attending the liturgy; listening to sermons preached both within and outside of church; performing the sacraments of confession and penance; and piously reciting the prayers in Books of Hours compiled especially for them.

✳

Paramount in Christianity was the idea that most forms of human anger were unrighteous, vicious, and sinful. That view followed fairly directly from the classical inheritance of Aristotle and Stoicism and the Jewish repudiation of human anger. Perhaps it stemmed as well from early attempts to rid Christianity of the idea of divine wrath. For example, in a list of the attributes of God, the early Christian Aristides (d.134) wrote, "Wrath and indignation he possesses not, for there is nothing which is able to stand against him." In effect Aristides claimed that God could not get angry because he was beyond slights and insults; he was nothing like human beings, who are "wrathful and covetous and envious, with other defects as well."[3] Even more radical was the Christian heretic Marcion (d.160) who, as we learn from his critics (our only source for his views), rejected the God of Hebrew Scriptures. Marcion wanted a purely good God, "who never takes offense, is never angry, never inflicts punishment, who has prepared no fire in hell, no gnashing of teeth in the outer darkness!"[4] These are his words as recorded by his enemy Tertullian (d.220). They were meant to mock the heretic, but they likely did indeed reflect his distaste for a furious God.

Without the legitimation of the God of the Old Testament, no anger whatever could be virtuous or even indifferent. However, as we shall see, most Christian thinkers were eager—or at least willing—to defend the wrath of God. But that did not affect their view of humans, and anger had a prominent place on every list of vices that they devised. The earliest such inventories were developed within communities of desert hermits—men and women who set their sights on heaven and rejected the world. Hermits were led by charismatic teachers like the fourth-century Evagrius of Pontus, who listed eight powerful "thoughts" that, if not immediately chased away, led to their corresponding vices. Essentially, these thoughts were the Christian version of the Stoic "first motions," the shocks and bites that the wise person judged to be of no account and refused to assent to. Evagrius no doubt learned about Stoicism as part of his education in the Greek-speaking region of Pontus, in Asia Minor. Translated into Christian terms, Stoic "bites" became "temptations."

Evagrius taught that temptations came from demons. Assenting to them meant falling prey to the demons and the particular vices that they brought with them, and that meant losing the chance to enjoy the tranquil foretaste of heaven. In Evagrius' systematization, the thoughts, each one associated with its own demon, had a particular order, starting with gluttony followed by lust, then avarice—all three desirous of material things—then sadness, anger, acedia (boredom or dull indifference), vainglory, and lastly pride. This made for a progression from temptations of the body to those of the soul.[5]

The Evagrian monk had to do constant cosmic battle against the demons. He was obliged to discern the demons' armaments with a keen eye and see through their flimsiness. In anger's case, the demon's weapon was the perception of injury, and it could be dis-armed by thinking a contrary thought—for example, "that was no injury at all." Counter-thoughts were the monks' slings, stones, and arrows.

Christians were at war, and their enemy was invisible. Roughly contemporary with Evagrius was the Latin poet Prudentius, whose poem *Psychomachia* introduced each virtue as a persona in close combat with its corresponding vice. Anger contended with a very militant Patience. In medieval illustrations of the poem, both Anger (*ira*) and Patience (*patientia*) were fully armed warriors, both females because of the gender of the Latin nouns that designated them. When Anger's sword shattered on Patience's bronze helmet, she turned on herself in fury and committed suicide (see Plate 5). Patience, whose well-protected body was able to resist every blow, thereupon said in triumph to the dying Anger, "We have overcome a boasting vice with our customary virtue, without risking any blood or life. This war of ours has a law: to wipe out the furies and their whole army of evils by enduring their raging violence."[6] Here we see a far more militant patience than the one counseled by the Buddha.

In the fifth century, John Cassian, founder and abbot of the monastery of Saint-Victor at Marseille and formerly a member of Evagrius' community, dispensed with considering the eight thoughts to be pre-emotions. Rather, they were themselves emotions—and they were bad. Cassian slightly reordered the Evagrian list.[7] All eight vices attacked on three different fronts of the soul. When the concupiscent part of the soul was taken over by an invading emotion, it spawned gluttony, lust, avarice, and other earthly desires. When the irascible part was affected, it disgorged rage, sulkiness, acedia, and cruelty. As soon as the logical part was conquered, it gave birth to vainglory, pride, envy, heresy, and other monsters.

Evagrius had the monks fight each demon one by one. Cassian thought that was too easy: the battle could not be won until all were defeated. The vices, Cassian said, were like the companies in an army battalion; no sooner was one overcome than the next attacked. At other times he likened the vices to a tree, with gluttony at its toxic root. To destroy the tree, the monk had systematically to cut down each malignant branch and then pull it out by the root. Yet Cassian worried that at the very moment of triumph, pride—because of the soul's very vanity in vanquishing the other vices—would be able to declare victory, and the battles would have to begin again.

The most influential scheme of the vices was conceived in the sixth century by Pope Gregory the Great. (He was also, at various times, a monk, a diplomat, and a popularizer of learned Christian thought.) Gregory solved Cassian's dilemma by making pride, rather than gluttony, the root of the Tree of Vices. The Seven Deadly Sins branched out from there, starting with the spiritual vices (vainglory, envy, anger, sadness) and moving on to the more concrete (avarice, gluttony, and lust). This was the regiment of vices that came to dominate the imagination of medieval men and women and still prevails today.

Regiment is the right word, for in addition to the tree, Gregory also used a military metaphor for the vices. The Christian soldier was in a battle with Pride, the queen of the vices. Her goal was to take over the soldier's citadel: the heart. Once she had it in her grasp, she handed it over to the "seven principal sins, as if to some of her generals." Anger was one of those generals, and Anger, like the others, had her own violent army following behind, including "brawls, swollen minds, insults, clamors, angry outbursts, and blasphemies."[8] (For Anger and her army springing from the Tree of Vices, see Plate 6.) Much later, as we have seen, the warriors in Anger's army were numbered among the "sins of the tongue."

Note how much more precise and militant this formulation was than that of the Buddha. The Buddha had plenty of lists—the Three Baskets and the "five faultless gifts" were just the tip of the iceberg. But his focus was less on the evil strategies of the vices than on the meditative methods that would free human beings from their clutches. In brief, the Christian sought to conquer the vices, the Buddhist to transcend them.

But, much like the Buddha—or Seneca—Gregory inveighed against anger. Commenting on a biblical passage, "Anger kills the fool (Job 5:2)," he castigated anger in passages worthy of the Stoics. When anger takes over our mind, it tears us apart: we can't think straight, we lose our sense of right and wrong, we imagine that everything that it prompts us to do is justified. We lose our friends, and "close the door against the Holy Spirit."[9] Our heart beats faster, our faces turn red, we can hardly speak and don't know what we are saying. We start spouting curses—maledictions. If words could kill, we would be murderers. Anger leads us to hell.

✷

Yet anger was not all bad. How could it be so, when God was so often angry in the Old Testament? We have seen that some early thinkers denied the continuity between the Old and New Testament God. But the mainstream Church Fathers were glad to speak of God's anger. Already before Evagrius' birth, Tertullian gave a strident defense of it in his polemic against Marcion, who wanted—Tertullian taunted—a god of "goodness"; but that would be an empty sort of god, "neither natural, nor rational, nor perfect, but wrong, and unjust." For God cannot be "simply and solely" good; that would be "some imperturbable and listless god" who would care nothing about mankind.[10] Instead, God issues commands, and he means to execute them; he forbids sins, and he intends to punish them. For Tertullian, God could not be just if he could not also be angry. But it was not the same sort of anger as the human brand. We read of God's "right hand" but we do not imagine that this is comparable to a human hand. So too God's anger. "Angry he will possibly be, but not irritated [. . .] [He will have] anger because of the wicked, and indignation because of the ungrateful, and jealousy because of the proud."[11]

In the early fourth century, Lactantius made a similar argument. The timing was crucial, for now the first Christian Emperor, Constantine the Great, held sway; and, while technically all the religions of the Roman Empire were tolerated under his rule, Christianity was for the first time fully empowered. As adviser and speech writer for the emperor,

Lactantius' political position was analogous to Seneca's two centuries before. But he took a very different philosophical stance on anger, and his words stuck.

Lactantius, like Tertullian, disparaged a God with no feelings; he would be uncaring, immobile, deaf to prayers. But Lactantius' treatise was not occasioned by the long-discredited Marcion and his heresy. It was, rather, addressed to those who still adhered to the ancient philosophies. Although Lactantius could have quoted the Old Testament, as Tertullian had done, he chose instead to make logic the foundation of his argument. He wanted to speak to the many pagans of the Roman Empire of his day, for even then they formed the majority of its citizens. He faulted Aristotle and other ancient philosophers for thinking that virtuous anger involved avenging injury. That could not be God's sort of anger, for nothing could harm God. Instead, God's anger was necessary to mete out due punishments. Lactantius faulted the Stoics for not realizing that there were two kinds of anger, and the right kind was "to correct faults."[12] This broke with most of the earlier ancient philosophies by legitimating anger in a new way.

There had always been a strain of thought in the ancient world that validated the anger of judges. That is why Seneca had felt the need to refute this argument by endorsing the idea of the dispassionate judge. What was new in Lactantius was his stress on the connection between God's just anger and human anger as its mirror. As the "desire for revenge," he said, anger was always a vice. But God rightly got angry at evil; and human beings had the obligation to do so as well. "We rise to take vengeance not because we have been hurt but to preserve discipline, to correct morals, to suppress lawlessness. This is just anger." Lactantius rewrote the old definition of Aristotle and Seneca, which defined anger as a response to injury. For Lactantius, "anger is the emotion that is aroused in order to restrain sins."[13] Even so, he was quick to contrast human with divine anger, for human anger was never so perfect as God's, nor was it so perfectly mingled with compassion.

Within a century of Lactantius the Roman Empire was officially Christian. Augustine (d.430), bishop of Hippo (on the coast of North Africa, today in Algeria) and the most influential theologian in the West for at least a half century, was free once again to rely on Holy Scriptures. But he, too, knew the old philosophical teachings and did not hesitate to revise them. Putting new stress on the human will, he made volition the equivalent or at least the driver of emotions. All emotions are good, he argued, when the will is turned the right way; all are evil when the will is turned awry. The right way is toward God, the city of God, the heavenly abode.

For Augustine, then, all emotions involved God (either turned toward or against him), and anger had a particularly important role. Without any perturbation, as a perfectly rational judgment, in a way that is entirely unlike human beings, God gets righteously angry at iniquity. His anger is expressed in Scriptures in words that humans can understand, and for that reason, it has a salutary effect on life on earth: "it uses such language to terrify the proud, to arouse the careless, to exercise the inquirer, and to nourish the intelligent."[14] As Michael McCarthy observes, for Augustine, God's anger was rather like that of the Stoic wise man: he "never suffers disturbance yet gives the impression of showing anger because of its salutary effect on others."[15] One such effect is to inspire people to get angry on God's behalf. Human anger, then, could be divinely sparked. Indeed, it might express God's anger itself: "God's anger is the emotion that occurs in the soul of one who knows the law [of God] when she sees that law transgressed by a sinner."[16] Note how careful Augustine is here. Righteous anger is not directed at the sinner but rather at the sin. Such anger is therapeutic and salutary, both for the sinner and for the one who sees and chastises the sin. It is beneficial to social life and justice on earth and a foretaste of the heaven to come.

Henceforth emotions, and anger in particular, were both execrated and praised. Even Gregory the Great, the thinker who put anger right in the middle of the seven deadly sins and who waxed eloquent about its horrible consequences, even Gregory conceded that anger was good when it helped to combat sin: "Anger stirred up by impatience is one thing; anger caused by zeal is another. The first is born of vice, the other of virtue."[17] We should get angry not only at our own sins but at those of our neighbors. It is true, admitted Gregory, that even good anger *feels* much like the bad sort, for we become confused and can't think straight as we rage over sins. But that confusion soon gives way to greater clarity. Like an eye salve, anger at first blurs our vision, but then it lets us see better than ever before. For anger to work in this way, it has to be the tool, not the master, of reason. Gregory was hesitant: he knew very well the force of anger—he felt it himself sometimes. And so, just as Cicero advised his brother to cool off, so Gregory told "those who are moved by righteous zeal" to wait until they had calmed down before they punished sin.[18] But that didn't mean that they should never get angry.

Originally, systematic thought about the vices and virtues was largely the preserve of monasteries, where men and women dedicated their entire lives to their religious vocation and secreted themselves away from the ordinary demands of society. But this changed as monastic life gained prestige, its ideas and practices gradually penetrating into the habits of the laity. Under Charlemagne, the Frankish king who in the year 800 became the first emperor in the West since the fifth century, biblical kings became the model for Christian rulership. Charlemagne said that he wanted to institute the laws of God in his empire; he employed advisers who envisioned him as a religious leader; and some of the regional officials whom he appointed wanted to know how to govern virtuously. This was the context of a treatise on the vices and virtues written for Wido, count of the Breton March, by Alcuin, one of Charlemagne's key advisers.

As count, Wido was charged by the emperor with keeping the peace, both as a warrior and as a judge. Apart from the fact that he himself fought in wars, his position was not so different from that long before held by a Roman provincial governor like Quintus, Cicero's irascible brother. "Restrain your tongue," Cicero had advised Quintus. Alcuin had much more to say on the topic, and this is the important point. He did not—he could not—simply condemn all anger. He had to also positively encourage it. So, in the midst of warning Wido against getting angry and asking him to tame it, Alcuin also talked about a good sort of anger that "is just and necessary when a person is angry about his own sins and indignant with himself when he acts wickedly. For the prophet says, 'Be angry and do not sin.' "[19] The "prophet" here was David, and the exhortation was from the psalms. It was important advice for a man whose misuse of power was restrained, if at all, mainly by his conscience. And it is a good example of how the words of the Hebrew Scriptures had already, by the years around 800, infiltrated the reading materials of an early medieval count.

Did Wido take heed? It is impossible to know. But Alcuin claimed that Wido himself had asked him to write the treatise so that in the midst of his "warlike occupations" he would have a handy guide to give him comfort and lead him to heaven. Already in the ninth century, then, even laypeople were worried about vice and virtue.

In the ensuing centuries and with growing enthusiasm, laypeople absorbed the gist of Christian ethics. The Church's emphasis on confession and penance, which the Fourth Lateran Council (1215) required of everyone at least once a year, meant that the devout had to keep track of their sins. They were aided in that endeavor by university scholars and members of the new mendicant orders—primarily the Dominicans and Franciscans—who itemized all possible sins and their evil effects. The professors wrote the treatises; the preachers—mainly mendicants—turned that learned thought into simple vernacular sermons that all could understand. Christian ethics were preached not only in churches but also on city streets and at aristocratic and royal courts.

The twelfth and above all the thirteenth centuries saw a remarkable proliferation of works treating the vices and virtues. Seneca, whose works had lain dormant from the sixth to the eleventh centuries, was read again; the extant works of Aristotle were translated, studied, and debated. William Peraldus, who created the special category of "sins of the tongue," was a particularly popular writer: his treatise on the virtues and vices survives today in over five hundred manuscript copies. It was often translated, sometimes adapted for "simpler" folk, and constantly cited by other scholars. Peraldus, refusing to be bound by the Gregorian seven, named nine capital vices. He began with gluttony, put pride near the middle, and located anger next to last.

Meanwhile, the newly commercialized economy of the High Middle Ages meant that some fortunes were now rooted in money rather than in land ownership. The moral issues connected with this development led some thinkers to make avarice rather than pride the root of all evil.[20] In a twelfth-century encyclopedia illustration, a plant named the "Tree of Evil; Synagogue" has as its root not pride but cupidity, the twin of avarice. (See Plate 7.) Its first fruits are homicide and brawl; next come branches laden with rivalry, anger, despair, dissension, and envy; its topmost fruits are fornication, impurity, lust, enmity, and contention. The scheme was "Gregorian" only in the sense that within the roundel signifying anger were the same monstrous offspring as Gregory had dubbed anger's warriors: brawls, swollen minds, insults, clamors, angry outbursts, and blasphemies. In other hands, the number of sins so proliferated that some commentators abandoned the Gregorian blueprint altogether, replacing it with the Ten Commandments. This was particularly the practice of Protestants, who sought to base their religion on Holy Scriptures alone. Even so, Gregory's notion of Seven Deadly Sins hung on, especially in Catholic countries and in the popular imagination.

✴

Ideas about anger's vicious and virtuous character were not just theories. They had an impact on the way people lived their lives, presented themselves to others, and judged those around them.

Consider the use of clamors, one of anger's unruly followers. Originally, clamors had a legal role: when Roman petitioners brought a complaint or request to a magistrate, this was known as "making a clamor." It certainly was a noisy affair, as crowds gathered around the magistrate's throne and shouted. But when Gregory the Great wrote about clamors, he had something different in mind: the chatter of ungoverned thoughts, the arguments that angry people carry on within themselves as they nurse their grudges and create "brawls and loud clamors in their heart."[21]

Clearly, the quiet of the monastery was no place for such noise. Yet in the eleventh and twelfth centuries, monks regularly made use of clamors to God and the patron saints of their monasteries, waging spiritual warfare against those who, they claimed, plundered their property and invaded their sanctuaries. They had a whole ritual for this. Prostrating themselves before the altar, the monks asked God for justice. Sometimes they cast to the ground the crucifix and reliquaries holding the remains of the saints. Evil people, they said, were "disturbing and disrupting" the monastery and its property. The monks prayed that "all the maledictions of God" befall their enemies. "May their lot and inheritance be perpetual flames. [. . .] May they be cursed in cities, may they be cursed in fields."[22] The monks wanted their enemies to be excommunicated—excluded from the Church and its salvific sacraments. They chanted the psalms that celebrated God's vengeance.

It's hard to say that the monks were angry in the normal sense. Their curses were chanted as part of rituals, they were written down, and monks were not supposed to get angry. But their words expressed anger on behalf of God, petitioning him to protect his own. They were meant to "correct the faults" of wicked invaders. Their anger, we might say, was the silent, militant anger of Prudentius' Patience. They meant it to overcome the vicious and violent knights who plundered sacred land and snatched the property of God. They were demanding not human expedients but the justice of God.

In short, unlike Buddhism which forbade anger altogether, Christianity admired a certain kind of anger directed against wronging God and his laws. It was not just legitimate anger, as Aristotle would have it. Rather, it was positively righteous. It was even more just than the anger of Seneca's Medea, who carried out the vengeance of the gods, for the Christian God's anger was understood to be constructive rather than vindictive.

Somewhat ironically, it was also the anger that was professed by the very knights who were the "enemies" cursed by the monks. At least the knights claimed their anger to be righteous. We see this best in the chivalric poetry of the period, which mirrored (as well as critiqued) the knightly ethos. Here, medieval warriors regularly got angry, and equally regularly they invoked God to reinforce their fury. Like the monks, their anger was often about land—estates taken away from them unjustly, properties promised to them but not received. While the monks cursed and called down the wrath of God, the knights waged bloody war. But both groups thought that they were doing God's work.

Consider Raoul de Cambrai, the hero of a late twelfth-century anonymous poem.[23] He expected to inherit some land, but the king granted it to someone else. The poem recounted Raoul's fury and his attempts to gain the inheritance of others by war and fire. While the poet thought Raoul's anger excessive and his acts of violence atrocities, he also showed how Raoul appealed to God as though his rage were righteous. Before burning down a whole city, for example, "he swore by God and his mercy" that he would do it. Afterward he vowed to continue the battle against his enemies "by the faith I owe Saint Géri,"—the saint particularly dear to his heart.

Poems like this reveal an emotional community of feudal lords very similar to that of the monks when it came to anger, except that knights went to war and monks (ordinarily) did not. Yet the two communities were alike in seeing God on their side. Nor did either simply wait for God to act. Warriors went to battle, plundered, and set fires. Monks called out to God, flung down Christ's crucifix and the reliquaries of the saints, and prostrated themselves before the altar. Indeed, there were good reasons for these emotional communities to overlap: monks came from knightly and lordly families; lords were the chief donors of property to monastic houses, and monks prayed for the souls of their benefactors. Monks and secular lords lived in the same neighborhoods and knew one another as both friends and enemies.

Monks and lords were medieval society's elite. Peasants might rage, but their anger was never appreciated as righteous. As Paul Freedman has noted, "anger was an essentially noble prerogative."[24] As in the world of Aristotle, so too in the Middle Ages, you needed status to be insulted; peasants lacked rank and therefore honor. In the traditional view of society there were those who prayed, those who fought, and then (on the lowest rung) those who worked. Medieval poems and tales depicted peasants as rough, stupid, and generally docile. They might fuss and fume about something, but when they did so, they were either impotent or comical—or both. On the other hand, sometimes they banded together and presented a terrifying threat, burning, pillaging, and murdering with such abandon that they might as well have been wild elephants.

Gradually, however, with the rise of towns and the creation of a new class of burghers, many of whom were wealthier than the richest lords in the countryside, the lower classes gained the right to get angry. During the fourteenth and fifteenth centuries, the dislocations caused by the Hundred Years' War led to numerous popular protests in French towns and countryside. At Paris, citizens stormed the royal palace. Even the provost of the merchants—normally allied with the royal family—joined the crowd. On his knees, he spoke to the future king, asking him to lift monetary imposts, for, he said, they "weighed down the people in many intolerable ways." Hardly had he ended his speech when the protestors made "a terrible clamor," vowing that they would no longer pay; they would "rather die a thousand times than suffer such shame and injury."[25]

This was "righteous anger." The citizens of Paris did not just think that they were "in the right"—even Seneca and the Buddha knew that angry people always think they are right—but also considered themselves to be part of a larger struggle for divine justice. In England a popular revolt around the same time featured a rhyme effectively anticipating Jefferson's "All men are created equal":

When Adam delved [dug]
And Eve span [spun]
Who then was the gentleman?

Insult, harm, and shame had always been anger's preludes. We saw that already with Buddhism. But to human humiliation, Christianity added the experience of Christ—whipped, denied, and crucified, pouring out his blood for sinful humanity. Christians thought of Christ when they experienced insult and harm, and they claimed to share in God's justice when they clamored for amends. When Pope Urban II preached the First Crusade, he bewailed the crimes that "an accursed race" had inflicted on Christians in the east. Turning to his audience, a crowd gathered outside the church at Clermont in France, he asked, "On whom therefore is the labor of avenging these wrongs and of recovering this territory incumbent, if not upon you?" He quoted the Gospel, in case anyone might be held back from the Crusade because of family ties: "He that loveth father or mother more than me, is not worthy of me." He told the gathered faithful that they must put aside their petty quarrels and go to war against "the wicked race." The crowd cried out "It is the will of God," and Urban responded, "Let this then be your war-cry in combat."[26]

The varieties of righteous anger in the medieval period were legion. But there were certain discernable patterns, emotional sequences. First came shame: in the case of the crusaders, shame was roused (so said Urban) by the destruction of churches and the torture, rape, and pillage of Christians. Then came vengeance to right these wrongs; that was God's, and the crusaders were called upon to help him. Similarly, when medieval monks clamored to God to consign their enemies to "perpetual flames," they acted out the shame of Christ himself by symbolically humiliating his saints and crucifix, casting them to the ground. Knights, princes, kings, and (eventually) citizens saw themselves as participants in the same supra-human drama. Humiliated, like the humble Christ, they, too, were in the right (or so they judged) when they protested or fought back, for they were fighting on God's side. This view of anger as righteous, passionate, virtuous, and productive would have a potent future in the modern world.

# 8

## MORAL SENTIMENTS

The tradition of theologically minded virtues and vices faded in the course of the sixteenth and seventeenth centuries. But the idea left important traces, not only in the fact that even today the "Seven Deadly Sins" have real frisson, but also in the form of "righteous anger." Peter Sloterdijk speaks of a "treasury of rage" left to the West by the Judeo-Christian notion of a just and avenging God.[1] We continue to spend the resources of that treasury on behalf of ideals and convictions that have taken on quasi-sacred status.

The savage wars that ripped Europe apart in the seventeenth century made clear that a united Christendom was a long-lost fantasy and that morality had to be put on a new footing, separate from the Church. It would, however, be wrong to think that the Christian religion disappeared from the ethical thought of Europeans. As J.B. Schneewind has pointed out, "To win wide acceptance, a moral philosophy would have to offer an account of at least the main points of what was taken by every confession as the core of Christian morality."[2] But how exactly could that be done?

Some philosophers looked to "natural law." Dutch political theorist Hugo Grotius (d.1645) argued that, although there might be a great variety of civil laws, some created for advantage rather than for justice, it is the "natural inclination of mankind to live in society" and in peace.[3] This natural law "is the fountain of right." It prescribes that we will not take that "which is another's," that we will fulfill our promises, and that we will provide for "the reparation of a damage done through our own [fault]." Grotius also intends for us to punish anyone who violates the natural laws. Clearly, those laws are close to the Ten Commandments, but for Grotius they are also "natural," followed by all, even people ignorant of the Mosaic tradition. He thought that anything that harms the fountain of right is contrary to our "natural inclination," even though he knew that among our inclinations are attractions to pleasure and "blind passion."[4] Those bad inclinations are why civil laws had to be written to concretize and ensure the natural law. Grotius had no good words for anger, which in its most ungovernable moments leads to murder, the antithesis of right and always a violation of civil law. The laws of the state are thus central to human morality; we are obliged to adhere to them. But Grotius thought that we also have some duties that cannot be enforced except out of our own inner volition, independent of religious or civil compulsion. We already see in infants "a propensity to do good to others [. . .] and compassion likewise discovers itself upon every occasion in that tender age."[5] All of this, said Grotius, would be true even if (which is not the case) there were no God.

By attributing some limited morality to the autonomous individual rather than to external law, Grotius joined a growing chorus of thinkers. Some of them, the so-called Egoists, argued that even human vice led to a kind of virtue. We have already seen a glimmer of this idea in Descartes. It was elaborated at greater length by Descartes' contemporary Thomas Hobbes (d.1679), who thought that human nature, left to itself, made human life untenable. In their pursuit of pleasure and avoidance of pain, people were in constant competition, not because they could never feel contented but because nothing in the state of nature ensured that they would be able to keep what they had. To escape the constant anxiety of life without laws, they had to create the Leviathan—society, the state, and its rules and regulations. In effect, the Leviathan, an outcome of vice, created virtue.

Anger figured in Hobbes' discussion in two ways. In the first place, he belittled it, rejecting the long and rich tradition initiated by Aristotle. The classical definition made no sense, Hobbes said. Anyone can see that anger is not a response to a slight but rather is rage at any obstacle in our way, even "things inanimate and without sense."[6] We see people kicking the table leg that they bumped into; stupid things like that are the causes of anger, and they happen all the time. In the second place, however, he took anger very seriously, claiming that "there are few crimes that may not be produced by anger." The Leviathan had to attend to the ill effects of anger by creating laws against crime and punishing those who violate them.[7] Like all the other vices, anger reveals the reasons why laws are necessary for virtue.

Both Grotius and Hobbes looked mainly to laws to teach us that it pays to be moral. But other philosophers around the same time, the Autonomists, were convinced that people did not need external laws; human beings had the autonomous capacity to guide themselves. In effect, these thinkers expanded the duties that Grotius said came out of our own volition to include most of morality.

The Autonomists were of two schools. One assumed that people must by nature have within themselves the simple knowledge necessary to lead them to ethical truths, because God would not create mankind in any other way. The other sought an entirely secular foundation for morality. They assumed that human nature was as uniform and predictable as Isaac Newton had shown physical nature to be. Just as Newton had had to imagine abstract "ideal conditions" in order to arrive at his three laws of motion, so these philosophers—especially David Hume (d.1776) and, following him, Adam Smith (d.1790)—created the fiction of an abstract human being who functioned according to certain laws.

Hume, the pioneer among these thinkers, began with perceptions, defined as everything that comes into the mind. Perceptions that are immediate are "of the senses and all bodily pains and pleasures." Those that involve reflection (that is, the admixture of an idea) are "the passions and other emotions resembling them."[8] Anger is one of these, and as in

Thomas Aquinas' scheme (though Hume would vigorously deny the similarities), it was often part of a sequence of feelings: "grief and disappointment give rise to anger, anger to envy, envy to malice, and malice to grief again, till the whole circle be completed."[9] Human nature is fickle and moves from one impression to another.

Fickleness doesn't sound very virtuous, and, indeed, Hume was aware that he would have to find virtue (and vice) in (or at least in spite of) the fact that our "original and natural instinct" is grounded in ourselves. As a result of that instinct, it is in our nature to associate virtue with pleasure and vice with pain. Hume proposed a thought experiment: "let us suppose I am in company with a person whom I formerly regarded without any sentiments either of friendship or enmity."[10] If I endow this other person with the pleasurable attribute of virtue, I feel love and benevolence toward him. If, however, I imagine that my companion has the disagreeable attribute of vice, that immediately makes me feel hate and anger—the desire for "the misery and an aversion to the happiness of the person hated."[11] In this way, my "selfish" pain at the viciousness of my companion becomes a source of my ethics. Why hatred and anger should work in this way Hume chalked up to "an arbitrary and original instinct implanted in our nature."[12] He had no interest in speculating about what or who might have implanted it. It was enough to know that anger exists and that it has consequences.

One of those consequences is that anger lets itself be known to others. All emotions do that: human beings resonate with each other's emotions through their innate propensity to sympathize. We not only communicate our feelings to others but we also tend to adjust our own emotions to those around us. The phenomenon of "sympathy" goes far to explain why there is "uniformity [. . .] in the humors and turn of thinking of those of the same nation." People take on the emotional coloring of those around them. The cheerful appearance of an acquaintance "infuses a sensible complacency and serenity into my mind; as an angry or sorrowful one throws a sudden damp upon me," writes Hume. "Hatred, resentment, esteem, love, courage, mirth, and melancholy; all these passions I feel more from communication than from my own natural temper and disposition."[13] Long before discovering "mirror neurons" or contemplating "emotional communities," Hume was arguing that we resonate and echo the feelings of those around us.

Because of our sympathetic capacity, when we think of people who are loving and agreeable, our eyes tear up and we feel pleasure, just as those loving and agreeable people themselves take pleasure in their feelings. Angry and hate-filled people give us pain and uneasiness, just as they themselves also feel disquiet. In both cases, when we enter into the feelings of others, we momentarily forget about ourselves. Our ability to sympathize leads directly to our approval and disapproval of other people, an ethical sense that has nothing to do with "utility and advantage."[14] Our feelings—not our reason—are the source of our morals.

Anger is essential for our ethical sensibilities. We need to be angry at vicious people, and we may even need to say so. When anger is felt and communicated judiciously, "in a low degree," it may be admirable. Even when its fury is intense, we must recognize that it is "inherent in our very frame and constitution."[15] It is true that when anger turns into cruelty, it is the worst of vices. But that very excess brings out the moral sensibilities in the rest of us: we feel pity and concern for cruelty's victims. We recoil from the "person guilty of [cruelty]," and we feel "a stronger hatred than we are sensible of on any other occasion."[16] Our moral sense needs anger to allow us to condemn, just as it needs love to allow us to approve. Without anger, we could not make moral judgments.

Superficially this sounds a bit like Lactantius, who said that God could not love the good if he could not also get angry at the wicked. But the foundation of Hume's argument is entirely different. Lactantius' God has divine knowledge of what is virtuous and what is not. Hume's morality is rooted in human nature and its ability to sympathize. Sympathy is the sentiment that creates and sustains human society. Let us imagine for a moment that we lived in the "state of nature." In that case, before the formation of society, we would be motivated only by self-love and have no other standard of moral judgment. Selfishness would then be a virtue. But we do not live in the state of nature, for enlightened self-love has led us to create a better form of selfishness—one with rules that allow us to live together in harmony. When we love the good, we love those who conform to those rules; when we are angry at the wicked, it is because they violate our salutary social conventions. Our morality stems from the society we humans have created, and anger is essential to it.

Very similar were the notions of human nature held by Adam Smith. Writing about a decade after Hume, he too saw sympathy, "our fellow-feeling with any passion," as the source of social harmony.[17] Nevertheless, he emphasized (more than did Hume) the ways in which our self-love keeps intruding. We have to make an effort of imagination to put ourselves in the position of another, and the effort can only be "momentary."[18] Anxious as we are to have our passions mirrored at the same pitch as we feel them, we learn to "flatten" them out so that others may more easily understand and feel them; we feel the need to lighten their task of "becoming us" imaginatively.

✳

Modern researchers seem to ratify Hume's and Smith's notions of sympathy with laboratory experiments on "emotional contagion." Most such studies involve face-to-face contact, or at least include voice and gesture. But a Facebook-sponsored study reported that words alone may also do the trick: when friends' newsfeeds were tweaked to contain only "negative emotions" (i.e. negative emotion words), viewers tended to express negative emotions in their own posts, while "positive" newsfeeds made their viewers more apt to reveal pleasant feelings. In this study, anger was considered a negative emotion.[19]

But the differences between modern notions of emotional contagion and the eighteenth-century theories of sympathy are as important as the similarities. Taking Smith as our model we see a *process* of adjustment that requires time: you sympathize with my feelings, but, because your feelings are not so intense as mine, I in turn adjust my own feelings to match yours. In addition, according to Smith, irate emotions are more demanding than others. We insist that our friends share our resentments more than we care about them sympathizing with our joys. Yet angry feelings are the hardest of all to resonate with, since our initial impulse is to feel sympathy for their *victims*.

Angry feelings are also hard to sympathize with because they are generally "disagreeable." Recall that Aristotle thought that anger was both painful and pleasurable. Hume and Smith had to take this into account. They limited the times when anger was pleasurable; but they admitted it some pleasure in its moral role when, in Smith's words, anger is "that noble and generous resentment which governs its pursuit of the greatest injuries." That sort of anger is godlike in its zeal for both vengeance and punishment. Impartial people observing such anger will also rejoice at it.[20]

Most modern psychologists consider anger to be a purely "negative" emotion. When they visualize its place on an axis that runs from misery to pleasure, they see it at the unpleasant end. But more recently one of the creators of this axis, James Russell, has proposed that a person may feel angry yet cognitively assess the stimulus for her anger as pleasurable. He has in mind a mixed emotion like being angry at the "bad guy" in a good movie.[21] That is a concession to anger's pleasure. But it is a far cry from Smith's "noble and generous resentment."

In eighteenth-century France, anger's ennobling possibilities were embraced by numerous writers. The discourse of "human rights," born in the Middle Ages, bloomed in this environment. In his novel *Émile*, Jean-Jacques Rousseau (d.1778) observed a child being hit by his nurse. "I thought [the child would be] intimidated," wrote Rousseau. "I said to myself: he will have a servile soul. [. . .] I was wrong: the poor boy was choking with anger; he could not breathe; I saw him turn purple. A moment later came shrill cries: all the signs of resentment, of fury, of despair of this age were in his tone. [. . .] Had I doubted that the sentiment of justice and injustice was innate in the heart of man, this example alone would have convinced me."[22] Later in the same work, Rousseau made clear that by "man" he also had women in mind. Sophie, his female exemplar, is like Émile, his male Everyman, in every way but her sex: "she has the same organs, the same needs, the same faculties."[23] True, sex matters: Sophie, like all women, was meant (thought Rousseau) to contribute to the common good by being subservient to men. But God gave her the same passions and the same sense of justice as he gave to men. When Émile, Sophie's lover, fails to come to a rendezvous, she feels betrayed and angry. Then she learns that he neglected her in order to help an injured man, and her anger melts away.

The next generation, brought up on Rousseau and others of his ilk, fused his sense of personal dignity (the child's indignation when he was hit; Sophie's when she was neglected) with righteous rage against the social injustices that denied rights to most of the population. The resulting fusion was, in the words of Patrick Coleman, "one great emotion endowed with quasi-sacred significance." That sort of anger helped to bring about and justify the French Revolution.[24]

During the French Revolution between 1789 and 1794, the place of anger in French discourse swelled markedly. A sample of many of the materials produced during that period shows a notable increase in the use of the term *colère*, the French equivalent of the English word "anger," as well as related words—*ressentiment, rage, fureur, furie*, and so on.[25]

The highest frequency in the use of *colère* occurred in September 1793, when the word appeared 12 times. That was also when *rage* reached its highest mark: 25. Together they were used just a bit more often than the word *liberté* (34 instances) that same month. Yet *liberté* was a rallying cry of the revolution. These are not large numbers, but they do suggest a trend. The context of this liberal peppering of anger in the Revolutionary archives included the Reign of Terror, which began in March, 1793; continual war against other European states; and the introduction of a general army draft in August. While at the beginning of the Revolution, in 1789, Honoré-Gabriel Riqueti, Count of Mirabeau, warned against the "often ill-founded anger" of the people,[26] by 1793 popular anger had become as sacred as the Ten Commandments. Thus, in a speech to the National Convention at the beginning of September, a spokesman for the Paris commune exhorted the "Mountain," the most radical members of the Parliament, to "be the Mount Sinai of the French." From their mountain top they should, god-like, "launch amid thunderbolts the eternal decrees of justice and the will of the people [. . .]. The hour of justice and of anger has arrived!"[27] Later in the same month a local representative addressed the citizens of his district: "The French people, bent over under the yoke of the most hateful slavery, worn out by the crimes and vexations of tyrants and their accomplices, rose all together on July 14, 1789, broke their chains, and, in their just anger, stormed the Bastille."[28] The term "just anger" was repeated often that year. So was "holy anger," as when, on August 20, at a pageant meant to celebrate the Republic, a banner representing the monarchy did not go up in flames quickly enough. An "indignant" official, "seized by a holy and patriotic anger," tore the banner to pieces.[29] Sloterdijk's "treasury" of righteous anger was, we might say, funding the show.

The word *rage* did not normally fare so well in these materials. It was usually associated with invading armies, despots, and traitors. Even so, it was sometimes possible to speak of "just rage," as did the "citizens of Coffinal" (a small hamlet in southern France) in a letter they sent to the National Convention in mid-September 1793 in the wake of the Girondist Charlotte Corday's murder of the Montagnard Marat. "Marat is dead! O, assassins! If you measure your trophies by the importance of the victims you massacre, you have never triumphed more brilliantly. [. . .] But let us temper our just rage: patriotism will always survive among the debris."[30]

Within a year, the Mountain was brought down, the Terror ended, and satirists were lampooning "The Great Anger of Père Duchesne." In Plate 8, probably dating from 1794, a young man, clearly crazed, tears at his hair; in his haste he has knocked over his seat; his jailer smiles gaily. The youth is about to be executed. In fact, this so-called Père Duchesne was Jacques René Hébert, a radical journalist whose work appeared in the radical newspaper *Le Père Duchesne*. His writings were scabrous, satirical, and enormously popular, full of scathing attacks on his contemporaries. "Oh, quick, fuck, prepare the guillotine," he wrote in a characteristic article in 1793, urging the execution of the "traitor" General Custine. His call was heeded.[31] But Hébert was himself guillotined the following year, the occasion for Plate 8.

For many in England, watching such events across the Channel, the French Revolution was proof that the anger of revolt was never ethical, never just, certainly never sacred. In an autobiographical poem, William Wordsworth (d.1850) wrote about how he felt as a resident in France during the Revolution. At first, he was enthusiastic about the end of privilege. But with the Terror and the war, he could think only of

The goaded land waxed mad; the crimes of few
Spread into madness of the many; blasts
From hell came sanctified like airs from heaven.

He faulted "the blind rage / Of insolent tempers."[32] Wordsworth was writing these lines in 1805, but he cast them back to the past, as if they had been his response to the events of July 1793. That was precisely when some revolutionaries were speaking of their "just anger."

In the wake of the Revolution, English writers bifurcated the emotion of anger into two sorts, one good (indignation) and the other bad (rage, fury).

In his influential *Reflections on the Revolution in France* (1790), Edmund Burke mentioned good anger only once: at the end of his diatribe against the excesses of the Revolution, when he characterized himself as "one in whose breast no anger durable or vehement has ever been kindled, but by what he considered as tyranny."[33] He denied any such passion to the revolutionaries, whom he accused of "fury, outrage, and insult" as they rebelled against their "mild and lawful monarch."[34] History, he said, if misused, becomes a storehouse of weapons, "supplying the means of keeping alive, or reviving, dissensions and animosities, and adding fuel to civil fury." He faulted human "pride, ambition, avarice, revenge, lust, sedition, hypocrisy, ungoverned zeal, and all the train of disorderly appetites" for the woes of every commonwealth.[35] In effect, this was Gregory the Great's list of anger's myrmidons: "brawls, swollen minds, insults, clamors, angry outbursts, and blasphemies." But now these vices brought ruin to the body politic rather than to the individual sinner.

Meanwhile, as Andrew M. Stauffer has noted, anger's virtuous side was often termed "indignation."[36] Burke had recourse to the human sympathies and sensibilities that Hume and Smith had identified. When change is needed, people will know it: "the wise will determine [it] from the gravity of the case; the irritable, from sensibility to oppression; the high-minded, from disdain and indignation at abusive power in unworthy hands." All this is virtuous. But a revolution must be "the very last resource of the thinking and the good."[37] Commenting on the confiscation of the estates of a French Catholic cardinal, Burke wrote: "Can one hear of the proscription of such persons and the confiscation of their effects, without indignation and horror? He is not a man who does not feel such emotions on such occasions."[38] For Burke, indignation was entirely different from fury, and although both might be subsumed under the catch-all "anger," they were not the same.

Burke's tirade against the rage of the Revolution unleashed a torrent of responses for and against the events in France, all claiming the high ground for themselves, all accusing the others of "a frenzy of passion," as

Thomas Paine (d.1809) put it in his long polemic against Burke.[39] As in the United States today, so some of Burke's contemporaries in Britain feared a body politic so polarized as to preclude rational discussion.

Paine himself had long before adopted the rhetoric of moral sentiments to promote American independence. In his *Common Sense* (1776), a best-seller among the colonists, he evoked the "power of feeling," as the natural endowment of "all mankind."[40] In so doing, he signaled an important shift in attitudes. The inhabitants of the American colonies were divided by class and race, and heretofore only the white, male property-owning classes had laid claim to honorable moral sentiments while denying that others felt them. The colonists took advantage of their large vocabulary of "heated feelings" to refer to themselves and others in terms both nuanced and judgmental. Nicole Eustace has carefully surveyed the evidence, particularly in colonial Philadelphia. "Those who displayed [anger-like emotions] could be judged according to a wide variety of standards, involving anything from 'servile' tantrums, to 'savage' aggression, to honorable judgment."[41] Each term expressed a particular social prejudice, though the vocabulary was always contested and fluid.

"Indignation," as was true in England, was reserved for those whose anger was dignified, honorable, and righteous. "Resentment" was another such term, almost always claimed by men of property. Women, on the other hand, even high-status white women, were rarely said to "resent." Few of them owned property, and fewer yet could claim the same sort of honor as their male counterparts. Much as in Aristotle's ancient Athens, anger of the indignant sort was the privilege of a man in a position to be insulted.

Anger "unbridled," "wanton," and "in a passion" were terms set aside for members of the lower classes, criminals, and black men. No one spoke at all about black women's anger; they had neither property nor honor, and perhaps their usual role in Philadelphia as domestics meant that recognizing their anger would have been inordinately threatening. Similarly, the possibility that Indians might be angry was hardly mentioned. Quakers repudiated anger absolutely, as fully as did ancient Buddhists—though for different reasons. Taking the Sermon on the Mount's admonition to love as a commandment never to get angry, Quakers lived (as one of their elders said) "in opposition to sensual lust, vanity, pride, bitterness of spirit, corruption, enmity, and wrath."[42]

But after around 1750, the ideas of the Scottish moral philosophers like Hume and Smith crossed the Atlantic. Their notion of one "human nature" sold books and slipped into the curriculum of the College of Philadelphia. It made all social classes equal and even hinted at the equality of races and genders. At the same time, anger itself was being reevaluated, its association with violence now rehabilitated to suggest strength, valor, and success in war. Indians were suddenly praised as angry, and settlers on the frontier began to credit themselves with fury, rage, and even wrath. The victorious British army (still at this point allied with the colonists) was applauded in a newspaper article in 1759 because its soldiers "drove the French out of their lines [. . .] [with a] furious attack."[43]

This sort of oscillation between anger as the energizer of high-minded undertakings (on the one hand) and as the destructive resort of divisive impulses (on the other) continues today. Modern moral philosophers try to sort this out, in the process attempting to adapt modern psychological findings to ethical concerns. A good example is Zac Cogley, who argues that anger is virtuous when (and only when) it fulfills well all of its three functions: correctly appraising wrongdoing, motivating appropriate action, and communicating accurately.[44] It is a vice when it goes to one of two extremes: meekness and passivity on one end; wrath and aggressivity on the other. Cogley's notion lies somewhere between Aristotle's narrow rationale for anger and the universal justification of the Scottish philosophers. For anger to be virtuous, Cogley says, it must correctly appraise "wrongful conduct," and its intensity must fit the seriousness of the injury. Frederick Douglass and Martin Luther King Jr are Cogley's "exemplars of virtue." Their anger was ethical because the injustice of the institutions against which they railed was so great.

But rage for the right reasons must also move people to act—to protest, to work for change, to "dissuade others from wrongful conduct and to encourage (through an implicit threat) beneficial actions." This is "assertive resistance," says Cogley, citing King's work of transmuting "the inchoate rage of the ghetto into a constructive and creative channel."[45]

Like Aristotle, like the Scottish philosophers, Cogley makes anger's judgment essential to morality. His appeal to action and communication harks back to Hume's and Smith's notion of sympathy. He too observes that we do not feel our emotions in a void but rather adjust them to those around us, and they to ours. Yet, in the end, Cogley reveals how far we are today from the original assumptions behind the theory of moral sentiments. Hume and Smith were convinced that all human beings shared the same passions which, when expressed within the laws and norms of society, were both similar and moral. They had no need for extraordinary heroes like Douglass and King to provide exemplars of virtuous anger.

In *After Virtue*, Alasdair MacIntyre mourns our loss of the "impersonal standard by which moral disagreements might be rationally resolved"—a standard, he says, that existed until nineteenth-century philosophy broke into competing schools of thought.[46] He blames these schools for our shrill and discordant voices today, all claiming our own outrage to be the righteous one. In MacIntyre's wake, Cogley is trying to find a new "impersonal standard" so that we can reclaim a certain kind of anger for virtue, another for vice.

But the very idea that "out there," somewhere, is an impersonal and universal standard of virtue may in fact be the cause of the strident din of anger today. The possibility of virtuous human anger, first theorized by Aristotle, was confounded in medieval theology with the righteous anger of God and our human role in feeling and expressing it against those who violate the divine law. Even when, much later, the Scottish philosophers separated virtuous anger from God's directives, it nevertheless retained that same sense of absolute righteousness that could admit of no error. (Aristotle, by contrast, thought virtue could be adjusted to particular cases.)

Let us also admit that the so-called impersonal standard was never impersonal. Aristotle's definition of virtuous anger might have been flexible, but even so, it applied to a very small, resolutely elite, and exclusively male subgroup within the ancient *polis*. The medieval notion pertained to a greater number of people, but they had to be Christians (and only a certain kind of Christian, one adhering to the Catholic Church), and for the most part, they had to be male and of free status: knights and lords, priests and bishops. When Hume and other moral philosophers broke from the God-defined standard of virtue, when they looked to human nature to offer a universal template, they were still thinking that the resulting morality would mirror the justice of God. It was not by chance that their "sympathy" was close to "Love thy neighbor as thyself."

The real problem is not that we have lost an impersonal standard; the problem is the very idea of righteous anger. Our voices would be far less discordant if we did not believe that our anger is just and virtuous while "theirs" is not, if we admitted that we might possibly be wrong. And indeed, this book offers many alternative ways to think about our anger that do not claim it must be virtuous to be rightly felt—a whole variety of traditions with which to feel our anger, understand it, and deal with it. Anger need not be righteous to be important, to demand attention, to merit our interest or concern. Anger as a virtue or a vice, as a moral or immoral sentiment, is but one inherited idea about anger among many and often the most deleterious.

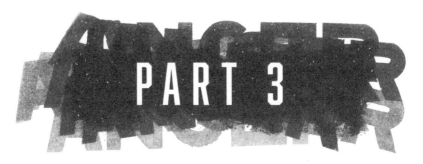

# PART 3

NATURAL ANGER

# EARLY MEDICAL TRADITIONS

If anger is natural—if it is part of human nature—then there is no point in imagining that we may reject it. There is not even much sense in endowing it with ethical value, whether good or bad. If anger is natural, then the best thing we may do is understand it: where it "resides," how it is produced, how it works, how we might control it.

As something occasionally detrimental to our bodies and minds, anger has long been a concern of medical practitioners. From the third to the eighteenth centuries in the West, the prevailing ideas about the role of anger in health derived largely from the many writings of Galen (d.216/17). In his *Art of Medicine*, this influential medical thinker and practitioner classified anger—along with all the other emotions—as one among the many factors that mattered to health, whether in helpful or harmful ways. These agents, which Galen called elements of "hygiene," were later codified as the "six non-naturals": (1) air and environment, (2) motion and rest, (3) sleeping and waking, (4) food and drink, (5) retention and elimination, and (6) "the affections of the soul"—the emotions, anger among them. All six change our bodies. In the right quantities and at the right times, they help preserve health. But when overabundant or insufficient, they make us sick. Galen considered it obvious that we should "keep away from the imbalance of all the psychic affections—anger, grief, joy, passion, fear and envy."[1]

Note that Galen did not say we should *avoid* the affections themselves but rather beware their "imbalance." He taught that bodies, like all matter, were composed of four basic elements—air, water, fire, and earth—each associated with a particular quality: air is cold, water wet, fire is hot, and earth dry. The human body has four humors related to those elements: the blood of the heart is hot and wet, the yellow (or red) bile of the liver is hot and dry, black bile from the spleen is cold and dry, and the phlegm of the brain is cold and wet. Bodily health is the product of the correct and harmonious mix of these humors and the elements that they represent. A normal male body is hot and dry; the normal female is, by contrast, cold and wet. However, each individual has his or her own "right" balance.

An emotion like anger is able to modify the body's hotness, coldness, wetness, and dryness. But how? Anger, Galen wrote, is "a kind of boiling of the hot in the heart." The heart beats violently, and anger moves outward via the blood and the vital spirit in the arteries, heating the body as it goes. In so doing, it changes the body's mixtures. This may be good for the body, but it may also cause serious diseases. When people get into heated arguments and rages, their humoral balances change; they become "more bilious"—glutted with the hot and dry bile of the liver that may bring on a fever, a dangerous condition. But too little anger is also harmful: when people never argue, never rage, their bodies become cold and phlegmatic, bringing on "obstructions in the liver [. . .] and epilepsy." Just as bad are the mental effects of deficient anger: "an idle intellect, mindlessness and a soul which is completely lacking in spirit."[2] We need some anger just to get up in the morning and make it through the day.

All the passions have the potential to upset the body's normal state. But each does so in a different way. The physician can generally diagnose the ones that are disordered by knowing the various kinds of pulses associated with them. A person with a hard and small pulse is rarely angry, but if he is at last driven to rage, he remains angry longer than usual.[3] "In rage," Galen wrote, "the pulse is big, vigorous, fast and frequent. [. . .] In fear which is sudden and violent [the pulse is] quick, agitated, disordered, uneven." But beware, cautioned Galen: some people wish to conceal their anger. They nevertheless give it away by their "uneven" pulse, which may be distinguished from the still *more* uneven pulse of anxious people.[4] Galen was not quite boasting that a trained physician could administer a pulse-based lie-detector test, but he was not far from doing so.

Given the potential of the non-naturals to change the mixtures of the body, it is small wonder that Galen wrote a lot about the proper way to eat, sleep, exercise, and so on. These things are fairly easy to control: you measure your food, count your hours of sleep, clock how much you exercise. Doling out the correct amount of anger is far less obvious. Galen borrowed much of his own advice for guaranteeing the right level of anger from Seneca and other ancient writers. He prescribed a proper upbringing, habitual self-control, reliance on the monitoring of a trusted supervisor, daily self-assessments, soothing music, salutary reading, sleep, and so on. In fact, in his ethical works, Galen took a stance remarkably close to the Stoics for a doctor who clearly thought that some anger was natural and necessary.

It is instructive to compare for a moment Galen's thinking with the more modern theory of Harvard philosopher and psychologist William James (d.1910). For James also located the passions in the body and gave thinking no constituent role in the making of an emotion. In James' view, we become conscious of our emotions only when we feel their "characteristic bodily symptoms." If we try to conceive of anger, for example, without imagining its bodily concomitants—"no ebullition of it in the chest, no flushing of the face, no dilatation of the nostrils, no clenching of the teeth, no impulse to vigorous action"—we end up with no conception at all.[5]

The "ebullition" in the chest, the "boiling" sensation around the heart, the rushing of the heated blood to the face, causing it to blush—all these are Galenic notions, still potent in 1884 when James was writing, even though Galen's writings had long since been removed from the medical curriculum. And for all that, English speakers today still use expressions like, "You make my blood boil," and "She got all hot and bothered."[6] But the most enduring inheritance from Galen today—one that, however, separates body from soul in ways that Galen would never have approved— is the idea that emotions are part of our physiology and that scientists can study emotions via changes in pulse, skin conductance, and the like.

✳

In the Middle Ages, Galen's theories were partly an aspect of medical practice, whether or not book-learned, and in part the subject of formal instruction in schools. Early on, short summaries reduced the Galenic system to a few handy axioms, with the humors taking an even more important role as the chief causes of human health and temperament. The various types of dispositions, including the irascible tendency to get angry, were defined by their prevailing humors. While Galen had appreciated a variety of humoral balances, medieval physicians tended to designate the "sanguine" (warm and wet) disposition as optimum. But they were not doctrinaire about it. For example, on the issue of anger, an early medieval "bullet-point" summary of medical knowledge, the *Wisdom of the Art of Medicine*, claimed that choleric people—that is, people whose "complexion" (their mix of humors) was dominated by yellow bile's heat and dryness—"are hot-tempered and changeable. But others are taciturn and are said to be reserved. [. . .] These have their health restored by cold water."[7] We see in even this brief passage that choleric people were only *sometimes* hot-tempered; at other times they were "reserved." Medieval humoral theory was not a theory of pre-determined personality types.

With the rise of universities in Europe at the end of the twelfth century, medicine gradually joined philosophy and theology as an academic discipline. In the Islamic world, Galenic theories had already by then gained a distinguished tradition of commentary and elaboration. We glimpse some of that sophistication in the writings of Moses Maimonides (d.1204), a celebrated Jewish rabbi and physician at the court of Sultan Saladin of Egypt. Writing about a healthy regimen, Maimonides stressed the importance of emotions, for they "produce changes in the body that are great, evident and manifest to all." He had complicated remedies for all sorts of personality types. For example, for those who were "temperate"—in other words, not prone to anger—he recommended a healthful concoction that included bits of pearl, amber, coral, burned river crab, and oxtongue (a type of herb); gold and dodder of thyme (a parasitic plant); musk, basil, and balm-mint seeds; saffron, cinnamon, and red roses, all compounded into pills or kneaded with honey.[8]

Because that concoction was excellent for "strengthening the heart," Maimonides advocated it as a sort of basic recipe that could then be adjusted to the particular needs of irascible patients. For those with a "bad hot temperament," he advised reducing the saffron and musk, omitting the thyme, and adding fumitory and senna (both flowering plants). Other people were like "kings suffering from melancholia, a disorder that tends toward mania, that is rage." Theirs was an anger mingled with despair. In such cases, it was necessary to add to the basic recipe "the weight of a dram of thoroughly pulverized jacinth [a gemstone] of exquisite pomegranate color." Other patients suffered from "palpitation and weakness of the heart because of the badness of their hot temperament."[9] Theirs was an anger tinged with anxiety, and they needed an entirely different compound. There was no one-size-fits-all solution.

Did these medicines really make a difference? Yes, said Maimonides, observing that some of his patients obtained great relief from them. However, in other cases, pills were not the answer: instead, relief from gnawing anger came from "practical philosophy, and from the admonitions and disciplines of the Law."[10] Here the rabbi Maimonides triumphed over the doctor.

Meanwhile, European physicians were elaborating their own variants of Galenism. Consider the ideas of Bartholomaeus of Salerno (fl. c.1175). In one section of his influential commentary on the *Isagoge*— a ninth-century text that was largely a summary of Galen's work— Bartholomaeus explained the movements of the heart in accordance with his understanding of Aristotle, whose writings and thought were gaining primacy by the end of the twelfth century.[11] The heart's operative power, wrote Bartholomaeus, is to move the heart and arteries to dilate and contract. In thus operating, it "brings about in the heart anger, joy, and the other passions of the soul." So far, so good; neither Aristotle nor Galen would object. But Bartholomaeus could not follow Aristotle in thinking that emotions *began* in the heart. Instead, he asserted that "their origin lies in the brain and their execution comes from the heart." This was neither Aristotelian nor Galenic.

How did Bartholomaeus arrive at this idea? From Aristotle, he knew that behind every emotion was a judgment. But he couldn't follow Aristotle in thinking that judgments were located in the heart; he was too good a Galenist not to know that judgments, imagination, and the interpretation of sense perceptions must originate in the brain because, as Galen had showed through his studies of animal anatomy, the nerves originate in the brain. Galen had given the brain only a bit part in the unfolding of the affections. Bartholomaeus put it at center stage. His understanding of how we get angry was remarkably close to many modern cognitive accounts. As he wrote,

> The origin of all emotions lies in extrinsic causes perceived by some sense or by the imagination. For example, we perceive with our eyes a wild beast charging, or an enemy passing by with a certain haughty and proud mien. These are causes respectively of fear and of anger or indignation. Similarly, when we perceive with our eyes the beauties

and dances of virgins, we are moved to joy. Likewise, when we hear insults or flattery, we become angry or we rejoice. Hence it is plain that the cause of any emotion whatsoever is first perceived by sense or imagination.

When Bartholomaeus says that emotions have "extrinsic causes," he means what modern psychologist Nancy Stein (see Chapter 2) terms a "sense experience." In the case of anger, says Bartholomaeus, the cause might be "an enemy passing by with a certain haughty and proud mien." That is equivalent to Stein's next step, the evaluation that what has been sensed signals "the failure of an important goal." Bartholomaeus' goal is for the enemy to recognize our honor and dignity. Finally, in Stein's sequence, comes the belief that the failure can be rectified, which for her is an idea that is part of the appraisal process. Bartholomaeus makes a similar point: "the thought of taking vengeance for injuries received precedes anger. This thought is a certain imagination of the brain, which the fervor of the heart follows with the desire for revenge." For Galen, anger had been physical: "a kind of boiling of the hot in the heart." For Bartholomaeus anger was mental: a kind of *thought* that causes the heart to boil. This idea nicely suited his Christian context, for, as we have seen already in Gregory the Great, the vice of anger came from without and assailed the citadel of the heart. In Bartholomaeus' commentary, the "outside" is the brain, and its cogitations rile up the heart to burning rage.

Thus did medieval physicians open Galenism to new ideas and formulations. In the wake of the breakup of a monolithic Church, the invention of the printing press, the increase in general literacy, the scientific triumphs of Newton, and (above all) the introduction of human autopsies that began at the end of the fifteenth century and corrected Galen's anatomy, the seventeenth and eighteenth centuries marked a turning point in medical thought.

William Harvey's demonstration of the circulation of blood, published in 1628, not only invalidated Galen's separation of arteries from veins but also gave the heart a different role: rather than the physical embodiment of a part of the soul, it was now basically a pump. What did the emotions have to do with a pump? Nothing. And what did heat have to do with anger? Nothing either, as a contemporary of Harvey, Santorio Santorio (d.1636), discovered after he invented the thermometer. He had hoped it would prove Galen's category of hot temperament. Instead, it substituted a measurement for what Galen had intended to be a personality trait. What did it mean for a man to be "hot-tempered" when his temperature, like everyone else's, was 98.6°F (37°C)? A new, mechanical model of the body started to take hold.

As Galenic theory began to lose its grip, new explanations took its place. Bartholomaeus' emphasis on the brain as the site of the emotions was seconded by newly accurate dissections. At the same time, the humors were downgraded in importance, and the spirits—which for Galen moved inside the arterial blood carrying anger's heat from the heart through the whole body—were, at least initially, granted new pride of place. Thomas Willis (d.1675) exemplifies both trends. In his *Anatomy of the Brain*, he put the spirits at the center of his discussion. Anger, like the other passions, indeed like all thoughts, is first "conceived" in the brain, but no sooner does that happen than it moves the spirits. These agitate the cerebellum, which, in turn, stirs up the nerves serving the heart, the viscera, the "muscles of the face," and even the eyes, which Willis considered to be transparent windows onto "the feeling and intimate conceptions of the mind," unmasking even the will to dissemble. This general bodily agitation is inevitable, said Willis, "because the [. . .] spirits, tending this way and that way" in the space between the brain and the chest, "do at once strike those nerves as the strings of a harp." In effect, the spirits had for Willis the connective role that instantaneous electrochemical communication via the nerves has for scientists today.[12] With his emphasis on the brain and its role in churning up the spirits, Willis was abandoning the "old-fashioned" talk of humors and hot tempers.

Another result of relocating the emotions to the brain was to demote the heart's role and, in effect, to sever emotions from most of the body apart from the brain. Emotions became (in the new view) almost purely mental, though of course they had to be communicated to the rest of the body in order to carry out the actions that they required. When the heart was seen as the center of emotions, when it was the cauldron where the blood was heated in anger or cooled in fear, there was no separation of body and emotion because the brain/mind/soul were part of bodily processes. Descartes is often blamed for divorcing body and mind. As we saw in Chapter 3, he did not do so directly, for, as he specifically pointed out, the soul is joined to every part of the body. But Descartes' soul was concerned only with conscious thinking—with active thoughts, like "the car behind me is honking," and with passive thoughts, like "that honking is insulting me," which is felt as anger. The Cartesian soul does not concern itself with bodily processes like digestion or breathing. Those movements work automatically, just as the hands of a clock turn because of its mechanism. As philosopher Susan James points out, "Descartes faces the task of explaining how a purely mechanical body and a purely spiritual soul can interact at all, and how they can do so, as he claims they can, at the pineal gland in the center of the brain."[13]

That interaction was made possible, so Descartes' thinking went, by the spirits that traveled within the nerves. Sometimes the spirits worked *automatically*, as reflexive responses to sense perceptions: we touch a hot stove, the spirits move to the brain, the motions in the brain push the spirits to the hand, and we take our hand off the stove. No thought is involved; the whole process is carried out by the body alone. But at other times, the spirits are moved by a sense perception that requires thought. We hear a honking horn, the sensation travels to the pineal gland via the spirits, the gland is moved, and we think. If we think, "That's a horn," then the spirits may not move again in that episode. But if we think, "That's an insult to my driving," then we may feel anger, which moves the spirits down the nerves to stir up our blood. We may "turn pale or tremble"; we may "flush or even cry."[14]

But if Descartes sought to locate emotions within the mind, others, although equally happy to separate mind and body, began to think of emotions as purely an aspect of the body's hydraulic and mechanical systems. The physician William Clark (d.c.1780) envisioned the body as a concatenation of fluids and solids. Early microscopes could not see any fluid in the nerves, but, by analogy with blood vessels and the lymphatic system (discovered by Jean Pecquet a century before), Clark thought it "highly probable" that "nervous fluid"—equivalent to the spirits—flowed through the nerves.[15] This was of the utmost importance, he said, for "every faculty of the mind depends on the nervous system."[16] The emotions themselves might determine the "distribution of the nervous fluid." Anger, then, like all the emotions, could "disturb the whole animal economy."[17] Clark quoted Lorenzo Bellini (d.1704), an earlier medical authority, who had all sorts of things to say about the role of anger in the body: it "increases the influxes of the nervous fluid," and it makes the muscles and the heart contract "more frequently, with more velocity and force," which causes changes in the pulse and "in the motion of the blood."[18] When the excess fluid is extreme, dire illness is the result.

✳

When my mother interpreted my doll-battering as an outburst of the anger within me, she drew on the many hydraulic metaphors proposed over the years by physicians: an excess of humors, an overabundance of nervous fluid. Commonplace expressions about anger these days echo these ideas: "Try to get your anger out of your system." "She was brimming with rage." "She could feel her gorge rising." "His pent-up anger welled up inside him." "He was bursting with anger."[19] The idea that anger is due to an excess or a deficiency has echoes in the scientific literature of today as well. "Reduced levels of serotonin [. . .] significantly influences PFC [prefrontal cortex]-amygdala circuits implicated in aggression and other affective behaviors," announces an article published in 2012.[20] In other words, the authors were declaring that a deficiency of serotonin in the brains of their volunteer subjects led to abnormal responses to angry faces. The authors concluded that their study supported the idea that serotonin "facilitates the PFC in suppressing the negative emotions, generated in the amygdala, that are associated with aggression and other emotional behaviors."[21] Why the authors thought that angry faces implied aggression, indeed why they thought that anger could be seen in faces and should inspire negative emotions in their viewers, is the subject of my next chapter. But, to conclude this one: not so unlike my mother, these scientists would have said of my childish self, "She hasn't enough serotonin in her system."

# 10

# IN THE LAB

Today, parents who are concerned about their child's anger will no doubt want to read what the experts say. Some of the most prestigious among our experts—certainly those most often in the news—are laboratory scientists. But worried parents reading the conclusions of such scientists will not find clarity, for there are numerous different and often conflicting opinions. Many articles offer images of faces posed to express a universally recognizable anger. Reading those, parents might earnestly scan the faces of their children to find matching traits. They might want to change the way their children look when angry, perhaps using a children's book that claims to help kids learn how to do just that. Other articles on anger are accompanied by gorgeously colored brain scans showing the regions of the brain where, the authors say, anger is "located." Concerned parents might well ask whether there is a way to "deactivate" that part of the brain. Indeed, some scientists have thought that there is: it's called amygdalotomy, a procedure that deactivates the amygdala nucleus. Needless to say, however, this operation poses numerous problems, not least because the nucleus is not always tied to angry responses and because it is certainly tied to other sorts of behaviors and brain functions.[1]

Yet other authoritative studies tell us to forget the brain scans and the faces. They deny that anger is a natural category, one that everyone feels and expresses. They repudiate those who say that anger shows up in some spots in the brain or as expressions on everyone's face. They say, instead, that anger is one of many constructs that the brain creates as it monitors and makes sense of the information that comes to it from the body and the external world. If in some cultures a mental category like anger is not useful for survival and flourishing, it will not exist as such.

These constitute the main schools of thought regarding anger that have been proposed by experimental science. There are others. Perhaps the most important is Alan J. Fridlund's approach. He argues that what we call "anger" is (like all the emotions) an intentional and strategic social gesture. In Fridlund's view, the "anger face" signals (depending on the context) something akin to "Back off or I'll attack."[2] Like Fridlund, but often for different reasons, many therapists concerned with anger also reject the major hypotheses offered by laboratory scientists, or they subscribe to them only in part. We have met some of those therapists in the course of this book. But here, in this chapter, we will consider the main theories that are based on laboratory experiments rather than focus on therapies. Of course, lab-based work also has important implications for therapy.

There are two crucial questions that divide these schools of thought. The dominant school, which we might call the Basic Emotions group, hardly bothers with the first and most fundamental question: is anger a natural entity, something real, something fundamentally biological, and one of a number of basic emotions? The scientists claiming Basic Emotions ignore these questions because they assume that the answer to all of them is yes. They focus on a second question: how best may anger be studied? Some members of this school say via faces and reactions to them. Others prefer via brain scans. Some combine both photos and scans.

But another school of thought, the members of which call themselves Psychological Constructionists, answers those questions in the negative. They present data, using both angry faces and brain scans, to argue that experimental scientists have been barking up the wrong tree. They, like many in the Basic Emotions school, are generally neuroscientists. But they say that the neural networks in the brain show that the *whole brain* is involved in the production of what we call anger. Our brains learn over time to put together certain feelings, expressions (including facial expressions and palpitating hearts), and reactions in ways that we call anger. Psychological Constructionists say that anger is not hard-wired in us genetically when we are born; it is learned—it becomes a concept—as neural patterns are formed with inputs from parents, schools, societies, and so on. When we see a baby screaming and her face getting red, it is we who interpret what she is feeling as anger, and as she grows up, she internalizes that category.

Finally, there is a group of scientists, the Enactivists, that thinks that the first, the most crucial questions, have been badly posed. They should not center on whether anger is a "basic" emotion. They should ask whether there are neural circuits in the brain that form the foundations of the feelings, thoughts, and actions that we connect to anger but that other societies may call something else, understand differently, perhaps express in ways hard for us to associate with anything like anger. These scientists believe that all of us have these hard-wired circuits. They are connected to our faces just as they are involved in many other things that we do—that we "enact"—in the world.

We should not be discouraged that there are conflicting schools of thought. To the contrary! This whole book is about different and often jostling ideas about anger. That is the point: the more facets of anger we see, the better we can understand, feel, and know what to do with our own. Let us, then, enter the lab.

＊

The Basic Emotions school claims to have its origins in Charles Darwin (d.1882) and his seminal book *The Expression of Emotions in Man and Animals*.[3] Darwin's purpose was to show that emotions were expressed with the same or related muscles and physiology in both human beings and animals. He wanted to counter the accepted view that human beings were somehow exceptional, as if they were endowed (as an earlier anatomist, Charles Bell, had declared) with a "special apparatus" for communicating their feelings.[4] Darwin thought that other animals had apparatuses homologous with those of people. Revenge and anger were "instincts" belonging to more than mankind. Playing on the Christian tradition in which the Devil had instigated man's fall from Paradise, Darwin joked that "our descent, then, is the origin of our evil passions!!—The Devil under [the] form of Baboon is our grandfather." And I suppose that, had he continued the jest, he would have noted that modern civilization was gradually overcoming the Devil's curse. For Darwin observed that in his day revenge and anger were generally kept under control and were even "slowly vanishing" in human society, although both had once been "necessary & no doubt were preservative."[5]

Since "civilized man" was normally too restrained, Darwin preferred to observe anger and other emotional expressions in infants, the insane, and—via detailed questionnaires to missionaries, landowners, teachers and others in England's far-flung empire—other "races of mankind." He also questioned more than "twenty educated persons of various ages and both sexes," asking them to identify the emotions shown on "the face of an old man, whose skin was little sensitive." He was referring to photographs made by French neurologist Duchenne de Boulogne (d.1875) while stimulating the man's facial muscles with an electrical probe to mimic various emotional expressions.[6] (See Plate 9.)

Darwin's use of Duchenne's photographs was the distant model and justification for many modern scientific experiments. He was convinced that the face was the chief organ of human emotional expression, and he speculated that this became especially true after people began to wear clothing. Darwin was not at all bothered by the fact that the man in Duchenne's photographs was probably not feeling the induced emotion at all.[7] He quoted Shakespeare on the reality of actors' "put on" feelings. This same assumption informs many scientific experiments using faces today. But now the faces are usually digitized and may even be manipulated to morph from one expression to another.

Darwin did not use the term "basic emotions," let alone say that there was any particular number of them. But he has been understood to have thought that. He certainly did not deny the old Western notion—persistent from at least the time of the ancient Greeks—that anger is a natural entity, a sort of species of the genus "emotion." Many scientists understand Darwin to have said that human emotional expressions have never changed and do not vary even within different populations. Thus, Lisa Feldman Barrett, who is a major proponent of the Psychological Constructionist school, calls Darwin an "essentialist," that is, someone who thinks that certain categories, such as anger and joy, or dogs and cats "have a true reality or nature. Within each category, the members are thought to share a deep, underlying property (an essence)." Barrett claims that Darwin "wrote that emotions were passed down to us, unchanging through the ages, from an early animal ancestor."[8]

She is right about Darwin thinking that our emotions have been "passed down." But she may not be quite correct in saying that Darwin considered them "unchanging." At least in the case of anger, Darwin pointed out how behaviors and even uses did indeed adapt over time. Anger originally had a role in survival; it prepared—and continues to prepare—an animal to attack, to act out the "fight" half of the fight or flight response. At the beginning of primate history, it probably had a similar function. But Darwin did not think that its expression in his own day remained as it had been originally. As he said, "Our early progenitors, when enraged, would probably have exposed their teeth more freely than does [today's] man, [. . . and] when indignant or moderately angry, would not have held their heads erect, opened their chests, squared their shoulders, and clenched their fists."[9] Those gestures were adaptations to our upright stance and our ability to fight using fists and clubs.

Darwin also suggested that anger could take on new functions. Philosopher Paul Griffiths has called these new purposes "secondary adaptations." Today anger has the secondary adaptation of signaling our displeasure, our indignation. It has become a mode of social communication, in its own way an adaptation suited to the needs of survival in the modern world.[10]

However, Darwin imagined that there were limits to change, for habits were inherited. Writing before the discovery of genes, Darwin was a convinced Lamarckian in believing that acquired characteristics were handed down to subsequent generations. For him, that explained why an angry person who had no intention of attacking anyone would nevertheless unwillingly experience a rapid heartbeat and fleeting betrayals of her feelings in "those muscles of the face which are least obedient to the will."[11]

✳

In the last sentence of his book on emotions, Darwin called on physiologists to continue his research. Reading Darwin as endorsing a Basic Emotions approach, some of his immediate successors looked for the particular and characteristic physiological signs of each emotion. Taking their subjects—whether human or animal—into their laboratories, they used new machines to measure pulse and respiration. They sought the objective, measurable record of each emotion. French physician Fernand Papillon (d.1874) reflected the optimism of his day when he said that the sphygmograph (see Plate 10), which measured blood pressure, could be used to produce tracings of the heart's motion "under the influence of the various passions." In his view, each emotion had "a curve of its own." He was thinking of the waves the pulse made as it was recorded by the device on a piece of paper.[12]

Inventions like the sphygmograph reflected the widespread assumption that machines could read people's emotions even better

1 Yamantaka, Destroyer of the God of Death (Tibet, early eighteenth century). With a head like a bull, three telescoping eyes, white fangs, and deep blue skin, this wrathful god is nevertheless thought to be hate-free. He tramples a corpse representing human self-regard, the origin of death. Painted on a large cloth, this image was used in tantric religious ceremonies.

2 Medea Contemplating Infanticide (House of the Dioscuri, Pompeii, first century). As her children play a game and their tutor watches over them, Medea, standing aloof, reaches for the hilt of her sword. Painted around the same time that Seneca wrote his drama, Medea's anger is here turned into melancholy, a feeling appropriate for a woman about to destroy all domestic tranquility. In its original context, the fresco decorated a private home, placed opposite another fresco that depicted Andromeda, the perfect wife and mother.

3 Saint Peter Hitting a Demon (England, eleventh century). As a benevolent angel looks on, Peter and a demon fight over a soul. Peter wins the tug-of-war by hitting the demon in the face with his enormous key. On the right, a winged demon drags two lost souls away.

4 Pieter Bruegel the Elder, *Anger* (Antwerp, 1557). Anger dominates a landscape teeming with brutal animals, brawling people, and violent demons. Her mouth holds a knife, a graphic representation of the sharp savagery of sins of the tongue. Beneath her, heavily armored figures haul a larger version of the knife, slicing through bodies as they go.

5 The Death of Anger (Southern Germany, ninth century). Illustrating a poem by
Prudentius, the action (reading from right to left and from top to bottom) shows Anger's
sword shattering on the helmet of Patience. Thus defeated, Anger falls on her spears,
committing suicide. At the bottom, Patience delicately tests to see whether Anger is
indeed dead by poking at the corpse with the tip of her spear.

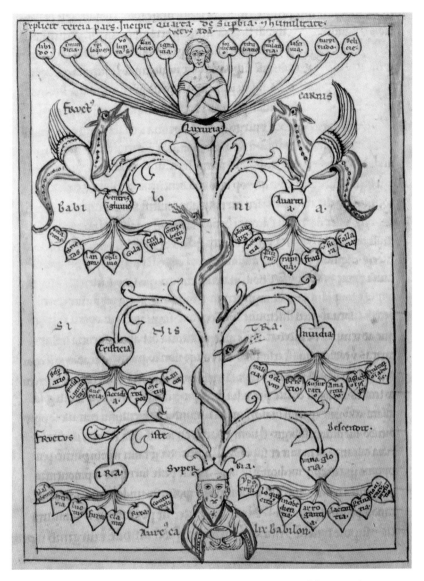

6 Tree of Vices (Germany, thirteenth century). In this depiction of the Tree of Vices, it is the "Golden Chalice of Babylon" (Rev. 17:4) that supports the tree's root, Pride (*Superbia*). Anger (*Ira*) is Pride's first vicious fruit (on the left), and it has itself spawned seven more bitter offshoots: blasphemy, impudence, grief, fury, clamor, brawling, and insult.

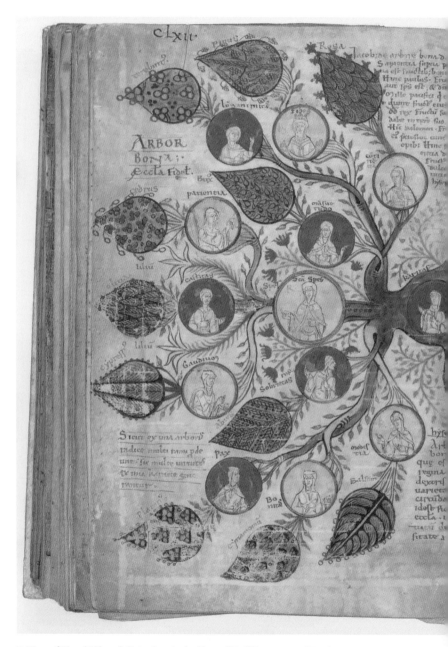

7 Tree of Good/Church Paired with the Tree of Evil/Synagogue (Northern France, twelfth century). On the left-hand page are all the flowering fruits of Charity, here identified with the Church.

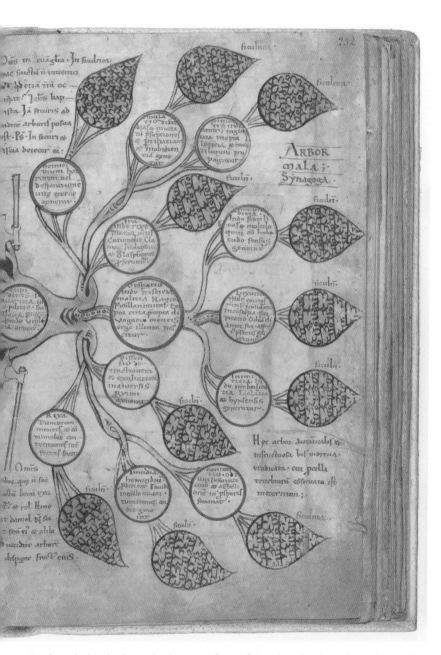

On the right-hand side are the desiccated fruits of Cupidity, already in this early period associated with the Jewish Synagogue. Anger (*Ira*) and all her progeny (brawls, clamors, and so on) are among Cupidity's first fruits. Two axes are poised to cut down the Tree of Evil at its roots.

*Il est bougrement en Colère le Père Duchene.*

8  Père Duchesne is Damn Angry (Paris, c.1794). Anger is lampooned here as fully as is "Père Duchesne," the pen name of Jacques René Hébert, whose newspaper violently scorned and berated the political figures of his day. The figure's disheveled hair and anguished look echo the persona of Anger in the Prudentius manuscript in Plate 5. The image represents a backlash against anger, now associated with the excesses of the French Revolution.

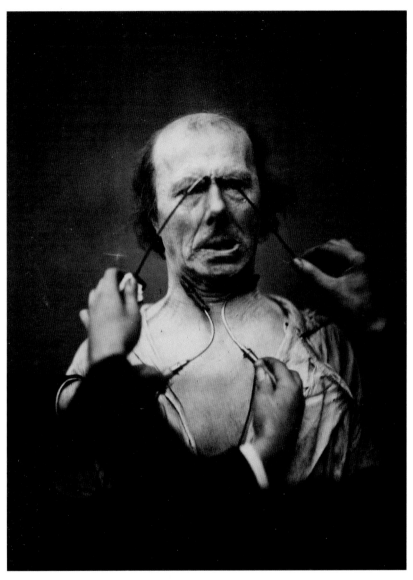

9 *Colère* (Anger) (Paris, nineteenth century). Working with a man whose face was insensitive to pain, G.-B.-A. Duchenne de Boulogne (d.1875) applied electrical stimuli to achieve what he considered authentic expressions of various emotions. With one set of probes he stimulates the muscles that make the eyebrows draw together, while with another, he contracts the *platysma* muscle between the face and neck. The effect, in his view, was the face of anger. Today, Paul Ekman and his group work with 46 "action facial units" based on facial musculature. Ekman's face of anger employs units 4 (lowered brow), 5 (raised upper lid), 7 (tightened lid), and (in one version) 23 (tightened lip).

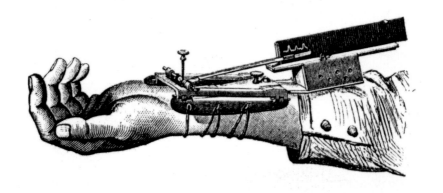

10 The Sphygmograph (Paris, 1878). The mid-nineteenth century saw the invention of a stationary device to measure blood pressure. Étienne-Jules Marey (d.1904) devised the portable version shown here. Fixed over the arm's radial artery, the Marey sphygmograph recorded waves corresponding to the pulse. Many scientists thought that various wave patterns would offer objective read-outs of emotions.

11 "Righteous Anger" Posed (New York, c.1914). This was one of eighty-six photographs of different "posed emotions" used by Antoinette Feleky in a study of emotional expression. For this pose, she asked the model, a woman identified as A.F. (the researcher herself?), to recollect thoughts and feelings of "righteous anger." In a later study, Feleky tested respiratory changes connected with various emotions. She was part of a scientific movement—still very active today—that sought predictable, measurable bodily signs of discrete emotions.

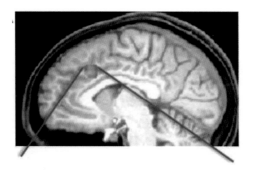

12  Brain Scan of the Location of the Subjective Experience of Anger (California, 2009). A normalized "brain" is here sliced to expose the cingulate gyrus (the white "snake" just above the brain stem) and nearby regions. The orange square shows the location (the left dorsal anterior cingulate cortex) that the authors of "The Angry Brain" found to be associated with general aggression and self-reports of anger after provocation. The provocations (insults) were given by the experimenters themselves, who argued that the study therefore closely mirrored the real world, even though throughout most of the test the participants were encased in padded foam head constraints and situated within a scanner that took whole-brain images.

13  "Mad as Hell" Sign (Washington, D.C., 2017). "Mad as Hell," a cry of madness and liberation in the 1976 movie *Network*, joins signs protesting "Tax Cuts for the Rich" and "Women Resist Tax Breaks for Billionaires" at a rally held before the Capitol building about a month before the Senate passed Trump's 2017 tax bill.

than people. Gone was Seneca's hope that by reviewing our angry moments at the end of each day we might do better the next. Our inner selves were open not to our conscious scrutiny but to objective measurements of our physiology. This idea laid the groundwork for the lie-detector. Indeed, one of its early inventors, Leonarde Keeler, called it an "emotiograph."[13] But already by the early twentieth century, the hope of finding "a curve" for each emotion was pretty well dashed. It was quite clear that the physiological markers for all strong emotions were very much alike.

What remained, however, were faces: were they the objective physical signs of discrete emotions? Experimental results were initially only somewhat successful. For example, Antoinette Feleky made photographs of a woman posing a variety of emotional facial expressions. One of them was meant to express "righteous anger" (see Plate 11). But none of the "one hundred reliable persons" shown that pose came up with the right identification, although four judged it to be an expression of annoyance and another three of alarm. Feleky was not discouraged, explaining that wrong answers were due in part to "ignorance of the meanings of real facial expressions and to ignorance of the accepted meanings of the terms used."[14]

Feleky was not yet working with the idea of biologically determined basic emotions. That was first proposed by Sylvan Tomkins (d.1991), a philosopher-turned-psychologist. He named eight—later nine—inherited and innate primary "affect programs." They were the "primary motives of human beings," corresponding to particular structures of the subcortical brain that instructed and controlled the body's muscular and glandular responses. Tomkins declared the face to be the "primary site" of these affects, and he offered a list of them (each consisting of a pair representing low and high intensity) alongside their "component facial responses."[15] To test his hypothesis, he developed a set of photographs of faces simulating "interest, enjoyment, surprise, distress, fear, shame, contempt, and anger" and asked a group of "readily available" firemen to label them.[16] Later Paul

Ekman would call six of these—happiness, sadness, fear, disgust, surprise, and anger—the "basic emotions" and develop a set of photographs for them. As Giovanna Colombetti notes, Ekman had very little rationale for limiting the number to six, other than that he and his collaborators could not find enough "good photos"—photos giving the expressions that they considered valid—for the others.[17]

They certainly found acceptable ones for anger, and armed with these and other photographs of faces simulating the remaining five, Ekman and his collaborators got people around the world to identify the facial expressions with emotion terms. The anger and happiness faces got the best results, even when the researchers went to New Guinea to question the Fore people, who had little contact with the West.[18] That study's conclusion, enshrined in almost all psychology textbooks, is that anger is one of six basic emotions, and it has a characteristic and recognizable facial expression. It is universal and hard-wired.

Except that the evidence is not so clear after all. I mentioned the Fore in Chapter 4 in connection with the "peaceable kingdoms" that anthropologists have explored. There I drew on the work of E. Richard Sorenson. This is the place to point out that Sorenson was one of the researchers who originally worked with Ekman. But his own test, which used the photographed faces with a different protocol, yielded results for anger no better than a guess. Far more interesting than the accuracy of the responses per se, Sorenson concluded, was the fact that the Fore tended to see anger in every face. Theirs was a culture, he suggested, far more sensitive than our own to the socially disruptive effects of anger. The Fore were inclined to read anger into any strong facial expression because their society depended on close personal relations and support, both of which required an even temper.[19] We have seen the same sort of social concerns among the Semai of Malaysia.

Despite Sorenson's and many other critiques of Ekman's work,[20] experimenters have confidently continued to use posed—and now digitized—faces in their work. Faces are extremely convenient, and at least in Western societies, the "anger face" actually does tend to be identified as angry. This fact may be used for both good and bad. For its good use, consider a study that seems to show that by learning to see more happiness in ambiguous facial expressions, people will feel less anger. The investigators manipulated images of the same face to morph it from "unambiguously happy to unambiguously angry, with emotionally ambiguous images in the middle." They found that by teaching a group of "high-risk youth" to see "happiness" in faces that had previously been identified as "angry," they were able to reduce the incidence of the youths' aggressive behavior.[21] This seems an exceedingly salutary use of faces!

On the other side of the ledger, however, is the conclusion that people who do not read the emotions in faces "correctly" are abnormal. There is even a word for this alleged deficiency: alexithymia. Young children are taught in school to give the right answers for each posed face. Books offer examples of how children should look when they feel a certain way. There is nothing wrong with the socialization of children; indeed, it is a necessity in every culture. But there is a problem when it comes to reading faces. There are some people whose facial muscles are paralyzed. They have emotions like everyone else, but because they seem "strange" to those of us accustomed to see feelings in facial expressions, they find themselves misunderstood and socially isolated.[22] Then, too, "abnormality" is a very dangerous word. In Nazi Germany, autistic children were labeled abnormal and therefore undesirable. Relegated to institutions, they were starved and fed barbiturates until they died.[23] We don't kill "autistic" children today, but the term is still in the DSM—the bible of "mental disorders."[24] The tests that Sorenson made with the Fore tell us that perfectly normal people can "misread" faces—that is, see emotions that Westerners do not see. Sorenson himself thought that the characteristic Fore facial expression of anger looked a lot like sadness, though other Fore, knowing their own culture, agreed it was anger. Westerners, too, can regularly make mistakes within their own society. D. Vaughn Becker found that students in a psychology class had an easy time reading female faces as "happy" and male faces as "angry." But they had trouble recognizing the "anger face" on a woman and the "happiness face" on a man.[25] We need to be wary of our impressions as we read the faces of others, and be willing to admit a healthy uncertainty lest our alexithymia be inscribed as a "disease."

Posed faces have seemed to ratify the view that each emotion has its individual, identifiable somatic marker. So, too, have many studies using brain-scan equipment. Let one example stand for all. In an article seeking the "neural correlates of anger," researchers using fEPI (functional Echo-Planar Imaging) reported that after subjects were insulted, their feelings of anger were correlated to "activity in the dorsal anterior cingulate cortex" (see Plate 12). "Activity" refers to oxygenation and blood flow; the orange square in the plate pinpoints the location in which abundant activity takes place.[26] The curve produced by the sphygmograph in Plate 10 is obviously far less sophisticated than the picture offered by the scan in Plate 12, but the two have a similar purpose: to show the characteristic trace of a single emotion in a measurement that corresponds to a bodily process, whether cardiac or neural.

Yet all along there has been another, very different scientific tradition, one that dissents from the view that each emotion is a natural kind with its own characteristic marker. It, too, sees itself as Darwinian. Recall that Darwin never said that there was a fixed number of basic emotions. He said simply that the expression of many emotions had such striking similarities in both people and animals that the human type must have evolved from a "lower form." In the case of anger, he thought quite a bit had to change when human beings started to go about on two legs. He used what he could from physiology as well as evidence from bodily postures and faces. When William James read Darwin, he concluded not that faces were particularly relevant but rather that human physiology marked each emotion. As James put it, "we feel sorry because we cry, angry because we strike, afraid because we tremble."[27] Once we feel the body reacting, we apply the "ordinary perceptive processes" of the mind. We scratch and then know we have an itch. We strike and call it anger.

James turned a lot of Western thought about anger on its head, though the Galenic tradition had always implied his view. The Psychological Constructionist school traces its distant origins to James' vision. It also credits the influence of the theory of German physician and philosopher Wilhelm Wundt (d.1920). Wundt postulated two basic "elements" of the mind: sensations and feelings. Angry feelings (he called them, like all the emotions, "affective processes") could range from slight arousal ("I am a bit annoyed") to highly aroused ("I am furious"). They could be pleasurable ("I am going to get back at him") or painful ("I'm furious, but there is nothing I can do about it"). While the mind buzzes with a whole variety of these affective processes, not all rise to the level of an "emotion." Emotions are both intense and complex; they are made up of many feelings plus something else, "some idea" about what they are. Constantly in flux, emotions cannot be pinned down as natural categories. Words like "anger" are our convenient label not for a thing but for a process that consists of a succession of feelings and that involves physical sensations as well, not only in the "heart, blood-vessels, and respiration, but [also in] the *external muscles*." Anger ends up as an action—perhaps a snub, perhaps revenge. Then it subsides, giving way to the "ordinary quiet flow of feelings."[28]

The Psychological Constructionist school has taken these ideas and applied them to the brain. They consider emotions to be produced by the brain in the course of its activities as the regulator, mediator, and predictor of our internal and external states. The brain is constantly receiving sensations from both our bodies and the outside world. The result is what these scientists call "core affect." There is no moment in life without some core affect; it represents the integration of sensory information from both outside and within the body that allows the brain "to safely navigate the world by predicting reward and threat, friend and foe."[29]

Indeed, Lisa Feldman Barrett, whom we have met in several of the previous chapters, says that prediction is the key job of the brain, which utilizes "neural conversations" to "anticipate every fragment of sight, sound, smell, taste, and touch that you will experience and every action that you will take."[30] In its predictive role, the brain makes sense of what it integrates. Barrett says that we may therefore think of the brain as "a situated conceptualization generator." It is "situated" because it is in both the body and the world. As it develops, it draws on language and culture to conceptualize—that is, organize and cope with—both worlds. Emotions are "conceptualized instances of sensations."[31] They are not natural kinds but rather ways the mind finds to group together a variety of sensations based on present and past experiences. Each culture may clump together life events and sensations rather differently. Anger is not a "something"; it is a concept, representing one sort of clumping. We in the Anglophone world use the term anger. Other cultures use different words. More important, their terms rarely signify quite the same thing, with the same range of meanings, as "anger." To be sure, anthropologists and linguists offer rough and ready equivalents, but that is because they need to communicate with their Western readers.

Psychological Constructionists draw their conclusions from neuroscience. How, then, do they deal with observations like the one that found anger correlated to a particular region of the brain, such as "activity in the dorsal anterior cingulate cortex"? (Recall Plate 12.) If anger has one "home" in the brain, it must be a "something." Psychological Constructionists debunk such studies. They point out that meta-analyses of neuroimaging (statistical analyses of many studies pooled together) suggest that no emotion is *always* connected to one brain location and that many emotions are connected to the *same* regions. While one study finds anger connected with the dorsal anterior cingulate cortex, others find it in the amygdala, a very different part of the brain.[32] Psychological Constructionists say that anger is the product of the brain across all of its regions, for the brain's circuitry works as a whole. It stands to reason that one study will find anger's activity in one place, and another study will find it elsewhere. It is, indeed, here, there, and everywhere in the brain because it is constructed by the brain as a useful concept.

The brain gets special attention from Psychological Constructionists because they see it as the mediator between the inner and outer self. But they are also interested in the rest of the body, even the face, even its physiology. The primary purpose of the brain's conceptions and categories is "to produce inferences."[33] Inferences prepare us for action both inside our body and in the world. You hear a horn behind you; you freeze, your heart beats more quickly, you step on the gas or you slow down to a crawl. Alternatively, you hear the sound and wonder what sort of car horn is so mellifluous. In all of these instances, your physical state changes, and therefore your core affect becomes more or less intense, more or less pleasurable. If your focus is on the sound of the horn, that's not an emotion; it's a perception, and your core affect will probably not be very intense—unless you are a composer like George Gershwin, who was so intrigued with the sounds of honking French taxis that he included them in his *An American in Paris*! If your focus is on the gorge rising in your throat, your pounding heart, and the intensity of your feelings, you say you are angry. The two cases differ precisely in how you conceptualize the event, and that will depend on your past experiences. But you are always learning from new incidents, which means that you can change your predictions and with them your bodily responses.

This, too, has underlying moral dimensions quite different from those connected with the Basic Emotions crowd. Now, it is true that scientists generally consider anger above all a natural given, not a moral issue. As human beings, they may agree with the Buddhists and the Stoics that anger is bad; or they may concur with the Christian tradition that anger is both bad (if directed against people) and good (if directed against sin, evil, or wrongdoing). But in their role as scientists, their overriding interest is in anger as a variable whose nature and effects may be understood objectively. In the modern period, they began to rely on machines to provide them with precise measurements and visualizations. Even so, scientific theories often have moral implications, and Psychological Constructionists know that. They point out that machine outputs have to be interpreted, and they think that many brain scans and facial expressions have been read out of context. When considered together, they say, the evidence shows that the brain as a whole constructs anger. This means that we are not slaves to some habit inculcated in the prehistoric past. We can open ourselves to new conceptualizations. We are always learning, and as adults we can evaluate, rethink, and unlearn. We are moral beings and can recalibrate our emotions to match. One very attractive aspect of this view is that it does not relegate anyone to the category "abnormal." On the other hand, it does condemn rigidity as morally problematic, which ought to seem all to the good for anyone convinced by the thrust of this book.

But now we have two competing points of views that seem to have no way to meet. On one side are those who say that anger is one of the universal basic emotions, expressed mainly on the face, recognized across cultures. They admit that cultures may overlay these expressions and try to mask them. They call these attempts "display rules." But the "real" emotions will nevertheless leak out through what they call "microexpressions"— tiny facial movements that they claim to be able to see and measure. That assumption was the basis of the TV show "Lie to Me" where, over the course of three seasons, a psychologist modeled after Paul Ekman helped law-enforcement agents by using Ekman's facial coding system to identify potential terrorists.

Pointedly contesting the idea of Basic Emotions are the Psychological Constructionists, who say that the brain creates certain categories to make sense of the body and the world. In our particular culture, anger is the word we use to categorize certain sensations, feelings, impulses, and actions. Anger is how we have learned to speak of an activation of core affect high in unpleasantness and intensity, but not as high in intensity as, say, fear.

Enactivists say that they have found a workable compromise. Like the Psychological Constructionists they think of the human brain as the mediator between the body and external world and thus filled with affect. But, following William James, they put more stress on the whole body, asserting that we are angry only after we feel the racing of our heart, the furrowing of our forehead, the reddening of our face.

Enactivists are willing to acknowledge that English "anger" may not perfectly match terms in other languages. But they consider this immaterial: it's hardly unusual for people to have feelings for which they have no precise word; this is simply a "lexical lacuna."[34] They look to the findings of psychobiologists like Jaak Panksepp (d.2017), who worked with mammals. Panksepp got around lexical lacunae by speaking of "prototype emotional systems." He used the all-capital-letter signifier RAGE to refer to what emerges in Semai culture as *lesnees*, Utku society as *urulu*, and Anglophone cultures as *anger*.[35] These words and the contexts in which they are used are not exactly the same, and Panksepp was happy to acknowledge that fact. He theorized that genetically determined subcortical systems like RAGE interact with higher cortical concepts—the words, social restraints, social conventions, and so on that reflect our emotional learning.

Contrary to many proponents of basic emotions, Enactivists accept that facial expressions may not be all that is necessary to "read" another person's feelings; they agree that emotions need to be understood in context. Nor do they think that there is any reason to limit the basic emotions to six—or any other number. Why even use the term "basic"?

The important point is that emotions are, for Enactivists, natural kinds at some subcortical level; they are *genetic* universals, but in the real world they are always modified by factors like culture, morals, and habits.

Enactivists criticize Psychological Constructionists for their inability to explain the "specific mechanisms that would accompany the transformation of *core affect* into a true emotion itself."[36] How exactly does something so nebulous as core affect coalesce into something as concrete as anger? They critique the findings of brain scans not because they are inconsistent but because they are not good informants of emotional brain activity. They show brain activity, sure. But when researchers tell subjects to look at angry faces and then correlate that with exceptional activity in the dorsal anterior cingulate cortex, they are making the questionable assumption that the brain neurons are responding to "anger." In fact, that is a leap of faith. Maybe the neurons are responding to the *size* of the photograph or to its *colors* or to the tone of voice of the researcher. There is no linguist who knows the "language" of the neurons. Far better than brain scans, says Enactivist Fausto Caruana, are studies that use electrical or chemical stimulation of particular brain areas, for then it may be possible to get real language feedback.

Caruana is drawing on experiments like that of Suresh Bhatt and colleagues, who found that both forms of stimulation of particular regions in the mid- and lower brains of cats caused the animals to exhibit signs of "defensive rage." The chief expression that the researchers looked for was hissing. The higher the level of electrical current stimulation, the more vigorous was the hiss. In a related experiment they injected a drug known to activate a certain type of receptor distributed along the brain stem. In that case, the cats hissed. Then, when they primed the receptor with an antagonist (a drug nullifying the receptor's action), the cat did not hiss.[37] Studies like this, Bhatt thinks, support Panksepp's thesis of a RAGE "brain operating system" in all mammalian species.[38] Caruana agrees, and he considers such studies to be crucial because hissing, unlike the oxygenation read-out of a brain scan, is a form of language. The cat is "telling" us that she is indeed enraged.

All of these approaches suggest different therapeutic possibilities. As we have seen, the Basic Emotions paradigm for anger might lead, for example, to training troubled youths to see happy faces where previously they had identified anger. Psychological Constructionist therapy is more cerebral. It asks us to open ourselves to other conceptions, other ways of imagining, feeling, and expressing anger (as, for example, the ones presented in this very book), and, as we do that, to revise our own experiences and attitudes. The Enactivist view—which accepts that the RAGE system may be deactivated by particular chemicals—suggests therapies that rely on drugs.

The one commonality that unites all of these positions is the laboratory itself. The advantage of the lab is its rigor: it can eliminate unwanted variables and test for particulars that are impossible to isolate in the real world. But that very advantage is equally the lab's weakness. Emotions are felt and expressed in contexts. I myself am very poor at identifying angry faces in photographs, but I have little trouble sensing that someone is angry *in my own society*. And even a cat's hiss may mean one thing when she is prodded by an electric goad and quite another when she is threatened by a predator. Anger in a laboratory is not the same as anger on the street.

# 11

# SOCIETY'S CHILD

The anger that we feel and express is a product of our society, say social constructivists. (In the lab, it is additionally and more immediately shaped by laboratory conditions and expectations.) The field of social constructivism, though not unprecedented before the 1980s, took off at that time with the growing recognition among anthropologists, philosophers, and sociologists that many essentialist assumptions were wrong. People are not divided into precisely two genders, races are not biological entities, rationality is not separate from emotionality, nature is not the opposite of nurture, Western emotions are not universal.[1] We are not born pre-wired for anger, but neither do we create it ourselves out of whole cloth. "People are not free to invent their own emotions any more than they are free to invent their own language—not if they wish to be understood," says James Averill, a pioneer in the field.[2] We learn about anger—and, as this book argues, many sorts of anger—as we make use of the values, ideas, and rules that we start to internalize from an early age.

Today, there is lively debate among social constructivists. They differ on how fully cultures or societies form or shape emotions. They ask whether the process of construction comes from the "top"—as rulers, elites, and various authority figures model and inculcate norms—or from the "bottom"—as face-to-face communities adjust and negotiate the feelings that their members have and express. They differ, too, about how (and how thoroughly) biological givens play a role in our emotions.

Nevertheless, what brings these schools of thought together is the conviction that emotions are not inborn entities. Many would agree that something like anger consists in a fuzzy set of behaviors, values, concepts, and feelings that accords more or less with a cultural prototype, a sort of Platonic idea of anger, that we English-speakers have learned to apply to ourselves. "anger" is not a pre-formed element in the mind. But it is also not simply given to us by some sort of monolithic society: any instance of anger is part of a process created *mutually* by ourselves acting within our society and the tools (conceptions, languages, opportunities) that our society offers to us.

We come close to the social constructivist position, then, when we imagine that our families, communities, and cultures offer us a variety of useful scripts that we might perform in any angry episode, but on which we can and always will improvise—not only in our behaviors but also our inner experiences. "Useful" is a key word here. In his classic study of anger, constructivist James Averill argues that in American society anger is generally paired with aggression.[3] That is not unique to America, but it is not invariably the case in other cultures. Averill points to a number of societies in which aggression has nothing to do with anger whatever. We have already seen some examples—though not his—among the peaceable and non-peaceable kingdoms discussed in Chapter 4. Given that fact, Averill says, we must ask what function the pairing has in America. One answer is obvious from anger's uses in the law: the assumption that anger leads to violence is advantageous for our society, in part because it lets aggressive people off the hook. Perpetrating a crime "in the heat of passion" is a handy excuse for people to say, in effect, "I wasn't in control." We saw in Chapter 5 how this idea was already used—and contested—in medieval and early modern legal circles.

But that is not the only use of anger. In American society, it is often directed against loved ones and friends. In some cases, it is a way for us to shed our own responsibility and foist it on our target: "You are making me angry," not "I am angry." In an early social constructivist essay on anger, philosopher C. Terry Warner made this function of anger the heart of his argument. He called anger a "delusion"—the illusion that we are passive in our anger. We may imagine, with Seneca, that we judged wrongly, that the driver who honked was not trying to "diss" us. But even then, we will never deny that the person who honked caused our anger. The anger is real and always true, whether or not the appraisal is correct. This is our delusion. Our anger always has "ulterior considerations," and those have to do with ratifying our dignity, asserting our victimhood, and claiming an ideal self. Because of this, anger resists its own demise, using everything it can to fuel its passion. Warner imagines an argument between husband and wife:

> Alison: "Look, I haven't said a single thing that's unfair to you."
> Brent: "Oh no, you're never in the wrong, are you? You're even too good to live with."[4]

But Warner leaves out a social function of anger that is not delusional at all: anger often helps to recalibrate relationships. In effect, it is one good way to signal our need to put a relationship on a new footing. We may imagine an exchange between Warner's imaginary couple a bit later in the argument:

> Alison: "Is it unfair for me to say that you don't help enough with the dishes?"
> Brent: "Yes, it's unfair. But ok. I'll take over the dishwashing from now on if you'll take out the garbage."

Other scenarios are possible as well:

> Alison: "You never help with the housework."
> Brent: "You are right. I apologize. Give me a list of what is needed; I'll get started."

As opposed to:

Alison: "You never help with the housework."
Brent: "What? Why *should* I help. You sit around all day while I work with no coffee break and a horrible boss."
Alison: "I can't stand this anymore. I don't sit around all day! I take care of the girls, cook, clean, *and* work part time . . . I've had it with you."

Anger, then, does not necessarily feed on itself; it is constructed "in the context of *moment-to-moment interactions*." After Brent apologized, Alison's anger was constructed very differently (descending from high to low in intensity and negativity) from its construction when he told her that she sat around all day (rapidly ascending along both axes).[5]

✻

Some examples from history enlarge and enrich the social constructivist argument. Medievalist Richard Barton discusses an early twelfth-century incident involving a feudal lord, Juhel, who wanted his "men"—his warriors and vassals—to donate land to his favorite monastery. At a formal gift-giving ceremony, one of Juhel's men refused to give anything. Juhel got angry and tried to "lay violent hands on" the miscreant, but witnesses dragged him away.[6] It turned out that nurturing his outburst was an earlier and more serious hurt: the ungenerous vassal was a former serf who had been freed from serfdom without Juhel's consent. Peace was patched up by a neighbor, who organized a series of gifts all around and negotiated a settlement: Juhel recognized the free status of the former serf, who in turn acknowledged the authority of his lord by giving land to the monastery. In this episode anger signaled a dysfunctional relationship, and its venting was an essential step in readjusting the bond between the two men.

Why should we care about this petty altercation? It shows that the social construction of emotions takes place not just during a moment (as we saw with Alison and Brent) but also within ongoing relationships that have a history and a future. Further, it illustrates how anger may work to reconfigure relationships, not only in our society but also in others in which angry confrontations are acceptable. Consider that in Utku culture an incident like Juhel's could not have occurred, not because there were no hierarchies (there were) or ongoing rivalries (those existed as well), but because anger was not tolerated. Finally, Juhel's case throws new light on norms about anger within medieval society at large, helping to revise our preconceptions about the connection between anger and violence in the Middle Ages. Barton's social constructivist interpretation of the event allows him to counter the widespread notion that the medieval period was full of bloody violence and little else. This stereotype is so widespread that it has made its way into the movies: "I'mma get medieval on your ass," says Marcellus to Zed in Tarantino's cult movie *Pulp Fiction* (1994), before dispatching his groveling victim. Barton points out that "getting medieval" could mean, to the contrary, anger defused and amity restored.

In general, historians have much to contribute to the social constructivist vision. The very first important study of the history of anger—by Peter and Carol Stearns—assumed that anger was a basic emotion that nevertheless changed in valuation, function, and expression over time. To understand how and why this happened, the authors undertook to analyze the changing needs of American society and to suggest how it shaped, but did not entirely construct, anger.

In the eighteenth century, the Stearnses argued, Americans began to wage "a long campaign to control anger."[7] Starting in the 1830s, the war gained a clear focus: the family. A flurry of magazines and advice books told middle-class people—men and women anxious to feel and behave properly—that, while anger might be acceptable in the workplace, home was "a sacred enclosure" where couples should "cultivate a spirit of mutual and generous forbearance, carefully avoiding anything like angry contention or contradiction."[8] The focus shifted, however, in the early twentieth century, when anger became counterproductive in the workplace. Above all, the service industries demanded cheerful faces. Recall Hochschild's study of airline stewardesses: no anger was allowed to cloud their smiling faces. The Stearnses put the starting date for this sort of workplace requirement around 1920. Many of us can attest to the cheeriness expected (and displayed) by waitresses, salesladies, cashiers—and of some men in these sorts of positions as well.

The Stearnses alert us not only to the changing standards of anger in American middle-class society, but also to how those norms relate to space. At first, the family was the place immune (ideally) to expressions of anger. A half century or so later, that attitude was extended to the workplace. Where then could anger be expressed? Perhaps on the political stage—my next chapter suggests that possibility.

The Stearnses were careful to distinguish the anger people might *feel* from the standards they tried to follow. But they also argued that, in time, the ideals came to influence emotional experience. Many historians, however, are wary of claiming that they can talk about anger other than as a "discourse." That accounts for titles like *Representing Women's Anger in Early Modern England* rather than, bluntly, *Women's Anger in Early Modern England*. But "discourse" is a way to skirt the key issue: is socially constructed anger "real"? Alison and Brent were admittedly engaged in a discourse: their argument had the social role of creating, modifying, exacerbating or soothing problems in their ongoing relationship. But that didn't make their anger feel any the less real.

Of course, Alison and Brent's dialogues are hypothetical. Let us turn from them to some modern real-world cases, beginning with Anthony M., who wanted help curbing his intense fury at those whom he loved or who did not meet his expectations. He certainly felt angry—subjectively, viscerally so. How would a social constructivist construe his anger? Assuming Anthony was not a social misfit, which is of course possible, his anger must have been created in and through his relationships, his culture, and his own methods for navigating them both. C. Peter Bankart, the Buddhist therapist whose comments on this case I discussed in Chapter 1, makes a social constructivist observation: Anthony lives in a society that values being "right, respected, and obeyed." These values belong to a set of "rigid sex-specific cultural norms. Thus, the angry man sees himself not only as the last bastion of what is right, proper, and acceptable but also as the pinpointed target of a myriad of moral infractions."[9] By this light, Anthony is drawing on a variety of cultural conventions, especially from the tradition, very much still with us, that men have the duty to express virtuous, godly anger.

Lundy Bancroft, a domestic consultant who works with men even more abusive than Anthony, has a relatively top-down view of how socialization works, creating values and beliefs in the child that, he says, persist into adulthood. Bancroft's abuser is created by "the family he grows up in, his neighborhood, the television he watches and books he reads, jokes he hears, [. . .] and his most influential adult role models." He is the product of his culture, and Bancroft's therapy is focused in large measure on changing the values inculcated by that culture.[10]

But it isn't as though abuse is embedded in all the institutions that socialize us—not even in those that seem to socialize abusers. Social influences do not work in one way only: they have a variety of meanings for and impacts on the children, adolescents, and adults who come under their influence. Bancroft thinks that segments of our society collude with abusers, giving them encouragement. He points out, for example, that the law has traditionally upheld the rights of men over their wives—prosecution for domestic violence "was uncommon before 1990." He faults prize-winning entertainers who ratify violence against women, citing Eminem's "Kim"—"Sit down bitch / If you move again

I'll beat the shit out of you."[11] But is he right to assume that legal definitions matter much in people's lives or that Eminem's verses are taken in the same way by all who hear them?

✳

The problem with analyses like Bankart and Bancroft's is that they are exceedingly general, as if everyone subject to the same cultural inputs will come away with the same emotions. But this is not really the case. We must go beyond grand abstractions in order to understand each individual's situation more fully and specifically.

Similarly, generalizing about a whole society means considering global social rules that apply only partially to all and probably fully to no one. Averill got around this methodological issue by looking at statistical averages and leaving outliers behind. He administered questionnaires to fairly homogeneous groups of people, asking them to record their moments of anger, and analyzing the commonalities in their replies. That is one strategy. Another is Hannelore Weber's, who asked people outright what caused their anger and what they thought were the appropriate responses. Her best results came when she inquired about *in*appropriate causes and responses. A surprising number of people made the cost-benefit analysis that anger was not worth the bother. In effect, they were Neostoics along the lines of Martha Nussbaum, who considered Medea's fierce anger to have been pointless and counterproductive (see Chapter 3).[12]

As a historian, I prefer to think in terms of emotional communities. That means looking in depth at the microcontexts in which people like Anthony—and all of us—live and feel. Done thoroughly and properly, this means exploring biographies, whole dossiers of writings, oral histories and interviews, creative works—not just of one person but of his or her friends, families, co-workers, and so on. It means deeply embedding people in the nitty-gritty of their lives to the fullest extent possible.

Only then can we begin to know what their—and their society's—many and sometimes contradictory emotional norms and values are. Different emotional communities may practice superficially similar sorts of anger; even so the feeling itself will have very different values and meanings—and therefore will be experienced differently. Let me illustrate what I mean by offering three very brief examples (all discussed more fully elsewhere) of co-existing emotional communities in medieval France.

Let us begin with knights. When a medieval warrior was beset by his enemies but unable to overcome them, he would go to his overlord to get help. He was expected to approach the greater man "dolefully, tearfully, and deferentially," in that way trying to arouse his anger.[13] When he was successful, his superior, too, became angry and carried out attacks on the same enemies. The episode typically ended with some sort of resolution, often a negotiated peace marked by rituals of friendship and love among all parties.

Now compare this with the clamors of the monks discussed in Chapter 7. The monks, too, had enemies. To deal with them, they humbled themselves before the altar of their church, alongside the relics of the saints and perhaps the crucifix, and they called out curses on their enemies in order to gain God's ear and his help in defeating his enemies. There are a number of similarities in these two angry patterns, but they do not make the experiences or meanings of anger the same. The monks, like the Semai of the Malay Peninsula, like the Utku in Northern Canada, did not "get angry." Rather they called down the wrath of God. How could the subjective feeling of their anger have been exactly the same as that of the warrior who went off to fight?

Finally, consider the anger of troubadour poet-singers at the court of the count of Toulouse around the same time. Their songs expressed their intense love for their lady, but that emotion was hedged about with fears and assertions of betrayal. While their own love was pure (they claimed), their lady's affections were fickle and false. The troubadours sang of their anger, though anger is not quite the right word. They used the word *ira*, which, in their language—the tongue of southern France called Old Occitan—meant both anger and sorrow and sometimes a mixture of the two. Often there is no way to translate it except with a compound idea: a sad anger, an angry sorrow. In the words of Raimon de Miraval,

> Because of the wrongs that the ladies do
> the service of Love turns to decadence.
> For they demonstrate so much deceit
> that the most faithful lover gets sorrowfully angry.[14]

At Toulouse, the anger that the troubadours sang about was mingled with sadness. We may well doubt that the troubadours were describing their own private feelings, though, even at the time, some people thought that their songs were autobiographical. Rather, let us say simply that their songs expressed a particular kind of anger that was generally understood and appreciated by their public—their patrons above all. In that sense, it was a constructed feeling in which the musicians, their benefactors, and various courtiers and hangers-on colluded. Philosopher Kathleen Higgins has explored the various ways in which music, including troubadour music and, for that matter, the hip hop lyrics of Eminem, may be considered culturally constructed as well as biologically grounded. The verdict is hardly in, but the idea of "attunement" among performer, audience, and members of the audience with one another seems fruitful. Dancing, nodding, and foot-tapping encourage (and are symptoms of) "feelings of solidarity" that depend on both culture and hard-wiring.[15] By the same token, people who are not attuned to the same sort of music in the same way find it alienating. But, to conclude our survey of some medieval emotional communities, the anger expressed during the entertainments at the court of Toulouse was very different from that of warriors ready to do battle and of monks earnestly petitioning God.

The ambiguity of the meaning of *ira* is the sort of fact that social constructivists take very seriously. Anger is a social construction in *our* society. It is theoretically possible that some societies have nothing like it. We have already seen that the Semai and Utku never—or hardly ever—get angry. Nevertheless, both cultures have a word for anger. In *Unnatural Emotions*, a study of the society of Ifaluk (a tiny island in the southwest Pacific), anthropologist Catherine Lutz wished to show that behind such terms are worlds of difference. Among her many goals was to question our easy use of the English word anger as the pure, real emotion. Why should other words, like Old Occitan *ira*, be explained with a compound? Why not consider *ira* the real emotion and our own word anger an eviscerated *ira*—an *ira* minus its sorrowful heart? On Ifaluk, no one speaks of "anger." Obviously not: no one speaks English. But when Lutz pointed that out, she meant more than the word. She meant that no word in Ifaluk quite matches the assumptions, metaphors, associations, causes, cures, behaviors, and everything else that goes along with "anger."[16]

The Ifaluk have a word, *song*, that may be roughly translated as anger. But, Lutz says, *song* is not the same as Western anger, which has the many meanings that this book has been at pains to describe. *Song* is always associated with a moral transgression: someone has upset the moral order, and someone else is *song* because she or he disapproves of that disruption. Lutz uses the term "justifiable anger" to roughly translate *song*'s meaning. (In this, she accedes to the English word.) She is perfectly aware that Western notions of anger include something like justifiable anger. But she carefully distinguishes between the two, arguing that on Ifaluk moral anger regulates relationships among people, whereas in the West moral anger is about individual rights.

As we have seen, Western anger also has a role in structuring relationships, but Ifaluk *song* is different because it is always connected to a moral judgment. Feudal lord Juhel was angry that he had not been consulted about freeing his serf, but he did not claim that the freeing itself violated a sacred taboo. *Song*'s connection to justice and social order elevates the person feeling it to a position of power. While *song* may be expressed by anyone, it is most often the prerogative of Ifaluk chiefs, imposing a top-down construction on the emotional life of others. This is accomplished without violence—by shunning the offender, through gossip, and so on. The one who has offended is expected to be (and is) afraid; he or she will eventually apologize and perhaps pay a fine or send a gift to the person who is *song*, ending the episode. As they daily carry out their many social obligations, people routinely try to avoid the *song* of others; in this way, the anger of *song* ironically makes Ifaluk a peaceable kingdom.

Lutz's insistence on *song*'s difference from English *anger* and her careful discrimination of the anger of *song* from the irritability felt during sickness (*tipmochmoch*) and the annoyance felt at slights (*tang*) suggest that linguists might lean toward a social constructivist view. Some do: Anna Wierzbicka argues that different words for emotions express something essential about how those emotions are experienced. She warns us "not to interpret another culture's categories of experience as just a subtype of this or that emotion recognized lexically by English."[17] On the other hand, Zoltán Kövecses argues that "many unrelated languages" share a key constructive metaphor for anger: "the angry person is a pressurized container." This generates the associated but more complex metaphor "anger is a hot fluid in a container." In English, the results of these analogies include:

—His pent-up anger *welled up* inside him.
—Billy's just *blowing off steam*.
—When I told him, he just *exploded*.
—I *blew* my stack.[18]

Some historical linguists, taking up the same idea, find different governing metaphors—those expressing affliction and swelling—for anger in Old English, the form of English dominant before the Norman Conquest of England in 1066.[19] Such studies mesh with social constructivism insofar as metaphors are key ways in which societies conceive of reality and consequently of the roles of emotions within the individual and the world. However, at least in the case of anger, Kövecses argues that the metaphor of "fluid under pressure" meshes with our "actual physiology." He cites studies by Paul Ekman and his colleagues that claim that "skin temperature and pulse rate rise in anger in both American and Minangkabau [West Sumatran] subjects."[20] With this, we are back to the Galenic body. But other scholars report that the angry person's heart rate and systolic blood pressure are not much different from those of the fearful person, and while facial skin temperature rises, finger temperature drops.[21]

How useful is social constructivism? It is certainly helpful for seeing purposes in feelings and behaviors that otherwise seem "irrational," such as cursing monks and quarreling husbands and wives. Furthermore, it fits very well with the theory of Psychological Construction, which ratifies the importance of social norms by postulating a constantly developing brain, always creating new neural pathways for fresh predictions and conceptualizations, including those introduced by families, schools, songs, and so on. But social constructivism also works with the theory of Basic Emotions—especially when the stress is on display rules rather than on the universality of facial expressions or brain regions. And it can agree as well with the Enactivists when they emphasize the role of the cortex in modifying the biologically grounded brain systems below.

Moreover, social constructivism reminds us that the dyad nature/ nurture is not a real opposition but rather the simplification of a far more complex reality. It is true that our bodies are biological entities that, to some extent, constrain who we are and how we can move, behave, speak, and feel. But it is also true that our bodies are shaped by our ambient environment. Epigeneticists have shown how external conditions may turn off some genes, turn others on, and modify still others. Some of these changes may be inherited. Anthropologists alert to the social implications of these findings speak of "phenotypic adaptations." In cities, for example, impoverished neighborhoods are tantamount to ecological niches "with [heritable] organism-shaping effects especially on behavior, cognition, and health." In Brazil, the consequences of poverty include "obesity, less skeletal robusticity, and certain psychological disorders."[22] Our emotive selves are as susceptible to ambient conditions as every other aspect of our body.

But social constructivism is also somehow unsatisfying to many. Although it recognizes the importance of individual agency in creating emotions, it tends to find even here some general formulas. Thus, Batja Mesquita and her colleagues interviewed Japanese and American subjects about how they experienced interpersonal confrontations, which in both cultures were linked to anger. Then they summed up their findings:

In North American contexts, offense situations were framed as threats to the individual's autonomy and self-worth [. . .] and were to be solved by reaffirming the self and by getting back at the other person. In Japanese contexts, on the other hand, offense episodes tended to be interpreted as threats to the relationship that call for a better understanding of the other person's motives [. . .]. The appropriate actions in these situations were to keep one's calm.[23]

Anthropologist Andrew Beatty objects to grand generalizations like these. He proposes that we think in terms of narratives that grasp individual instances in their full particularity, with their backstories and histories, populated by living people who may not be "representative."[24] He describes incidents in Java in which a Westerner would expect anger, yet were not experienced that way by the people involved. Beatty resists the impulse to conclude that "The Javanese do not get angry." He insists on treating each situation in all its singularity. He tells the story of one such event. One afternoon a neighbor—a plowman—welcomed Beatty into his house with a broad smile. Yet shortly before that, as Beatty found out later, the poor man had discovered that his only source of livelihood, his buffalo, had been poisoned. Although (as the plowman eventually explained to Beatty) he did consider who might have done the deed, he decided that the loss was his "due, a blow destined to make him 'aware.'" He was relieved that his daughter had been spared. Beatty does not infer that the plowman felt angry but refrained from showing it. Rather, the plowman achieved a "kind of disengagement, a refusal to feel. Caring, but not feeling."[25] He did not try to restrain his anger (as Seneca would advise) or abandon it (as the Buddha would have) or make a Transition (as Martha Nussbaum would like) because, in Beatty's view, he bypassed anger altogether. To come to this conclusion, Beatty had to see the whole episode as it unfolded with this particular man at this particular time, and he had to know the man pretty well. Beatty is an anthropologist who thinks like a novelist and wants others to do so as well.

In the plowman's case, the anger was missing. In other instances, anger is very much in evidence, yet here, too, social constructivism has been faulted precisely for erasing the feeling's force and passion. For years, anthropologist Renato Rosaldo could not understand why, among the Ilongot of the Philippines, bereavement was one of the motives that led to killing other human beings. After much planning and preparation, grieving Ilongot men went off to await a victim—any victim—in order to cut off his or her head and toss it on the ground. In this way, they said, they "threw away" their anger. Even though headhunting was the Ilongot's "most salient cultural practice," Rosaldo could find no key to this behavior in social needs or functions, generalizations that are the usual anthropological explanation. Instead, he discovered the reason for Ilongot headhunting in his own individual experience, when his wife—also a brilliant anthropologist—died in a freak accident. Then Rosaldo was overcome by rage, grief, and a host of other "powerful visceral emotional states." While he did not himself go headhunting, he now understood the powerful anger that lay within Ilongot grief.[26]

With this as his starting point, Rosaldo critiques certain kinds of social constructivism as particularly unemotional ways to think about emotion. Like Beatty, he asks anthropologists to look at the non-structured, spontaneous activities that take place outside of rituals; he wants them to look at the "platitudes" that unfold over time, always keeping in mind the exceptional force of feelings.

Finally, social constructivism has also been criticized for its moral neutrality. This is William Reddy's complaint. He is himself close to being a social constructivist in claiming that people in power always impose their emotions on the rest of us: "emotional regimes," he says, are "the set of normative emotions" that prop up those in power.[27] Furthermore, he sees bottom-up social construction taking place via what he calls "emotional refuges," where people carve out spaces in which they are relieved of the strictures of the regime. Yet Reddy rejects the ethical implications of social constructivism because it offers no way to critique any society or political order. If everything is socially constructed, then the observer has no objective perch on which to stand and declare moral judgment—first, because her own judgment is constructed; and second, because nothing gives her the moral authority to condemn or praise other societies and their mores. Reddy claims to have found an objective perch for moral judgments. It is not that such and such an emotion is good or bad, nor that emotions should be expressed in this or that way. It is, rather, that "emotional liberty" is good. This is the freedom to change our own emotions, to rethink and reformulate them as we learn, grow, and change our life's goals. Societies that offer room to feel many different ways are freer—and, for Reddy, better—than those that do not.

But even here, it is the observer who must make the judgment about which societies are free. If Americans are freer than the Semai to express anger, but the Semai are freer to express fear, which society has the greater liberty? And is freedom to express shame as morally excellent as the freedom to express love. Of course, Reddy means freedom in more than just expression. He means the liberty "to change goals [. . .] to undergo or derail conversion experiences." While these are mental processes, most of them entail some action in the world. An observer might legitimately ask, however, whether a society in which everyone were entirely free to change their goals, and thus their commitments, would not be so socially chaotic as to be morally worse, not better, than others.

Social constructivists argue against the general view that anger is a natural—indeed, elemental—aspect of human nature. Consider the recent rise of attacks on immigrants in Germany. The authors of an article in the *New York Times* blamed the aggression on Facebook's practice of tapping "into negative, primal emotions like anger or fear."[28] From the perspective of a social constructivist, however, far from drawing on anything "primal," Facebook was itself imposing the socially constructed assumption that anger and fear are easily tapped. The social network was taking emotions created by a few people and amplifying them in such a way as to make them seem majoritarian. It was Facebook that manufactured this emotional regime of the few.

# 12

## ANGER CELEBRATED

Whenever I mention to friends and acquaintances that I am writing a book on anger, their response almost invariably is, "How timely!" or, "We could certainly use that!" The idea that we live in an Age of Anger, as Pankaj Mishra calls it, is widespread these days.[1] But the same thing was true in the 1980s, when Peter and Carol Stearns wrote their book on the declining acceptance of anger in America. The Stearnses demurred, calling any seeming "freewheeling ventilation of anger" simply misreading "cues from a few atypical sources." They considered the campaign against anger begun by the Victorians to be continuing apace in their own time.[2]

It is likely that something similar is true today. Even if everyone in the public eye seems to be angry or is declared to be angry, older standards persist as well: few advice books today advocate anger, and anger management classes are legion. Nevertheless, there is good reason to think that anger is currently much valued and, in some circles at least, even celebrated. And although this is not entirely new, it is newly amplified by the media with which we are surrounded today.

That it is not entirely new must be emphasized. Mishra begins his book with the example of the poet, futurist, and proto-fascist Gabriele D'Annunzio (d.1938), who founded the "Free State of Fiume" and advocated the recovery of "masculinity" through violence, death, and sacrifice. D'Annunzio was, in Mishra's words, "an opportunistic prophet for angry misfits of Europe."[3]

But did those misfits glorify their anger? Did they celebrate it? Or was it simply the unspoken emotion behind their adulation of D'Annunzio? Mishra argues that the movements of political nationalism and economic globalization around the year 1900 were the precedents to our own age of anger, and he thinks that D'Annunzio was a forerunner of the populists of our own time. Uffa Jensen's book on the "angry politics" in Germany today makes much the same point. In the nineteenth century, modernity, both authors assert, uprooted Westerners from their traditional cocoons of sociability—villages, communities, families—and threw them into a maelstrom of fears, anxieties, and resentments.[4] Today, the same forces have affected every nook and cranny of the inhabited world. ISIS and D'Annunzio's men are cut from the same cloth, according to Mishra; nineteenth-century anti-Semitism was the dress rehearsal for the far right today, argues Jensen.

I generally agree, and I will gesture toward these arguments here from time to time. But for the most part I want to concentrate on something a bit different: today we have a discourse that does not just employ anger but also lauds it, demands it, ratifies it, and celebrates it. And I will argue that this sort of anger, although rooted in the past, derives not just from the rootlessness, unhappiness, and anxiety that is part of our modern lives, but also from something little noted: the sense that our honor has been insulted and maligned, and we need to assert it and demand that it be recognized. We no longer have duels, and the very use of the word honor has greatly declined, except, perhaps, when referring to "honor killings" in cultures far away. But the sense of honor dismissed, disregarded, disrespected—dissed—seems widespread. In many ways it takes us back to the ancient definition of anger as a response to a hurt that is perceived as deliberate by someone who has no right to inflict it. With the internet, cable TV, misinformation campaigns, and radio chatter amplifying our sense of injury and encouraging us to get angry, we are beginning to lose sight of the other long traditions, outlined in this book, of abandoning, controlling, and critiquing anger.

In the past, anger was mainly decried or, at best, justified under certain strict circumstances. But was it lauded? Yes, a bit, but only when it was felt by people "worthy" to feel and express it—mainly men, mainly elite men. Other people might fuss and rage, but theirs was not true anger, not dignified and just. It is true that the medieval clerics who termed anger one of the seven deadly sins also thought that people, all people, should rightly get angry at sin. But when we stop to ask precisely who *in practice* had the right to get justly angry, the answer is male clerics or male warriors. Some medieval women got righteously angry, but we know about them mainly from hagiographies: they numbered among the most elite of all people, the saints.

That situation changed. Protest movements increasingly claimed anger as their birthright, as we saw with the popular outcries of the later Middle Ages. Eventually, in the philosophies of Hume, Smith, and other Enlightenment thinkers, anger was given a moral role. In the writings of Rousseau, anger against injustice was the right and duty of all men— and of all women too. In effect, anger was theoretically democratized during the seventeenth and eighteenth centuries. By the time of the French Revolution, writers could claim that the whole "French people" had exercised their "just anger" when they stormed the Bastille. Even so, this was pretty isolated. For the most part, the rhetoric of the French Revolution concerned the "rights of man and citizen."

"Passion is the gale," said the American revolutionaries. They had much the same point in mind as did British punk rock singer John Lydon (Johnny Rotten) when, in 1986, he recorded the song "Rise," with the constantly repeated refrain "Anger is an energy." It didn't matter who you were, whether wrong or right, whether black or white, sang Lydon, you needed to know that "the written word is a lie," you had to fight the "shitstem," you needed to rise and get on the road: you required the energy of anger.[5] "Anger is an energy" became the theme of his autobiography.[6]

It may seem frivolous to compare the passions invoked by American revolutionaries with Lydon's lyrics. But I would argue that it is not.

Lydon was thinking of South Africa under apartheid; that's the significance of the lines "They put a hotwire to my head / 'cause of the things I did and said / And made these feelings go away / Model citizen in every way." These words, Lydon explains, "are a reference to the torture techniques that the apartheid government was using."[7] In short, Lydon converted the pain of a tortured person in South Africa into his own personal hurt. That made him angry, and he told others to get angry in "Rise," his very public, loud, and hard-driving song. The 1960s women's movement made popular the slogan "the personal is political."[8] With Lydon and many others today, personal anger is the term, metaphor, and style of choice for demanding a political voice. All across the political spectrum, people want their voices heard.

In September 2018, when President Donald Trump's nominee for Supreme Court Justice Brett Kavanaugh was accused of sexual misconduct, he testified before the Senate Judiciary Committee with an evident show of anger. At times he modeled an Ekmanesque face: mouth curled in a sneer and brows knitted together. He expressed his "outrage." He blamed the Democrats for orchestrating a "political hit, fueled with apparent pent-up anger about President Trump and the 2016 election."[9] After Kavanaugh's presentation, Trump, himself a follower of the dictum "never show weakness," was evidently very pleased.[10] Others joined in the praise.

People at the other end of the political spectrum, dissenters from Trump, were also feeling angry, for opposite reasons. This was particularly true of women who identified with Kavanaugh's accuser, Christine Blasey Ford. "As a woman, as a loving parent [. . .] I am angry. I'm beyond angry," wrote author Jennifer Weiner on the front page of the *New York Times Sunday Review* as she contemplated the upcoming Senate hearing. "I find myself [. . .] stuck in a simmer of rage. My hands furl into fists. My jaw clenches. My teeth grind in the night." Her description of anger might as well have been straight out of Galen or Darwin. However, unlike the anger they were thinking of, Weiner's was directed against a system—the "old frat boys," as she called them, the men who run our society and engage in or at least wink at sexual harassment. She was not angry about a particular person—not Donald Trump nor Brett Kavanaugh, nor even the Republican Senators who seemed likely to confirm him. She wanted to "burn down" (as she put it) the whole fraternity house that is our society.[11]

✻

How did we get to the point where all sides are praising anger? In the late nineteenth and early twentieth centuries, states were obliged in the name of nationalism to integrate numerous hitherto independent local cultures into one ideally homogeneous people. Working against that unaccustomed unity were deeply rooted prejudices. These were bolstered by new pseudo-scientific notions of race that made religion, too, a racial category. That is why nineteenth-century Germans could confidently write about a Jewish "people's spirit" (*Volksgeist*), something that Jews could never shed, not even if they converted to Christianity. They could never integrate with the rest of German society because they were strangers to it by their very nature.

The ancients had talked about different races and disdained those beyond their borders. But the idea that race is inherited, that it is responsible for an indelible (inferior or superior) culture, that it marks every individual who belongs to it, that it is biological and inescapable— that was a European invention. "Purity of blood," was the slogan used by the fifteenth-century Spanish Inquisition (with lots of support from popular sentiment) to prevent converted Jews from assimilating with the rest of Spanish society. Racial profiling became more pressing in the nineteenth century, as the European aristocracy gradually lost its standing in the wake of the French Revolution. Arthur de Gobineau (d.1882) argued forcefully and influentially that "all civilizations derive from the white race, that none can exist without its help, and that a society is great and brilliant only so far as it preserves the blood of the noble group that created it, provided that this group itself belongs to the most illustrious branch of our species."[12] Gregor Mendel's (d.1884) discovery of genetic inheritance led eugenicists to argue that mental health, criminality, intelligence, and morality were inherited and distributed in characteristic and unvarying fashion within the various races. Eugenicists made both "controlled breeding" and "culling" of human races part of their program.

A long campaign to eradicate the myth of race by anthropologists, scientists, and many others has had only limited success. The United States Census Bureau asks people to identify their race, but it at least gives lip service to the idea that "race" is a socially constructed, not biologically grounded, category: "the racial categories included in the census questionnaire generally reflect a social definition of race [. . .] and not an attempt to define race biologically, anthropologically, or genetically."[13] It is therefore possible to tick off more than one race on a census form. Even so, the idea of fixed races permeates our perceptions.

Racial thinking has inexorably led many people to identify themselves with one race, to feel that theirs is not accorded the honor due to it, and to assert that the very presence of other races hurts their own dignity. This is the prelude to the white nationalist chant, "You will not replace us!" repeated constantly by alt-right demonstrators at rallies, most infamously at a 2017 demonstration against the removal of a statue of Confederate General Robert E. Lee in Charlottesville, Virginia, where it was sometimes transmuted to "Jews will not replace us."[14] To the alt-right, Lee was a champion of "white people," and taking down the statue was therefore an affront to the "white race."

The "You will not replace us!" chant derives from an idea propounded by French far-right writer Renaud Camus and popularized in his book, *The Great Replacement* (*Le Grand Remplacement*, 2011). Camus argued that French society was being "replaced" by Middle Eastern immigrants. The same sort of thing was happening in the United States: the "descendants of those who built the nation suddenly find themselves to be in the minority." Everyone loves the abstract ideas of "integration," "assimilation," and "multiculturalism" in theory, wrote Camus, but everyone is horrified when they actually are put into practice.[15]

Indeed, this "horror" takes on visual punch in a YouTube video by Lauren Southern, a Canadian alt-right activist. She shows images and cites statistics to prove "insanely high growth rates" in immigrant populations. She shows images of hordes of people jumping barriers and flooding over borders. Our "Western values," she laments (without saying what they are!), will disappear. Southern is angry, but hers is anger with a very pretty face; unlike Seneca, she would not be embarrassed by looking in a mirror. Her anger is delivered in the guise of pity for and perplexity at those benighted people who do not see that "we" are about to be replaced by "them." Hers is a long-term, durable anger. It will continue at a slow burn for as long as the immigrants are visible. As Uffa Jensen points out, anger today is "a permanent condition that is at once unleashed by an injustice—whether real or imagined—and that we ever afterward want to put right." But, as Jensen also points out, this durable anger seeks to "break out into a full emotion."[16] We saw that eruption in the strident chant of the white nationalist demonstrators at Charlottesville. Their anger was fueled by the moral outrage of injured honor. It traded on the idea that whites are "disrespected" by everyone— everyone, that is, who belongs to a non-white race or who is white but politically liberal. In this same mode, Jared Taylor, the founder of *American Renaissance*, a white supremacist magazine, railed against the *New York Times* for promoting an Asian, Sarah Jeong, to its editorial board. "Miss Jeong's appointment memorialized the double standard: Disrespect for protected classes is vile but contempt for whites is fine."[17]

The "disrespect" that Taylor felt, the contempt that he perceived coming from the *New York Times* and elsewhere, is also the hurt at the core of the anger explored by Arlie Hochschild in her book about the emotions of a group of far-right adherents living in Louisiana.[18] Their anger is fueled by what they see as their denigration in the "elite press." They bristle at the term redneck. They are proud of their Christian values and way of life, which they feel are under siege. They believe that they have worked hard, they have sacrificed, they are men and women of tough moral fiber. And yet they are little appreciated. Hochschild discovers their "deep story" in a sort of myth: they feel as if they have been waiting patiently in line for their turn at the American Dream only to find that others, far less worthy, have cut into the line ahead of them: people on welfare, who are getting the money that Hochschild's interviewees have paid in taxes; people promoted because of affirmative action, who are getting ahead simply because they are black; people who are upstarts, like "women, immigrants, refugees."

But why are her Louisianan informants not angry about the hurts they have endured at the hands of the industries that have sickened them and polluted their environment, laid them off their jobs and cut their dwindling wages and pensions? They are certainly aware of these things; they deeply mourn the loss of the clear waters in which they once fished, the once pristine land now foul and toxic. The answer is that they bear these hurts because they do not experience them as dishonors. They believe in progress and accept that it comes with a price. They see polluting companies as neighbors with the same goals in mind. Indeed, they think of themselves as businessmen too—though their enterprises are on scales unimaginably small compared to the oil and other industries they work for. The real insults to these Louisianans come from the "liberals" and the federal programs that liberals support. The government, as they see it, dismisses their honor—the honor of hard-working, white, heterosexual, Christian men and women.

Europe and the United States are not alone in engendering groups that harbor the fears, hatreds, and angers that motivate the "You will not replace us!" refrain. In Myanmar, Buddhists are, as I write, killing, raping, and expelling Rohingya Muslims from Rakhine province. Although within Buddhism itself there is a long tradition—entirely independent of the Western chant—that made a virtue of killing or expelling others (see Chapter 1), nevertheless, Myanmar has been strongly influenced as well by Western racism and its slogans.

In his book on Myanmar, journalist Francis Wade points out that when Muslims first arrived in Rakhine in the ninth century, they were easily absorbed. Borders in those days were porous; Rakhine's populations moved westward into the neighboring Bengali polities, and immigrants from the other direction moved in. In those days, Rakhine was an independent kingdom, and its ruler, though favoring Buddhism, nevertheless welcomed all sorts of ethnicities and religions. That diversity was eroded by the British, who ended the monarchy and Rakhine's independence when they took over Burma in the nineteenth century. Again (as in Europe and the Americas) national unification meant absorbing and assimilating hitherto separate local cultures—and again the "solution" was only half-hearted. Convinced that races were biological entities, and eager to impose divisions that would facilitate their rule, the British named—created, really—139 ethnic groups, or "races" in Burma. Although unprecedented before the colonial take-over, the racial divisions constructed by the occupiers were accepted and naturalized, even by the anti-colonial independence movement, whose revolutionary rallying cry was "Race, Language, the Buddhist religion!"

Rohingya Muslims were stripped of their citizenship in 1962, when the military took power and entrusted only the "superior race"—the so-called "Buddhist race"—with official duties. But it was not until 2012, one year after Myanmar's military junta transferred partial power to civilian rule, that violence directed specifically against the Rohingya began. When Wade interviewed Buddhists about the violence, one monk declared, "we need to defend ourselves by building a fence with our bones."[19] It was not they who were doing the killing, in other words; it was the Muslims who were trying to kill Buddhism itself. "Buddhism stands for the truth and peace," the monk went on. "Therefore, if the Buddhist cultures vanish, truth and peace would vanish steadily as well. [. . .] It can be the fall of Buddhism. And our race will be eliminated."[20] A Rakhine villager who participated in the burning of a Rohingya settlement explained, "If I don't protect my race then it will disappear."[21]

In essence these people were echoing the white supremacist chant: "You will not replace us!"

✳

Democracy by its very nature sets up expectations of being heard and counted. But since 1990, in the wake of the fall of the Berlin Wall, Pankaj Mishra observes, these hopes were energized. A "democratic revolution of aspiration [. . .] swept across the world, sparking longings for wealth, status and power. [. . .] Egalitarian ambition broke free of old social hierarchies."[22] Such ambitions lent themselves to the language of victimization on all sides. The chant "You will not replace us!" reflects the far right's urgent need to be recognized as well as its desire to be avenged on those who, in the view of its adherents, insult them simply by being different.

For many women, the "democratic revolution" began many years before Mishra's turning point—with women's fight for the right to vote and later with the women's liberation movement of the 1960s. But only very recently has it merged with both an angry rhetoric and a new form of anger more in keeping with the male style.

This is only very recent in part because, although anger may be an energy, it is not the only way to get energized. Just as the American and French Revolutions emphasized "rights," so too did the nineteenth- and early twentieth-century suffragette movement. Its first convention in its American guise began with a "Declaration of Sentiments" that left out anger altogether. Echoing the Declaration of Independence, it began with the "self-evident" truths "that all men and women are created equal." It spoke of the "patient sufferance" of women under a government of "absolute despotism." It listed the "repeated injuries and usurpations on the part of man toward woman," and it asserted that women felt themselves "aggrieved, oppressed, and fraudulently deprived of their most sacred rights." Energized by the language of rights as well as the "great precept of nature," these women certainly spoke of their degradation, but they countered it by "buckl[ing] on the armor that can best resist the keenest weapons of the enemy—contempt and ridicule." They urged adopting the "religious enthusiasm" and courage of Joan of Arc.[23]

Rights, nature's precept, religion, the courage of a saint: these are old-fashioned appeals indeed. Today, we have other energizing models, again not always anger. When Tarana Burke started the Me Too campaign in 2007, she simply wanted to "reach sexual assault survivors in underprivileged communities."[24] Even after the movement was turned into a Twitter hashtag and was popularized by actress Alyssa Milano in 2017, it involved the emotions of pain, grief, healing, and empathy far more than it did anger. But the Me Too movement—along with the election of Donald Trump, of whose sexual violence against women he himself boasted in a recording from 2005—is the context within which the current groundswell of women's wrath must be understood.

Again, a comparison with the suffragette movement may be useful to see what has changed and what has not. A broadside published in 1911 by the Women's Political Union, pointed out that in New York State ex-convicts, unlike women, had the power to vote. The illustration showed two clearly virtuous ladies (one holding a baby, the other wearing a graduation cap and gown) held back from the ballot box by an officer who at the same time gestures to a line of men in prison garb to come forward and hand in their votes. Were the women of the Political Union angry? They explicitly were not: they declared themselves not "prompted by a spirit of vindictiveness." They agreed that convicts who had served their time had the right to vote. But "with confidence we challenge every voter in the State of New York to give one sound reason why the four men who committed rape on women should be made the political rulers of the victims of their lust."[25]

The broadside was angry, we would say, for that is how we assess such things. But it did not celebrate women's anger—to the contrary. And this was to be expected, as these women wanted to woo supporters, and a show of anger would have been counterproductive. Recall the English "scold": the word referred to an angry woman and always disparaged her. Recall the image of the "angry black woman": it was always negative. When the stewardesses observed by Hochschild got angry, they had to do hard emotional labor to suppress those feelings and smile instead. Even Lauren Southern, the far-right Canadian, never frowned, never scowled in her YouTube video. Indeed, she was the very picture of geniality. The accuser of Brett Kavanaugh before the Senate Judiciary Committee, Christine Blasey Ford, calmly stated that, when both were teenagers, Kavanaugh had attacked her, forced her onto a bed, and held his hand over her mouth to prevent her screams. But she never said that she was angry about the incident or its traumatizing effect on the rest of her life. Indeed, she admitted to only one emotion: her "terror" at speaking before Congress. She was conciliatory, and if her voice trembled a bit, she did not cry. She quipped with a smile that she might need some caffeine after giving her opening statement, adding politely, "if that is available." When Senator Chuck Grassley asked her to pull the microphone nearer to her and she could not, she obliged even so: "I'll lean forward." When asked how she knew her memory of the attack was true, she answered with a short science lesson about the nature of memory, "indelible in the hippocampus."[26]

"That is how women have been told to behave when they are angry; to not let anyone know, and to joke and to be sweet and rational and vulnerable," wrote Rebecca Traister on the front page of the *Times Sunday Review* the weekend following the hearing. By contrast, she asserted, men are admired when they bellow, snarl, pout, and weep "furiously."[27]

Traister was describing different anger display rules for women and men in American culture. She was also advocating that women act more like men. Her complaint was not so different from that of the suffragettes: men have trampled on women's equality and dignity. But she did not use the rhetoric of rights so much as she employed the discourse of anger. Women, she was saying, have the same anger as men, and they should use it as men do.

It is not invariably the case that women and men have different rules for emotional expression. Among the Semai, Utku, and Fore, neither men nor women are expected to show anger. But such gender parity is not true in the United States, with its deeply rooted traditions of anger management that the Stearnses unearthed. Men are allowed to be— even admired for being—more strident than women. For men, expressing anger is, in certain settings, an effective tool for getting their way and accomplishing their goals. Consider the behavior of Republican Senator Lindsey Graham at the Senate judicial confirmation hearing. Demonstrating the "male model," Graham yelled at Diane Feinstein, one of four women on the judiciary committee and a Democrat, for her perfidy. He jabbed his finger at her, grimaced, and called the hearing a "sham." He teared up as, addressing Kavanaugh, he imagined what "you and your family have gone through."[28] Now consider the comportment of Feinstein: she said nothing. People everywhere follow feeling rules. But in the context of democratization, when male anger is voluble and confrontational, and when it has prestige and is associated with power, then some women will want to claim the same rights to combative angry expression as men have.

In other words, anger, among other things, has become a metaphor for power. And, again, recurring to the classical definition, we may say that many women today not only feel insulted by male privilege and power in general (as did the suffragettes), but they want to adopt the male mode of anger comportment in order to express themselves and regain their honor. That is why it is significant to these women that two of them riding in an elevator with Senator Jeff Flake, after the Kavanaugh hearing, shouted at him. One pointed her finger, the other demanded he look her in the face and accused him of "telling all women that they don't matter."[29]

Of course, there are precedents to such celebrations of women's anger. Already the *Year of the Woman* (1973), a documentary by Sandra Hochman, showed women at the Democratic National Convention of 1972 singing,

187

"Mine eyes have seen the glory of the flame of women's rage / Kept smoldering for centuries, now burning in this age. [. . .] / Our anger eats into us, we'll no longer bend to kings."[30] Similarly, Audre Lorde's keynote speech at the National Women's Studies Association Conference in 1981 began with a definition of racism and continued, "My response to racism is anger. [. . .] Anger of exclusion, of unquestioned privilege, of racial distortions, of silence, ill-use, stereotyping, defensiveness, misnaming, betrayal, and co-optation."[31] This is the justified and righteous anger of God at sin, taken on as a human duty by the virtuous. The anger that women then invoked and today encourage is in many ways the secular counterpart, the distant grandchild, of that Christian tradition. But in the echo-chamber of today's media, it is amplified to a chorus.

In her book on women's political anger, *Good and Mad*, Traister distinguishes this kind of rage from the anger endemic in personal relationships, the sort that has occupied most thinkers since the time of the Buddha. The anger that she is talking about is John Lydon's; she praises it for its ability to inject "energy, intensity, and urgency into battles that must be intense and urgent if they are to be won."[32] For Traister, every movement for social change, every lawsuit filed on behalf of women's rights is and has been fueled by socially productive anger. This would surprise the suffragettes. Nonetheless, it is true that a sense of righteous anger is behind many of today's women's movements.

Most of the current celebration of women's anger has been shaped as praise of public rage for public causes. But the line between public and private is often blurry. Consider Esther Kaplan's memories of the 1970s movement of "feminist consciousness raising." She rightly stresses that "those women *left their husbands*"; social movements have the potential— in her words—"to radically change us, not just radically change the world."[33] Even when anger is a public matter, its expression infiltrates and fills all facets of our private, inner, and domestic lives.

Conversely, in our age of Twitter and Facebook, private angers may become matters to celebrate publicly. At Georgetown University a professor of Security Studies was enraged by the male culture of the Senators at the Kavanaugh hearing. Afterward she tweeted: "Look at [this] chorus of entitled white men justifying a serial rapist's arrogated entitlement. All of them deserve miserable deaths while feminists laugh." Later she explained that "I aim to create language that creates as much discomfort as I am forced to feel in this regime. I cannot tell you the rage and hurt it feels as all of those men on that Judiciary Committee kicked sexual assault survivors in the gut."[34] Here, the language of hurt and the anger that it engenders takes us back not so much to the wrath of God as to the virtuous anger of the offended Aristotle.

This is the case as well for Giulia Sissa, a classicist at Berkeley, who has in effect rewritten the figure of Medea, making her heroic not because she is righting the cosmic wrongs committed by Jason but because she is unafraid—indeed proud—of her anger. Sissa celebrates women's jealousy, the amorous, erotic anger of every woman jilted by her lover. She berates Seneca for condemning anger and for making Medea a monster: "Now I am Medea!" Sissa proudly proclaims.[35] She is beside herself with rage. As she argues in great detail in her book, men have always been "allowed" to be jealous, but women's jealousy has been ridiculed, condemned, even forbidden throughout the course of Western civilization. Sissa renounces that tradition. She takes her own private anger and makes it public in order to dignify, redeem, and glorify anger. In the process, she hopes to give the "forbidden," shameful jealousy of women the same honor that men's jealousy has always commanded.

✳

At the first Women's March on Washington D.C. in early 2017, called to protest the election and inauguration of Trump, the first speaker, America Ferrera, linked the women's movement to Black Lives Matter: "We demand an end to the systemic murder and incarceration of our black brothers and sisters. [. . .] Together, we, all of us will fight, resist and oppose every single action that threatens the lives and dignity of any and all of our communities," she declared.[36] In fact, however, the fighting, resisting, and opposing rhetoric in Black Lives Matter is relatively muted. Certainly in the first appearance of that movement, in 2013, its emotional theme was love. "Black people. I love you. I love us. Our lives matter," posted Alicia Garza, a California-based writer and activist, when she learned that the killer of an unarmed black high school student, Trayvon Martin, had been acquitted.[37] Garza's friend Patrisse Cullors created the hashtag #blacklivesmatter. The movement took off in the wake of yet another killing of a young black man, Michael Brown, by a police officer in Ferguson, Missouri.

"Enraged by the death of Trayvon Martin and the subsequent acquittal of his killer [. . .] we took to the streets. A year later, we set out together on the Black Lives Matter Freedom Ride to Ferguson," reads the Black Lives Matter website.[38] In fact, it is not clear that the Black Lives Matter movement was all that prominent in the Ferguson protests, in part because, as Jelani Cobb has pointed out, the organization of the movement is decentralized and disputed.[39] Although there was anger at Ferguson, there were many other emotions as well, and the underlying theme was community spirit. In the words of one protestor from nearby St. Louis, "We all had the same pain and anger about this. We all came together that day."[40] Reporting on her own participation in the protests, a local civil rights activist spoke of the trauma of seeing Brown's blood on the street. Marching in front of the police department, "everyone was angry. I was angry. [. . .] This was the first time I had ever seen police dogs ready for attack in real life. [. . .] I tried to remain as calm as possible in such a volatile situation but seeing those police dogs snarling at young Black children filled me with anger and rage. [. . .] I decided to yell directly at the police."[41] Anger is certainly one emotion in the recent protests in which Black Lives Matter participates. This has to do—as one chronicler wrote in 2016—with the "deep anger among ordinary Blacks who have been beaten, imprisoned, humiliated, and abused."[42]

Even so, that deep anger is not particularly *celebrated* by this group. The movement's website talks about healing, about commitment to "a culture where each person feels seen, heard, and supported." Its stated values are inclusion, bonding, empathy, respect for differences.[43]

In a conversation about Traister's book *Good and Mad*, moderated by Garza, the two agreed that they were angry and that lots of women were angry, and they celebrated that fact.[44] But what sorts of anger were they talking about? Indeed, Garza asked Traister the key question, "Why anger? Why not just organizing or advocacy or activism?" Traister answered that anger—modeled on her own, which she described as a "bubbling, boiling" in her brain before she started to write—turned out to be the organizing principle of what was going on. When she decided to write about anger, "everything fell into place about the stories that I suddenly felt that were really important to tell." Garza, however, was not so sure: from her point of view, and that of Black Lives Matter, "there was a different realm of anger that folks were operating in [. . .] and those different realms of anger were not in synch."

Garza was right: not all anger is the same, and not even all political angers are the same. They have very different origins and goals, and therefore they feel—must feel—different. "You will not replace us!" is not the same anger as "We will be powerful," and those are distinct from "You will not cut in ahead of me." The first is exclusionary and mingled with hate; the second potentially inclusive and melded with courage; the third is a compound of nostalgia, sadness, and mourning. What they do have in common, however, is their sense of righteousness, the feeling that God is on their side. For that reason, all these celebrated angers generally seem good and right to the people feeling them. That helps make them unshakable—very different from the short-term and oft-regretted anger that dominates that emotion's long history.

Even within these separate groups, the angers are not quite the same. Consider the "we will be powerful" position of women on the left. Traister sees anger as a tool of power and wants the powerless (or less powerful) to assume its manner and its force. She longs for democracy to work, for people (in particular women) to be energized, to vote, to run for office, to organize and strategize with other women. Anger, she says, can be a "productive or catalytic force."[45] But cultural critic Laura Kipnis says that she is "angry" not so much because women lack power, or that men often escape blame for their sexual violence against women, but because public resources are not being disbursed for social programs.[46] Soraya Chemaly thinks women should be angry on the domestic front as well as about political causes.[47] Garza is mainly interested in building a movement "that is impactful and accountable, and effective," and if anger is a tool for that, well and good.[48] And if not, well, anger is not the real issue.

Similarly, on the right, the feelings of the Louisianans interviewed by Hochschild were not exactly the same. Some of her subjects were inspired by their sense of loyalty not to challenge the companies that provided local jobs, even when those jobs came with terrible dangers. Others resigned themselves to accepting and accommodating to the needs of the polluting corporations in their midst. Finally, others made their heroic masculinity, their dare-devil attitude, a good reason not to voice any complaint. The angers that buttressed these various but equally hard-won values were their own.

In *Good Anger*, religious philosopher John Giles Milhaven says that he will not discuss "any of the kinds of anger that are purely constructive." That's because "we do not need to ask a value question about such anger. There is no question that anger for change or liberation has good in it."[49] For him the ethical good of such anger is obvious. Now, it is true that anger has traditionally been considered a moral matter, whether to be utterly rejected (as with Seneca and the Buddhists) or judiciously embraced when expressed at the right time and in the right way toward the right people (as with Aristotle and his heirs). But only when it was connected with godly anger did it become a rigid, permanent, unshakable stance. Every political group today claims that their anger is "purely constructive," that all they want is "change or liberation." The problem is that they have extremely different notions of justice, betterment, and freedom. We seem to have come to an impasse, when many (generally secularized) notions of sin compete with one another for anger's badge of righteousness.

This issue was highlighted for me at the Women's March, when America Ferrera did more than link the women's movement to the causes of black people in the United States. Speaking on behalf of both immigrants and women, she lamented her pain and asserted her dignity and rights. She bewailed the "platform of hate and division" that had just assumed power. "But the President is not America. His cabinet is not America. Congress is not America. We are America, and we are here to stay."[50]

With this, we may sadly observe that both the left and the right are using much the same language. Both mourn their lost honor, seeing it dismissed, disregarded, disrespected. Ferrera's rhetoric is a mirror image of the chant of the demonstrators at Charlottesville, the harangue of the far-rightist Lauren Southern, the words of French theorist Renaud Camus. Ferrera's "The President is not America, [. . .] Congress is not America. We are America" is dangerously close to "Muslims will not replace us," "Jews will not replace us." And her "We are here to stay" is precisely the pledge that the far-right fears, abhors, and rejects. In fact, President Trump, Congress, and so on *are* America, or at least part of America, precisely because they seem to many Americans to represent the way for them to recover their honor and dignity.

And so, although the angers are not the same, they all seem to tend toward a common denominator, a common discourse, that to some degree blurs the very real differences that separate the left and the right, the one fighting for social justice for the oppressed and the other looking to preserve their turf. Both sides seem to be glad to hark back to a slogan first popularized in the 1976 movie *Network*, which foresaw and satirized the coming valuation of anger. The phrase "I'm mad as hell," famously pronounced by actor Peter Finch in the film, has taken on a life of its own in popular culture. It has become the title of a documentary about the web series "The Young Turk"; the title of songs by U.S. Girls, The Funkoars, and Thor; and the refrain of "Not Ready to Make Nice," by the Dixie Chicks. A short clip from Peter Finch's rage in the newsroom is the subject of numerous GIFs. Australia's ABC network airs a program called "Shaun Micallef's Mad as Hell," a satirical look at current news. The words "Mad as Hell" are written on protest signs (see Plate 13). They show up constantly in newspaper headlines. What does the phrase mean? In fact, it is meaningless: "Mad as Hell" celebrates anger at everything and nothing. It can be stuck as a label onto any opposition to anything.

✳

If it is useful to return to the Aristotelian definition of anger to see what might be behind the various political angers of today, it is equally useful to differentiate ours from his. Aristotle considered anger both pleasant and unpleasant. It was unpleasant because it was a painful desire for revenge on those who slighted us. It was pleasant because the contemplation of vengeance was sweet. The realistic likelihood of vengeance was why no one could get angry "with those who are much our superiors in power" for, in those cases, there was little prospect of getting even.[51] Furthermore, said Aristotle, anger was the wrong word if one felt it toward people or groups in general rather than toward particular people.

Aristotle's anger, then, was quite short term and practical. Someone slights you, you insult him in turn and move on; or you plan your insult and then carry it out another day. But the anger of "You will not replace us!" is not short term, for it is directed against too many groups. Indeed, if taken to its logical conclusion, its "you" is everyone who is not "us." For very different reasons, the anger of women against Trump is also enduring, in their case because it is directed not just against him but against what Trumpism stands for: ending abortion rights, curtailing immigration, denying climate change, defunding education, and so on.

Aristotle may help us see that what unites the various angers of our age is the sense of damaged honor. But he takes us only so far, and we cannot rely on him alone. Consider, then, the social constructivist notion of anger to understand its current celebration. Our society and we mutually construct our anger. Today, we have a wide variety of useful anger scripts, and we may also elaborate new ones to fit new goals and purposes. Since anger is traditionally linked to aggression in American society, a new script, claimed by some women, is to get angry in "the American way." Since anger also traditionally has had the role of signaling that something is wrong in a relationship, all the angry people we have seen in this chapter may indeed be getting ready for a negotiation on the public stage that will involve many groups.

The danger remains that factions that see themselves "on the side of God" will freeze in stances that can never be modified. Even Traister, an ardent fan of female anger, warns that anger "does have limits, perils; of course it can corrode. Anger at injustice and inequality is in many ways exactly like fuel. A necessary accelerant, it can drive—on some level *must* drive—noble and difficult crusades. But it is also combustible explosive."[52] It's too bad that she uses the metaphor of a crusade; does she not know how obscene it is for many Muslims? But the really important point is that even Traister's putative enemies—men in power, the alt-right—think that they, too, are working toward justice. The problem is that their definitions of that word are not hers. Even so, her point is well taken. The key challenge for today's celebration of so many angers is to step back from the flash point of their combustible explosivity and begin to talk.

# CONCLUSION

## MY ANGER, OUR ANGER

For one last time, please consider the little girl that I was, hitting my doll. Was I angry? From the point of view of my American mother in the twentieth century, yes, I was; my aggression proved it, and my mother didn't like it. But maybe I was not angry. Perhaps my doll had peed on the rug and I was, as Seneca might have put it, carrying out a "reasoned punishment." Or perhaps I was angry, but for good and righteous reasons, as if I were a young Saint Augustine committed to correcting the sins of my doll for her own salvation. Equally possibly I, as a little girl, was gaining the necessary experience of anger that philosophers like Descartes and Hume thought people needed if they were to develop their mature ethical sensibilities.

As these examples show, morality has been at the center of most discussions of anger. Is anger good or bad? Is it right or wrong? Even social scientists, convinced that society constructs or at least participates in the construction of our anger, think about its moral dimensions. When they theorize that anger is created by local communities, from the bottom up, they inevitably approve of it more than when they argue that it is imposed from the top down. Many see anger as something positive when it works to readjust relationships or to right the world's injustices. Others deplore the emotional labor that goes into being cheerful yet admire people who are able to control or contain their anger about things that would seem to invite outrage.

Most scientists consider anger to be an ineradicable element of human nature; even so they also think about the purposes it serves. With Galen, anger was caused by what we would today call the autonomic nervous system; in his terms, it was a manifestation of the spirit that animated the body. When anger was too strong, it caused physical harm. But some anger was always needed; a living human being required a bit of fire in her blood. With Darwin, however, a new and compelling theory—that anger played a role in the origin and evolution of species—overwhelmed all others. Every scientific theory about anger from then on—whether postulating Basic Emotions, Psychological Constructionism, or Enactivism—has claimed to be fully Darwinian.

There is, therefore, no escaping anger's moral meanings and the wide range of attitudes toward it, extending from absolute rejection to the warmest of welcomes. And it is precisely in the existence of this wide spectrum that we may find some guidance for our own anger. For it suggests that anger is no one thing. The anger that is part of hatred (as the Buddha theorized) is not the same as the anger mingled with pleasure and pain (as Aristotle thought of it), nor are those angers identical to the mournful rage of the far-right Louisianans that Hochschild interviewed.

All of these angers co-exist in our society today, even though we tend to mash them together in our minds and common parlance, labeling every part of the mixture "anger." This is a great pity. Indeed, the purpose of this book has been to see the many sorts of anger that existed in the past and remain with us today. Anger's morality lies in its very variety. By this I mean two things, one political, the other personal.

During the debate over the United States Constitution, before its adoption in 1789, James Madison argued that uniting the various states would provide "a safeguard against domestic faction."[1] By faction he meant a group of people jointly animated "by some common impulse of passion or of interest" that put them at odds with other groups or with "the permanent and aggregate interests of the community." He did not want to stamp out factionalism in the only way possible—by taking away liberty—for he was a "friend of popular government." But he also didn't imagine that there was any realistic way to give everyone "the same opinions, the same passions, and the same interests." His solution was a system of government that would prevent any one faction from imposing its will on the others.

By speaking of a group united "by some common impulse of passion or of interest," Madison was all but saying what I mean by emotional communities. I would change only his "or" to "and": passions and interests go together. Today we find ourselves fractured by groups animated by a great variety of angers and interests. Each considers itself right, just, and even inspired. Each would like to impose its interests, its notion of how to resolve its anger, on everyone else. This is a dead end: it is not possible without stifling all freedom, and that is hardly a solution. People must be free, and that will inevitably mean that they will have their various angers. But it doesn't inevitably mean that they must disapprove of all the others. Madison had an institutional fix to check and balance the different passions and interests. I want to suggest that we may invigorate this political system by recognizing that anger is not one thing, by understanding the values and roots of the many angers that exist today, and by appreciating—as did Darwin—the sheer value of variety itself as a condition for evolution and change.

What would this entail in practice? It would mean that we would be willing to teach our children that anger is expressed by more than one facial expression and that it comes in various forms and in combination with other feelings. Radio, television, the internet, video games—all the media that help shape us today—would be alert to the possibilities inherent in a pluralist view of anger. We ourselves would become aware of the sorts of angers that we harbor and be open to learning about and even adopting and adapting the angers and interests of others.

To rephrase the aphorism, the political is personal. We are the products (mediated by our own proclivities and temperaments) of our homes, schools, experiences, and so on. I know that we think that we know what anger feels like, and that it doesn't seem amenable to change. But that knowledge is itself a matter of schooling, labeling, and noticing that which accords with what we have received. William Reddy has defined emotions as "goal-relevant activations of thought material that exceed the translating capacity of attention within a short time horizon."[2] We might consider our particular anger at any one moment to be a goal-relevant activation of angry thought material that is larger and deeper and more complex than we can imagine it to be at the flash point of that anger. We ourselves are full of factions struggling to be recognized. Knowing and thinking about our many varieties of anger is one good way to increase our attention's capacity.

Hence this book. The angers of the past are still with us today, not only in the numerous anger therapies practiced by modern psychologists, some of which I have discussed in the foregoing chapters, but also in the many emotional communities that surround us, whether in books, our neighborhoods, the cacophony of the internet, or elsewhere in the world. All the many psychological self-help books on the shelves of bookstores, all the blogs that give us advice online: none of these presents ideas that are wholly newborn. All rely on past traditions. The more we know about these traditions—the more we understand where they came from, what they imply morally, and what their limitations are—the better we will be able to navigate our own lives. Do I really believe this? Does knowing about Seneca or Galen or James Averill really help me? Yes, it does. It helps me be less ashamed of beating my doll (and my many other similar moments), more willing to face the fact that I am not always right when I feel angry, and newly capable of recognizing what sort of anger I'm dealing with in a particular circumstance without assuming that it exactly matches the one I had on other occasions.

Similarly, can I really claim that this sort of knowledge will be of use to the body politic? Again, if Madison was right about the nature and dangers of faction, then the more aware we are about the makeup of our divisive angers the more we will be willing to negotiate and find resolutions. In the seventeenth century, Lord Halifax (George Savile, d.1695) offered the notion of "the Trimmer"—someone who modifies her position much as a sailor trims his sails, in accordance with circumstance. He meant the Trimmer to defy the logic of the absolute state (much in vogue in his day) and to keep the ship of state on course without giving in to despotism on the one hand and "the strife and contention [of . . .] men's passions and interests" on the other. People can be trimmers only by being compromisers; they see the way the wind is blowing and make use of it by tacking and jibing. Yes, we want our goals to be met, and yes, our anger may be one handy tool to reach it. But our goals are in this world, and to navigate its waters we need to understand the underlying issues that roil it. I argue with Halifax that our factional "struggles [. . .] support and strengthen [rather] than weaken or maim the Constitution; and the whole frame, instead of being torn or disjointed, [comes] to be the better and closer knit by being thus exercised."[3]

We are generally comfortable within our own emotional community, but we need not be locked in. Indeed, to be enclosed in that cocoon means denying our own reality and its personal and political potential. Let us rejoice (and not be too angry) about that larger picture.

# NOTES

## INTRODUCTION

1. Emily Katz Anhalt, *Enraged: Why Violent Times Need Ancient Greek Myths* (New Haven: Yale University Press, 2017).

## – PART 1: ANGER REJECTED (ALMOST) ABSOLUTELY –

### CHAPTER 1: BUDDHISM

1. "Akkosa Sutta: Insult," in *Samyutta Nikaya: The Grouped Discourses*, 7.2, ed. Access to Insight, at https://www.accesstoinsight.org/tipitaka/sn/index.html. Here and for all other references to the *Tipitaka: The Pali Canon*, see Access to Insight (BCBS Edition), 30 November 2013, at www.accesstoinsight.org/tipitaka. Most are trans. Thanissaro Bhikkhu.
2. "Kakacupama Sutta: The Simile of the Saw," in *Majjhima Nikaya: The Middle-length Discourses*, 21, ed. Access to Insight, at https://www.accesstoinsight.org/tipitaka/mn/index.html.
3. "Anapanasati Sutta: Mindfulness of Breathing," in *Majjhima Nikaya*, 118.
4. "Pacittiya: Rules Entailing Confession," in *Bhikkhu Pāṭimokkha: The Bhikkhus' Code of Discipline*, 8.75, ed. Access to Insight, at https://www.accesstoinsight.org/tipitaka/vin/sv/bhikkhu-pati.html#pc-part8.
5. "Kodhavagga: Anger," 221, in *Dhammapada: The Path of Dhamma*, XVII, ed. Access to Insight, at https://www.accesstoinsight.org/tipitaka/kn/dhp/index.html.
6. See "Yoga Sutta: Yokes," in *Anguttara Nikaya: The Further-factored Discourses*, 4.10, ed. Access to Insight at https://www.accesstoinsight.org/tipitaka/an/index.html.
7. "Kakacupama Sutta," in *Majjhima Nikaya*, 21.
8. *The Mahavamsa or the Great Chronicle of Ceylon*, trans. Wilhelm Geiger, quoted in Michael Jerryson, "Buddhist Traditions and Violence," in *The Oxford Handbook of Religion and Violence*, eds. Michael Jerryson, Mark Juergensmeyer and Margo Kitts (Oxford: Oxford University Press, 2013), Oxford Handbooks Online (www.oxfordhandbooks.com).
9. "Murder with Skill in Means: The Story of the Ship's Captain," trans. Mark Tatz, in *The Skill in Means (Upayakausalya Sutra)* (New Delhi: Motilal Banarsidass, 1994), 73–4.
10. Thich Nhat Hanh, *Anger: Wisdom for Cooling the Flames* (New York: Riverhead, 2001).
11. C. Peter Bankart, "Treating Anger with Wisdom and Compassion: A Buddhist Approach," in *Anger-Related Disorders: A Practitioner's Guide to Comparative Treatments*, ed. Eva L. Feindler (New York: Springer, 2006), 231–55.

12. Francis Wade, *Myanmar's Enemy Within: Buddhist Violence and the Making of a Muslim "Other"* (London: Zed Books, 2017), 269.

## CHAPTER 2: STOICISM

1. Seneca, *Letters on Ethics to Lucilius* 12, trans. Margaret Graver and A.A. Long (Chicago: University of Chicago Press, 2015), 48.
2. Seneca, *On Anger*, trans. Robert A. Kaster in *Anger, Mercy, Revenge*, trans. Robert A. Kaster and Martha C. Nussbaum (Chicago: University of Chicago Press, 2010), 3–129, at 14.
3. Ibid., 91.
4. The term "command center" is Margaret R. Graver's, whose *Stoicism and Emotion* (Chicago: University of Chicago Press, 2007) is a definitive guide to the topic.
5. Seneca, *On Anger*, 20.
6. Ibid., 18.
7. Ibid., 19.
8. Ibid., 24.
9. Ibid., 37.
10. Ibid., 36.
11. Nancy L. Stein, Marc W. Hernandez and Tom Trabasso, "Advances in Modeling Emotion and Thought: The Importance of Developmental, Online, and Multilevel Analyses," in *Handbook of Emotions*, eds. Michael Lewis, Jeannette M. Haviland-Jones and Lisa Feldman Barrett, 3rd ed. (New York: Guilford Press, 2008), 578.
12. Seneca, *On Anger*, 15.
13. All quotations are from Seneca, *Medea*, ed. and trans. A.J. Boyle (Oxford: Oxford University Press, 2014), 5–79.
14. William V. Harris, *Restraining Rage: The Ideology of Anger Control in Classical Antiquity* (Cambridge: Harvard University Press, 2001), chap. 9.
15. M. Tullius Cicero, *Letters to his brother Quintus*, ed. and trans. Evelyn S. Shuckburgh, at https://bit.ly/2ZxzxxZ.
16. Sallust, *The Catilinarian Conspiracy* 51, at https://bit.ly/2IPsZoh, my translation.
17. M. Tullius Cicero, *Against Catiline*, ed. and trans. C.D. Yonge, at https://bit.ly/2ZpT1V7.
18. Cicero, *For Marcus Caelius* 21, ed. and trans. C.D. Yonge, at https://bit.ly/2Ztz5AF.
19. Martin of Braga, *Anger*, in *Iberian Fathers, Volume 1: Writings of Martin of Braga, Paschasius of Dumium, Leander of Seville*, trans. Claude W. Barlow (Washington: The Catholic University of America Press, 1969).
20. Gregory of Tours, *The History of the Franks*, trans. Lewis Thorpe (London: Penguin, 1974) offers a lively translation.

## CHAPTER 3: VIOLENCE AND NEOSTOICISM

1. Justus Lipsius, *On Constancy: De Constantia translated by Sir John Stradling*, ed. John Sellars (Exeter, Devon: Bristol Phoenix Press, 2006), 37.
2. Johann Weyer, *De ira morbo*, in *Ioannis Wieri Opera Omnia* (Amsterdam: Petrum vanden Berge, 1660), 770–875. See Karl A.E. Enenkel, "Neo-Stoicism as an Antidote to Public Violence before Lipsius's *De constantia*: Johann Weyer's (Wier's) Anger Therapy, *De ira morbo* (1577)," in *Discourses of Anger in the Early Modern Period*, eds. Karl A.E. Enenkel and Anita Traninger (Leiden: Brill, 2015), 49–96. All translations from *De ira morbo* are my own.
3. Weyer, *De ira morbo*, 804.
4. Ibid., 807.
5. René Descartes, *The Passions of the Soul*, §65, trans. Stephen H. Voss (Indianapolis: Hackett, 1989), 55.
6. Ibid., §28, 34.

7. See Michael Krewet, "Descartes' Notion of Anger: Aspects of a Possible History of its Premises," in *Discourses of Anger*, 143–71.

8. Descartes, *Passions*, §204, 129.

9. Ibid.

10. Timothy J. Reiss, "Descartes, the Palatinate, and the Thirty Years War: Political Theory and Political Practice," *Yale French Studies* 80 (1991): 108–45, at 109.

11. Susan C. Karant-Nunn, "'Christians' Mourning and Lament Should Not Be Like the Heathens'": The Suppression of Religious Emotion in the Reformation," in *Confessionalization in Europe, 1555–1700: Essays in Honor and Memory of Bodo Nischan*, eds. John M. Headley, Hans J. Hillerbrand and Anthony J. Papalas (Aldershot: Routledge, 2004), 107–30, at 107, 111.

12. The information about word frequency here is gleaned from the Ngram browser provided by Early English Books Online.

13. John Warren, *Mans fury subservient to Gods glory: A Sermon preached to the* Parliament *at* Margarets Westminster *Febr. 20, 1656* (London: Nathanael Webb and William Grantham, 1657), 1, 7, 8, 16, spelling and punctuation updated, but italics in original.

14. Helkiah Crooke, *Microcosmographia: A Description of the Body of Man* (Barbican: W. Jaggard, 1616), 272.

15. *Jane Anger her Protection for Women. To defend them against the scandalous reportes of a late Surfeiting Lover* (London: Thomas Orwin, 1589), A, B4, C.

16. Gwynne Kennedy, *Just Anger: Representing Women's Anger in Early Modern England* (Carbondale: Southern Illinois University Press, 2000).

17. Howard Kassinove and Raymond Chip Tafrate, *Anger Management: The Complete Treatment Guidebook for Practitioners* (Atascadero: Impact Publishers, 2002), 1 (italics in original).

18. Raymond Chip Tafrate and Howard Kassinove, "Anger Management for Adults: A Menu-Driven Cognitive-Behavioral Approach to the Treatment of Anger Disorders," in *Anger-Related Disorders: A Practitioner's Guide to Comparative Treatments*, ed. Eva L. Feindler (New York: Springer, 2006), 115–37, at 118–19.

19. Ibid., 132.

20. Martha C. Nussbaum, *Anger and Forgiveness: Resentment, Generosity, Justice* (Oxford: Oxford University Press, 2016).

21. Ibid., 7.

22. Ibid., 118. The title of chap. 4 is "Intimate Relationships: The Trap of Anger."

23. Seneca, *On Anger*, 19.

24. Nussbaum, *Anger and Forgiveness*, 124.

## CHAPTER 4: PEACEABLE KINGDOMS

1. *Visio Baronti monachi Longoretensis*, trans. J.N. Hillgarth, in *Christianity and Paganism, 350–750* (Philadelphia: University of Pennsylvania Press, 1969), 195–204.

2. Dante Alighieri, *The Divine Comedy: Paradiso*, canto XXVII, 1.52–55, 1: *Italian Text and Translation*, trans. Charles S. Singleton (Princeton: Princeton University Press, 1975), 305.

3. Robert Knox Dentan, "'Honey Out of the Lion': Peace Research Emerging from Mid-20th-Century Violence," in *Expanding American Anthropology, 1945–1980: A Generation Reflects*, eds. A.B. Kehoe and P.L. Doughty (Tuscaloosa: University of Alabama Press, 2012), 204–20, at 204; Idem, "Recent Studies on Violence: What's In and What's Out," *Reviews in Anthropology* 37 (2008): 41–67, at 46.

4. Robert Knox Dentan, *The Semai: A Nonviolent People of Malaya* (New York: Holt, 1968), 55.

5. Clayton A. Robarchek, "Frustration, Aggression, and the Nonviolent Semai," *American Ethnologist* 4/4 (1977): 762–79, at 776.

6. Clayton A. Robarchek, "Conflict, Emotion, and Abreaction: Resolution of Conflict among the Semai Senoi," *Ethos* 7/2 (1979): 104–23, at 109–10.

7. Clayton A. Robarchek and Robert Knox Dentan, "Blood Drunkenness and the Bloodthirsty Semai: Unmaking Another Anthropological Myth," *American Anthropologist*, new series 89/2 (1987): 356–65, at 361.

8. Jean L. Briggs, *Never in Anger: Portrait of an Eskimo Family* (Cambridge: Harvard University Press, 1970).

9. Ibid., 47.

10. Ibid., 42.

11. Ibid., 181, 335.

12. E. Richard Sorenson, "Cooperation and Freedom among the Fore of New Guinea," in *Learning Non-Aggression: The Experience of Non-Literate Societies*, ed. Ashley Montagu (Oxford: Oxford University Press, 1978), 12–30, at 15, 24; Idem, *The Edge of the Forest: Land, Childhood and Change in a New Guinea Protoagricultural Society* (Washington: Smithsonian Institution Press, 1976), 143.

13. Carol Zisowitz Stearns and Peter N. Stearns, *Anger: The Struggle for Emotional Control in America's History* (Chicago: University of Chicago Press, 1986), 211.

14. Michael Potegal and Gerhard Stemmler, "Cross-Disciplinary Views of Anger: Consensus and Controversy," in *International Handbook of Anger: Constituent and Concomitant Biological, Psychological, and Social Processes*, eds. Michael Potegal, Gerhard Stemmler and Charles Donald Spielberger (New York: Springer, 2010), 3.

15. Primo Levi, *If This Is a Man*, trans. Stuart Woolf, in *The Complete Works of Primo Levi*, ed. Ann Goldstein, 3 vols. (New York: Liveright, 2015), 1:129.

16. Ibid., 159.

17. Ibid., 39.

18. Ibid., 41.

19. Ibid., 12.

20. Ibid., 50.

21. Ibid., 63.

22. Ibid., 113.

23. Ibid., 69.

24. Ibid., 86.

25. Ibid., 101.

26. Ibid., 112.

27. Varlam Shalamov, *Kolyma Stories*, trans. Donald Rayfield (New York: New York Review of Books, 2018).

28. Ibid., xv, 204.

29. Ibid., 206, xvi, 170, 174–5.

30. Ibid., 16, 13, 15–16, 12, 22.

31. Ibid., 20–21, 25.

32. Ibid., 19, 20.

33. Jason Horowitz, "Italy's Populists Turn Up the Heat as Anti-Migrant Anger Boils," *The New York Times* (February 5, 2018), at https://nyti.ms/2nF8cbM.

## CHAPTER 5: ANGRY WORDS

1. William M. Reddy, *The Navigation of Feeling: A Framework for the History of Emotions* (Cambridge: Cambridge University Press, 2001), 128.

2. *The Instructions of Amenemope*, chaps. 3 and 9, in *Ancient Egyptian Literature: A Book of Readings*, ed. Miriam Lichtheim, vol. 2: *The New Kingdom* (Berkeley: University of California Press, 2006), 156, 158–9.

3. Alex Ross, "True West: California Operas by John Adams and Annie Gosfield," *New Yorker* (December 11, 2017), 82.

4. *The Digest of Justinian* 48.16.1 (5), ed. and trans. Alan Watson (Philadelphia: University of Pennsylvania Press, 1985).

5. *The Theodosian Code and Novels and the Sirmondian Constitutions* 9.1.5, trans. Clyde Pharr with Theresa Sherrer Davidson and Mary Born Pharr (Princeton: Princeton University Press, 1952).

6. *Digest of Justinian* 50.17.48.

7. *Codex Justinianus* 4.20.14, trans. Fred H. Blume, at https://bit.ly/2XEBN4o.

8. *Theodosian Code* 9.39.3.

9. Robert Mannyng, *Robert of Brunne's Handlyng Synne*, lines 1252–84, ed. Frederick J. Furnivall (EETS, rpt. 2003), at https://bit.ly/2GH0pUu.

10. William Peraldus, *Summa de vitiis IX: De peccato linguae*, in William Peraldus, *Summa on the Vices: An Outline*, prepared by Richard G. Newhauser, Siegfried Wenzel, Bridget K. Balint and Edwin Craun at http://www.public.asu.edu/~rnewhaus/peraldus (all quotes are my translations from this source).

11. Quoted in Sandy Bardsley, "Sin, Speech, and Scolding in Late Medieval England," in *Fama: The Politics of Talk and Reputation in Medieval Europe*, eds. Thelma Fenster and Daniel Lord Smail (Ithaca: Cornell University Press, 2003), 153. I have modernized the Middle English.

12. *Select Cases on Defamation to 1600*, ed. R.H. Helmholz (London: Selden Society, 1985), 1:4–5.

13. Ibid., 6–12.

14. Fay Bound [Alberti], "'An Angry and Malicious Mind'? Narratives of Slander at the Church Courts of York, c.1660–c.1760," *History Workshop Journal* 56 (2003): 59–77, at 69.

15. Richard Allestree, *The Ladies Calling in Two Parts*, 4th printing (Oxford, 1676), 11–12, 48–9.

16. R.H. Helmholz, "Canonical Defamation in Medieval England," *American Journal of Legal History* 15 (1971): 255–68, esp. 256.

17. Cases in Bound [Alberti], "'An Angry and Malicious Mind'?" 70–2.

18. Henry Conset, *The Practice of the Spiritual or Ecclesiastical Courts*, 2nd ed. (London: W. Battersby, 1700), 335.

19. J.H. Baker, *An Introduction to English Legal History*, 4th ed. (Oxford: Oxford University Press, 2007), 530.

20. *Select Cases*, 1:22.

21. Allyson F. Creasman, "Fighting Words: Anger, Insult, and 'Self-Help' in Early Modern German Law," *Journal of Social History* 51/2 (2017): 272–92, at 277.

22. Allyson F. Creasman, *Censorship and Civic Order in Reformation Germany, 1517–1648: "Printed Poison & Evil Talk"* (Farnham: Ashgate, 2012), 28.

23. Katie Rogers and Maggie Haberman, "Trump's Evolution From Relief to Fury Over the Russia Indictment," *The New York Times* (February 18, 2018), at https://nyti.ms/2C7hgPg.

24. Vanessa E. Jones, "The Angry Black Woman: Tart-Tongued or Driven and No-Nonsense, She Is a Stereotype That Amuses Some and Offends Others," *Boston Globe* (April 20, 2004), at https://bit.ly/2GBAfBp.

25. Wendy Ashley, "The Angry Black Woman: The Impact of Pejorative Stereotypes on Psychotherapy with Black Women," *Social Work in Public Health* 29 (2014): 27–34, at 28.

26. Trina Jones and Kimberly Jade Norwood, "Aggressive Encounters and White Fragility: Deconstructing the Trope of the Angry Black Woman," *Iowa Law Review* 102 (2017): 2017–69, at 2037, 2044, 2056–8.

27. Gregory S. Parks and Matthew W. Hughey, *12 Angry Men: True Stories of Being a Black Man in America Today* (New York: New Press, 2010).

28. Adia Harvey Wingfield, "The Modern Mammy and the Angry Black Man: African American Professionals' Experience with Gendered Racism in the Workplace," *Gender and Class* 14 (2007): 196–212, at 204.

29. Arlie Hochschild, *The Managed Heart: Commercialization of Human Feeling* (Berkeley: University of California Press, 1983).

30. Benjamin Chew, *Journal of a Journey to Easton*, quoted in Nicole Eustace, *Passion Is the Gale: Emotion, Power, and the Coming of the American Revolution* (Williamsburg: University of North Carolina Press, 2008), 151.

## – PART 2: ANGER AS A VICE BUT ALSO (SOMETIMES) AS A VIRTUE –

### CHAPTER 6: ARISTOTLE AND HIS HEIRS

1. Aristotle, *Nicomachean Ethics* 2.6.20, in Aristotle, *Complete Works*, ed. Jonathan Barnes (Oxford: Oxford University Press, 2014). All references to Aristotle's works are from this edition.
2. Aristotle, *Rhetoric* 2.2.14.1370b1.
3. Aristotle, *Nicomachean Ethics* 4.5.1125b1–1126a1.
4. Aristotle, *Rhetoric* 1.1.15–25.1354a1.
5. Ibid., 2.1.20.1378a1.
6. Aristotle, *On the Soul* 1,10,403b1.
7. Aristotle, *Problems* 2,26,869a1; ibid. 27,3,30.
8. For this and further examples, see Barbara H. Rosenwein, *Generations of Feelings: A History of Emotions, 600–1700* (Cambridge: Cambridge University Press, 2016), chap. 4, here 136.
9. Aelred of Rievaulx, "A Rule of Life for a Recluse," trans. Mary Paul Macpherson, in *The Works of Aelred of Rievaulx*, I: *Treatises; The Pastoral Prayer* (Spencer: Cistercian Publications, 1971), 81, 88.
10. Thomas Aquinas, *Summa Theologica*, Ia-IIae, question 46, article 5, at http://www.newadvent.org/summa/2046.htm#article5.
11. Magda B. Arnold, *Emotion and Personality*, vol. 1: *Psychological Aspects* (New York: Columbia University Press, 1960), 171–2.
12. Ibid., 257, italics in original.
13. Lisa Feldman Barrett, Christine D. Wilson-Mendenhall and Lawrence W. Barsalou, "The Conceptual Act Theory: A Roadmap," in *The Psychological Construction of Emotion*, eds. Lisa Feldman Barrett and James A. Russell (New York: Guilford Press, 2015), 86.
14. Aristotle, *Rhetoric* 1.1.15.1354a1.
15. Lisa Feldman Barrett, *How Emotions Are Made: The Secret Life of the Brain* (Boston: Houghton Mifflin, 2017), chap. 11.

### CHAPTER 7: FROM HELL TO HEAVEN

1. I use here *The Schocken Bible*, vol. 1: *The Five Books of Moses*, trans. Everett Fox (New York: Schocken, 1995).
2. Michael C. McCarthy, "Divine Wrath and Human: Embarrassment Ancient and New," *Theological Studies* 70 (2009), 845–74, at 847.
3. Aristides, *Apology on Behalf of Christians* 1, 7, trans. D. M. Kay, at http://www.earlychristianwritings.com/text/aristides-kay.html.
4. Tertullian, *Against Marcion* 1:27, trans. Peter Holmes, rev. and ed. Kevin Knight, at http://www.newadvent.org/fathers/03127.htm.
5. Robert E. Sinkewicz, *Evagrius of Pontus: The Greek Ascetic Corpus* (Oxford: Oxford University Press, 2006), 98.
6. Prudentius, *Psychomachia* ll. 155–59, ed. Jeffrey Henderson, in *Prudentius*, vol. 1, Loeb Classical Library (Cambridge: Harvard University Press, 1949), 290.
7. John Cassian, *The Conferences of John Cassian*, I, conference 5, chap. 2, 135, trans. Christian Classics Ethereal Library, at http://www.agape-biblia.org/orthodoxy/conferences.pdf.
8. Gregory the Great, *Moralia in Job* 31.45.88–89 (*Corpus Christianorum Series Latina* 143B), 1610.
9. Ibid., 5.45.78, 276.
10. Tertullian, *Against Marcion* 1:25, trans. Peter Holmes, at http://www.newadvent.org/fathers/03122.htm.
11. Ibid., 2:16.
12. Lactantius, *On the Anger of God* 17.20, in Lactance, *La colère de Dieu*, ed. and trans. Christiane Ingremeau (Paris: Cerf, 1982), 180.

13. Ibid.

14. Augustine, *The City of God against the Pagans* 15.25, trans. Henry Bettenson (Harmondsworth: Penguin, 1972), 643.

15. McCarthy, "Divine Wrath," 867.

16. Augustine, *Enarrationes in Psalmos, Psalmus* 2, 38.4, line 10, eds. E. Dekkers and J. Fraipont (1956), online at *Library of Latin Texts - Series A* (Turnhout: Brepols, 2017) http://www.brepolis.net.

17. Gregory, *Moralia* 5.45.82, 279.

18. Ibid., 5.45.83, 280.

19. Alcuin, *De virtutibus et vitiis* 24, in *Patrologia Latina*, ed. J.-P. Migne (1863), 101:631.

20. Lester K. Little, "Pride Goes before Avarice: Social Change and the Vices in Latin Christendom," *American Historical Review* 76 (1971): 16–49, at 16.

21. Gregory, *Moralia* 4.30.57, 201.

22. Lester K. Little, *Benedictine Maledictions: Liturgical Cursing in Romanesque France* (Ithaca: Cornell University Press, 1993), 22–3.

23. *Raoul de Cambrai*, ed. and trans. Sarah Kay (Oxford: Clarendon Press, 1992).

24. Paul Freedman, "Peasant Anger in the Late Middle Ages," in *Anger's Past: The Social Uses of an Emotion in the Middle Ages*, ed. Barbara H. Rosenwein (Ithaca: Cornell University Press, 1998), 171–88, at 171.

25. *Chronique du religieux de Saint-Denys, contenant le règne de Charles VI, de 1380 à 1422*, ed. M.L. Bellaguet (Paris: Crapelet, 1839), 1:20.

26. Urban II's speech at Clermont (1095), as reported by Robert the Monk, *Historia Hierosolymitana*, in *The First Crusade: The Chronicle of Fulcher of Chartres and Other Source Materials*, ed. Edward Peters (Philadelphia: University of Pennsylvania Press, 1971), 2–5.

## CHAPTER 8: MORAL SENTIMENTS

1. Peter Sloterdijk, *Rage and Time: A Psychopolitical Investigation*, trans. Mario Wenning (New York: Columbia University Press, 2010), 81.

2. J.B. Schneewind, "Seventeenth- and Eighteenth-Century Ethics," in *A History of Western Ethics*, eds. Lawrence C. Becker and Charlotte B. Becker, 2nd ed. (London: Routledge, 2003), 78.

3. Hugo Grotius, *The Rights of War and Peace*, Book 1, eds. Jean Barbeyrac and Richard Tuck (Indianapolis: Liberty Fund, 2005), 1:79, at https://bit.ly/2UXbJod.

4. Ibid., 85–7.

5. Ibid., 83–4.

6. Thomas Hobbes, *The Elements of Law Natural and Politic*, part 1: *Human Nature*, ed. J.C.A. Gaskin (Oxford: Oxford University Press, 1994), 52.

7. Thomas Hobbes, *Leviathan*, ed. J.C.A. Gaskin (Oxford: Oxford University Press, 1996), 197.

8. David Hume, *A Treatise of Human Nature* 2.1.1.1, eds. David Fate Norton and Mary J. Norton (Oxford: Oxford University Press, 2000). I have modernized spelling and punctuation.

9. Ibid., 2.1.4.3.

10. Ibid., 2.2.2.2.

11. Ibid., 2.2.6.3.

12. Ibid., 2.2.7.1.

13. Ibid., 2.1.11.2.

14. Ibid., 3.3.3.4.

15. Ibid., 3.3.3.7.

16. Ibid., 3.3.3.8.

17. Adam Smith, *The Theory of Moral Sentiments*, eds. D.D. Raphael and A.L. Mafie (Oxford: Clarendon Press, 1976), 10, 22.

18. Ibid., 21.

19. Lab studies: see Elaine Hatfield, John T. Cacioppo and Richard L. Rapson, *Emotional Contagion* (Cambridge: Cambridge University Press, 1994), 79–127; Facebook: Adam D.I. Kramer, Jamie E. Guillory and Jeffrey T. Hancock, "Experimental Evidence of Massive-Scale Emotional Contagion through Social Networks," *Proceedings of the National Academy of Sciences of the United States* 111/24 (2014): 8788–90.
20. Smith, *Moral Sentiments*, 24.
21. James Russell, "Mixed Emotions Viewed from the Psychological Constructionist Perspective," *Emotion Review* 9/2 (2017): 111–17.
22. Jean-Jacques Rousseau, *Émile ou de l'Éducation. Livres I, II et III* (1762), 34, digitized Jean-Marie Tremblay, at https://bit.ly/1PiOj3T.
23. Rousseau, *Émile ou de l'Éducation. (livres 3 à 5)*, 307, at https://bit.ly/2XKO7QN.
24. Patrick Coleman, *Anger, Gratitude, and the Enlightenment Writer* (Oxford: Oxford University Press, 2011), 7.
25. Source: French Revolution Digital Archive, at https://frda.stanford.edu.
26. *Archives parlementaires de 1789 à 1860: recueil complet des débats législatifs & politiques des chambres françaises*, eds. J. Madival, E. Laurent et. al. (Paris: Librairie administrative de P. Dupont, 1862), 8:275, at https://bit.ly/34GkiEB.
27. Ibid., 73:410, repeated in similar terms at 412.
28. Ibid., 75:281, "just anger" was repeated frequently.
29. Ibid., 72:490.
30. Ibid., 74:88.
31. "La grande colère du Père Duchesne," No. 266 (1793), at https://bit.ly/2voivEu.
32. William Wordsworth, *The Prelude 1805* 10:312–24, in *The Prelude 1799, 1805, 1850*, eds. Jonathan Wordsworth, M.H. Abrams and Stephen Gill (New York: Norton, 1979), 374–6.
33. Edmund Burke, *Reflections on the French Revolution*, at https://bit.ly/2GGn6Iu, 244.
34. Ibid., 36.
35. Ibid., 138.
36. Andrew M. Stauffer, *Anger, Revolution, and Romanticism* (Cambridge: Cambridge University Press, 2005).
37. Burke, *Reflections*, 29.
38. Ibid., 111.
39. Thomas Paine, *The Rights of Man; Being An Answer to Mr. Burke's Attack on the French Revolution* (London: W.T. Sherwin, 1817), 1, at https://bit.ly/2vlShlZ.
40. Thomas Paine, *Common Sense*, at https://bit.ly/2L5LSGj.
41. Eustace, *Passion Is the Gale*, 152 and see esp. chap. 4, "Resolute Resentment versus Indiscrete Heat: Anger, Honor, and Social Status."
42. Ibid., 167.
43. Ibid., 183.
44. Zac Cogley, "A Study of Virtuous and Vicious Anger," in *Virtues and Their Vices*, eds. Kevin Timpe and Craig A. Boyd (Oxford: Oxford University Press, 2014), 199–224.
45. Ibid., 210–11.
46. Alasdair MacIntyre, *After Virtue: A Study in Moral Theory*, 3rd ed. (Notre Dame: University of Notre Dame Press, 2007), x.

– PART 3: NATURAL ANGER –

CHAPTER 9: EARLY MEDICAL TRADITIONS

1. Galen, *The Art of Medicine*, ed. and trans. Ian Johnston (Cambridge: Harvard University Press, 2016), 249.
2. Quoted in P.N. Singer, "The Essence of Rage: Galen on Emotional Disturbances and their Physical Correlates," in *Selfhood and the Soul: Essays on Ancient Thought and Literature in*

*Honour of Christopher Gill*, eds. Richard Seaford, John Wilkins and Matthew Wright (Oxford: Oxford University Press, 2017), 161–96, at 162, 191–92.

3. See Heinrich von Staden, "The Physiology and Therapy of Anger: Galen on Medicine, the Soul, and Nature," in *Islamic Philosophy, Science, Culture and Religion: Studies in Honor of Dimitri Gutas*, eds. Felicitas Meta Maria Opwis and David Reisman (Leiden: Brill, 2011), 63–87, at 75–6.

4. Quoted in Singer, "Essence of Rage," 177–8.

5. William James, "What is an Emotion?" *Mind* 9 (1884): 188–205, at 193, online at https://psychclassics.yorku.ca/James/emotion.htm.

6. See the long list of these and similar phrases in George Lakoff, *Women, Fire, and Dangerous Things: What Categories Reveal about the Mind* (Chicago: University of Chicago Press, 1987), 380, 382.

7. "The Wisdom of the Art of Medicine," trans. Faith Wallis, in *Medieval Medicine: A Reader*, ed. Faith Wallis (Toronto: University of Toronto Press, 2010), 18, 22.

8. Ariel Bar-Sela, Hebbel E. Hoff, Elias Faris, ed. and trans., "Moses Maimonides' Two Treatises on the Regimen of Health,' *Transactions of the American Philosophical Society* 54/4 (1964): 3–50, at 36.

9. Ibid.

10. Ibid., 25.

11. I owe the following observations and translations to the kind permission of Faith Wallis, who allowed me to see part of her edition of Bartholomaeus' commentary now in preparation for the Edizione Nazionale La Scuola Medica Salernitana (Florence: SISMEL).

12. Thomas Willis, *The Anatomy of the Brain*, in Thomas Willis, *Five Treatises*, trans. Samuel Pordage (London, 1681 [orig. pub. 1664 in Latin]).

13. Susan James, *Passions and Action: The Emotions in Seventeenth-Century Philosophy* (Oxford: Clarendon Press, 1997), 89.

14. Descartes, *Passions*, §200, 126.

15. William Clark, *A Medical Dissertation Concerning the Effects of the Passions on Human Bodies* (London, 1752), 37.

16. Ibid., 38.

17. Ibid., 40.

18. Ibid., 40–1.

19. Lakoff, *Women, Fire, and Dangerous Things*, 383–5.

20. Luca Passamonti et al., "Effects of Acute Tryptophan Depletion on Prefrontal Amygdala Connectivity While Viewing Facial Signals of Aggression," *Journal of Biological Psychiatry* 71 (2012): 36–43.

21. Ibid., 40.

## CHAPTER 10: IN THE LAB

1. Edward Hitchcock and Valerie Cairns, "Amygdalotomy," *Postgraduate Medical Journal* 49 (1973): 894–904.

2. Alan J. Fridlund, *Human Facial Expression: An Evolutionary View* (San Diego: Academic Press, 1994), 129.

3. Charles Darwin, *The Expression of Emotions in Man and Animals* (1872), in *From So Simple a Beginning: The Four Great Books of Charles Darwin*, ed. Edward O. Wilson (New York, 2006), 1255–477.

4. Charles Bell, *The Anatomy and Philosophy of Expression as Connected with the Fine Arts*, 3rd ed. (London, 1844), 121.

5. Charles Darwin, "M Notebook," line ref. 122–3, at *Darwin Online*, https://bit.ly/2UDNAyi.

6. Darwin, *Expression of Emotions*, 1267.

7. On the sources he drew upon, ibid., 1267–70.

8. Barrett, *How Emotions Are Made*, 157.
9. Darwin, *Expression of Emotions*, 1474.
10. Paul E. Griffiths, *What Emotions Really Are: The Problem of Psychological Categories* (Chicago: University of Chicago Press, 1997), 65.
11. Darwin, *Expression of Emotions*, 1301–2, 1338.
12. Fernand Papillon, "Physiology of the Passions," trans. J. Fitzgerald, *The Popular Science Monthly* 4 (1974): 552–64, at 559–60.
13. Geoffrey C. Bunn, *The Truth Machine: A Social History of the Lie Detector* (Baltimore: Johns Hopkins, 2012), 118.
14. Antoinette M. Feleky, "The Expression of the Emotions," *Psychological Review* 21/1 (1914): 33–41, at 36.
15. Silvan S. Tomkins, *Affect, Imagery, Consciousness*, ed. Bertram P. Karon, vol. 1: *The Positive Affects* (New York: Springer, 1962), 111–12, 204–5, 244, 337. In vol. 3: *The Negative Affects: Anger and Fear* (1991), xviii, he proposes nine by separating contempt and disgust.
16. Silvan S. Tomkins and Robert McCarter, "What and Where are the Primary Affects? Some Evidence for a Theory," *Perceptual and Motor Skills* 18/1 (1964): 119–58.
17. Giovanna Colombetti, *The Feeling Body: Affective Science Meets the Enactive Mind* (Cambridge: MIT Press, 2014), 39.
18. Paul Ekman and Wallace V. Friesen, "Constants across Cultures in the Face and Emotion," *Journal of Personality and Social Psychology* 17/2 (1971): 124–9.
19. Sorenson, *The Edge of the Forest*, 140–2.
20. The fullest critique is Ruth Leys, *The Ascent of Affect: Genealogy and Critique* (Chicago: University of Chicago Press, 2017). See also Jan Plamper, *The History of Emotions: An Introduction*, trans. K. Tribe (Oxford: Oxford University Press, 2012), 147–63.
21. Ian S. Penton-Voak, Jamie Thomas, Suzanne H. Gage, Mary McMurran, Sarah McDonald and Marcus R. Munafò, "Increasing Recognition of Happiness in Ambiguous Facial Expressions Reduces Anger and Aggressive Behavior," *Psychological Science* 24/5 (2013): 688–97.
22. Kathleen R. Bogart, Linda Tickle-Degnen and Nalini Ambady, "Communicating without the Face: Holistic Perception of Emotions of People with Facial Paralysis," *Basic and Applied Social Psychology* 36/4 (2014): 309–20.
23. Lisa Appignanesi, "Dr. Death," *New York Review of Books* 65/12 (2018): 32–4.
24. Today autism is called "Autism Spectrum Disorder" and is classed among Neurodevelopmental Disorders in *Diagnostic and Statistical Manual of Mental Disorders*, 5th ed. (=DSM-5) (Arlington: American Psychiatric Association, 2013), 50–9.
25. D. Vaughn Becker, "Facial Gender Interferes with Decisions about Facial Expressions of Anger and Happiness," *Journal of Experimental Psychology: General* 146/4 (2017): 457–63.
26. Thomas F. Denson, William C. Pedersen, Jaclyn Ronquillo and Anirvan S. Nandy, "The Angry Brain: Neural Correlates of Anger, Angry Rumination, and Aggressive Personality," *Journal of Cognitive Neuroscience* 21/4 (2008): 734–44.
27. James, "What is an Emotion?" 190.
28. Wilhelm Wundt, *Outlines of Psychology*, trans. Charles Hubbard Judd, 3rd rev. Engl. ed. from 7th rev. German ed. (Leipzig: Wilhelm Engelmann, 1907), 191, 205 (emphasis in the original).
29. Lisa Feldman Barrett and Eliza Bliss-Moreau, "Affect as a Psychological Primitive," *Advances in Experimental Social Psychology* 41 (2009): 167–208, at 172.
30. Barrett, *How Emotions Are Made*, 59.
31. Barrett, Wilson-Mendenhall, Barsalou, "The Conceptual Act Theory," 86–7.
32. Yinan Wang, Feng Kong, Xiangzhen Kong, Yuanfang Zhao, Danhua Lin and Jia Liu, "Unsatisfied Relatedness, Not Competence or Autonomy, Increases Trait Anger through the Right Amygdala," *Cognitive, Affective, and Behavioral Neuroscience* 17 (2017): 932–8, with references to some earlier work. Although dealing with "trait anger"—what earlier thinkers would have called "irascible personalities"—the authors were seeking locations for momentary anger rather than for the personality trait.

33. Barrett, Wilson-Mendenhall, Barsalou, "The Conceptual Act Theory," 89.
34. Colombetti, *The Feeling Body*, 30.
35. Jaak Panksepp, "Neurologizing the Psychology of Affects: How Appraisal-Based Constructivism and Basic Emotion Theory Can Coexist," *Perspectives on Psychological Science* 2/3 (2007): 281–96, at 286.
36. Fausto Caruana and Marco Viola, *Come funzionano le emozioni. Da Darwin alle neuroscienze* (Bologna: Il Mulino, 2018), 85.
37. Suresh Bhatt, Thomas R. Gregg and Allan Siegel, "NK$_1$ Receptors in the Medial Hypothalamus Potentiate Defensive Rage Behavior Elicited from the Midbrain Periaqueductal Gray of the Cat," *Brain Research* 966/1 (2003): 54–64, at 56.
38. Jaak Panksepp and Margaret R. Zellner, "Towards a Neurobiologically Based Unified Theory of Aggression," *International Review of Social Psychology/Revue internationale de psychologie sociale* 17/2 (2004): 37–61, at 42–4.

## CHAPTER 11: SOCIETY'S CHILD

1. For its deeper roots, see Plamper, *History of Emotions*, 80–98.
2. James R. Averill, "What Should Theories of Emotion Be About," in *Categorical versus Dimensional Models of Affect: A Seminar on the Theories of Panksepp and Russell*, eds. Peter Zachar and Ralph D. Ellis (Amsterdam: John Benjamins, 2012), 203–24, at 208.
3. James R. Averill, *Anger and Aggression: An Essay on Emotion* (New York: Springer, 1982).
4. C. Terry Warner, "Anger and Similar Delusions," in *The Social Construction of Emotions*, ed. Rom Harré (Oxford: Basil Blackwell, 1986), 148, 163.
5. Michael Boiger and Batja Mesquita, "The Construction of Emotion in Interactions, Relationships, and Cultures," *Emotion Review* 4/3 (2012): 221–9, at 221. (Italics in original.)
6. The incident and its documents are discussed in Richard E. Barton, "'Zealous Anger' and the Renegotiation of Aristocratic Relationships in Eleventh- and Twelfth-Century France," in *Anger's Past*, 153–70.
7. Stearns and Stearns, *Anger*, 36.
8. Ibid., 39, quoting advice literature from 1846 and 1874.
9. Bankart, "Treating Anger," 244.
10. Lundy Bancroft, *Why Does He Do That? Inside the Minds of Angry and Controlling Men* (New York: Berkley Books, 2002), 319.
11. Ibid., 321–22; Eminem, "Kim," at http://bit.ly/2DGGVxq.
12. Hannelore Weber, "Explorations in the Social Construction of Anger," *Motivation and Emotion* 28/2 (2004): 197–219.
13. Stephen D. White, "The Politics of Anger," in *Anger's Past*, 127–52, at 144.
14. Rosenwein, *Generations of Feelings*, 134.
15. Kathleen M. Higgins, "Biology and Culture in Musical Emotions," *Emotion Review* 4/3 (2012): 273–82, at 281.
16. Catherine A. Lutz, *Unnatural Emotions: Everyday Sentiments on a Micronesian Atoll and Their Challenge to Western Theory* (Chicago: University of Chicago Press, 1988), 3–4.
17. Anna Wierzbicka, "Emotion and Culture: Arguing with Martha Nussbaum," *Ethos* 31/4 (2004): 577–600, at 580.
18. Zoltán Kövecses, "Cross-Cultural Experience of Anger: A Psycholinguistic Analysis," in *International Handbook of Anger: Constituent and Concomitant Biological, Psychological, and Social Processes*, eds. Michael Potegal, Gerhard Stemmler and Charles Spielberger (New York: Springer, 2010), 157–74, at 161.
19. Summarized in Heli Tissari, "Current Emotion Research in English Linguistics: Words for Emotions in the History of English," *Emotion Review* 9/1 (2017): 86–94, at 89.
20. Kövecses, "Cross-Cultural Experience of Anger," 161.
21. Gerhard Stemmler, "Somatovisceral Activation during Anger," in *International Handbook of Anger*, 103–21.

22. Greg Downey, "Being Human in Cities: Phenotypic Bias from Urban Niche Construction," *Current Anthropology* 57, suppl. 13 (2016): S52–S64, at S53–54.
23. Boiger and Mesquita, "The Construction of Emotion," 226, quoting an unpublished study made in 2010.
24. Andrew Beatty, "Current Emotion Research in Anthropology: Reporting the Field," *Emotion Review* 5/4 (2013): 414–22.
25. Andrew Beatty, "The Headman's Defeat," unpublished MS kindly provided by the author.
26. Renato Rosaldo, *Culture and Truth: The Remaking of Social Analysis* (Boston: Beacon Press, 1989), 3–4, 9.
27. Reddy, *The Navigation of Feeling*, 129.
28. Amanda Taut and Max Fisher, "Facebook Fueled Anti-Refugee Attacks in Germany, New Research Suggests," *The New York Times* (August 21, 2018), at https://nyti.ms/2JfNsD4.

## CHAPTER 12: ANGER CELEBRATED

1. Pankaj Mishra, *Age of Anger: A History of the Present* (New York: Picador, 2017).
2. Stearns and Stearns, *Anger*, 211.
3. Mishra, *Age of Anger*, 2.
4. Uffa Jensen, *Zornpolitik* (Berlin: Suhrkamp, 2017).
5. The lyrics of "Rise" are at Public Image Ltd, https://genius.com/Public-image-ltd-rise-lyrics.
6. John Lydon, with Andrew Perry, *Anger is an Energy: My Life Uncensored* (New York: HarperCollins, 2014), 3 for "shitstem."
7. Ibid., 1.
8. On the origin and history of the phrase, see https://bit.ly/2DB8BUm.
9. Kavanaugh hearing: Transcript (September 27, 2018) at https://wapo.st/2PwCnyl.
10. Ben Riley-Smith, Gareth Davies and Nick Allen, "Brett Kavanaugh, Supreme Court Nominee, Gives Evidence—Latest Updates," *The Telegraph* (September 27, 2018), https://bit.ly/2voMaxc. For Trump on weakness, see Bob Woodward, *Fear: Trump in the White House* (New York: Simon & Schuster, 2018), 175.
11. Jennifer Weiner, "The Patriarchy Will Always Have Its Revenge," *New York Times. Sunday Review* (September 23, 2018), https://nyti.ms/2N0V6iY.
12. Arthur de Gobineau, *The Inequality of Human Races*, trans. Adrian Collins (New York: Howard Fertig, 1967), 150.
13. U.S. Census Bureau, "Race," https://bit.ly/1sjmNd1.
14. See http://bit.ly/2IOG9Te.
15. Renaud Camus, *Le Grand Remplacement (Introduction au remplacisme global)* (Plieux: Renaud Camus, 2017), 22.
16. Jensen, *Zornpolitik*, 115–17.
17. Jared Taylor, "NYT: The 'Religion of Whiteness' is a Threat to World Peace," *American Renaissance* (August 31, 2018), https://bit.ly/2vpiEaw.
18. Arlie Russell Hochschild, *Strangers in their Own Land: Anger and Mourning on the American Right* (New York: The New Press, 2016).
19. Wade, *Myanmar's Enemy Within*, 1.
20. Ibid., 5–6.
21. Ibid., 12.
22. Mishra, *Age of Anger*, 12.
23. "The First Convention Ever Called to Discuss the Civil and Political Rights of Women," Seneca Falls, July 19, 20, 1848, at Library of Congress website, http://www.loc.gov/resource/rbnawsa.n7548.
24. Alanna Vagianos, "The 'Me Too' Campaign Was Created by a Black Woman 10 Years Ago," *Huffpost* (10/17/2017), https://bit.ly/2gO4j0F.
25. "Votes for Women Broadside," January 28, 1911, at Library of Congress website, http://www.loc.gov/item/rbcmiller002522.

26. Kavanaugh hearing: Transcript, https://wapo.st/2PwCnyl.
27. Rebecca Traister, "Fury Is a Political Weapon. And Women Need to Wield It," *New York Times*. *Sunday Review* (September 30, 2018), https://nyti.ms/2IrmuWF.
28. For Graham's outburst, see https://cnn.it/2XDfiNk.
29. Christina Prignano, "A Northeastern graduate confronted Jeff Flake in an Elevator," *The Boston Globe* (September 28, 2018) https://bit.ly/2GGCUv0.
30. Sandra Hochman, *Year of the Woman: A Fantasy* (1973), at https://www.youtube.com/watch?v=yYKi5pk4eyk&t=1s (no permanent url).
31. Audre Lorde, "The Uses of Anger: Women Responding to Racism," 1981, at BlackPast, http://bit.ly/2J7qKwA.
32. Rebecca Traister, *Good and Mad: The Revolutionary Power of Women's Anger* (New York: Simon & Schuster, 2018), xxviii.
33. Quoted in ibid., xxx.
34. See https://nyp.st/2E3xWcy.
35. Giulia Sissa, *Jealousy: A Forbidden Passion* (Cambridge: Polity Press, 2017), 37.
36. Quoted in Aleena Gardezi, "America Ferrera at Women's March: We Are All under Attack," *Diverge* (January 23, 2017), https://bit.ly/2ZC19BN.
37. Jenna Wortham, "Black Tweets Matter: How the Tumultuous, Hilarious, Wide-Ranging Chat Party on Twitter Changed the Face of Activism in America," *Smithsonian Magazine* (September 2016), http://bit.ly/2ZN11je.
38. At https://blacklivesmatter.com/about/what-we-believe.
39. Jelani Cobb, "The Matter of Black Lives: A New Kind of Movement Found its Moment. What Will Its Future Be?" *The New Yorker* (March 13, 2016), https://bit.ly/2k6Am0a.
40. Joel Anderson, "Ferguson's Angry Young Men," *BuzzFeed.News* (August 22, 2014), http://bit.ly/2PGZrdL.
41. Johnetta Elzie, "Ferguson Forward," *Ebony* (2014), https://bit.ly/2Vsx5JI.
42. Keeanga-Yamahtta Taylor, *From #Blacklivesmatter to Black Liberation* (Chicago: Haymarket Books, 2016), 189.
43. At https://blacklivesmatter.com/about/what-we-believe.
44. Rebecca Traister and Alicia Garza: Good and Mad Women, video at http://bit.ly/2PO2fpT.
45. Traister, *Good and Mad*, 209.
46. Laura Kipnis, "Women are Furious. Now What?" *The Atlantic* (November 2018), https://bit.ly/2voMufo.
47. Soraya Chemaly, *Rage Becomes Her: The Power of Women's Anger* (New York: Atria, 2018).
48. Rebecca Traister and Alicia Garza: Good and Mad Women, video at http://bit.ly/2PO2fpT.
49. J. Giles Milhaven, *Good Anger* (Kansas City: Sheed & Ward, 1989), 62–64.
50. Quoted in Aleena Gardezi, "America Ferrera at Women's March," https://bit.ly/2ZC19BN.
51. Aristotle, *Rhetoric* 1.9.15.1370b1.
52. Traister, *Good and Mad*, xxiii.

## CONCLUSION: MY ANGER, OUR ANGER

1. *The Federalist Papers: No. 10*, at https://bit.ly/1L3guuV.
2. Reddy, *The Navigation of Feeling*, 128.
3. George Savile, Marquess of Halifax, *The Character of a Trimmer*, in *The Complete Works*, ed. Walter Raleigh (Oxford: Clarendon Press, 1912), 63.

# BIBLIOGRAPHY

Alberti, F. B., 2003, "'An Angry and Malicious Mind'? Narratives of Slander at the Church Courts of York, c.1660–c.1760," *History Workshop Journal*, 56: 59–77.

Anderson, J., 2014, "Ferguson's Angry Young Men," *BuzzFeed.News*. https://bit.ly/2PGZrdL.

Anhalt, E. K., 2017, *Enraged: Why Violent Times Need Ancient Greek Myths*, New Haven: Yale University Press.

Appignanesi, L., 2018, "Dr. Death," *New York Review of Books*, 65/12: 32–4.

Arnold, M. B., 1960, *Emotion and Personality*, vol. 1: *Psychological Aspects*, New York: Columbia University Press.

Ashley, W., 2014, "The Angry Black Woman: The Impact of Pejorative Stereotypes on Psychotherapy with Black Women," *Social Work in Public Health*, 29: 27–34.

Averill, J. R., 1982, *Anger and Aggression: An Essay on Emotion*, New York: Springer.

Averill, J. R., 2012, "The Future of Social Constructionism: Introduction to a Special Section of *Emotion Review*," *Emotion Review*, 4/3: 215–20.

Averill, J. R., 2012, "What Should Theories of Emotion Be About," in P. Zachar and R. D. Ellis (eds.), *Categorical versus Dimensional Models of Affect: A Seminar on the Theories of Panksepp and Russell*, Amsterdam: John Benjamins, 203–24.

Baker, J. H., 2007, *An Introduction to English Legal History*, 4th ed., Oxford: Oxford University Press.

Bancroft, L., 2002, *Why Does He Do That? Inside the Minds of Angry and Controlling Men*, New York: Berkley Books.

Bankart, C. P., 2006, "Treating Anger with Wisdom and Compassion: A Buddhist Approach," in E. L. Feindler (ed.), *Anger-Related Disorders*, 231–55.

Banks, A. J., 2014, *Anger and Racial Politics: The Emotional Foundation of Racial Attitudes in America*, Cambridge: Cambridge University Press.

Bardsley, S., 2003, "Sin, Speech, and Scolding in Late Medieval England," in T. Fenster and D. L. Smail (eds.), *Fama: The Politics of Talk and Reputation in Medieval Europe*, Ithaca: Cornell University Press, 145–64.

Barrett, L. F., 2017, *How Emotions Are Made: The Secret Life of the Brain*, Boston: Houghton Mifflin.

Barrett, L. F. and Bliss-Moreau, E., 2009, "Affect as a Psychological Primitive," *Advances in Experimental Social Psychology*, 41: 167–208.

Barrett, L. F., Wilson-Mendenhall, C. D. and Barsalou, L. W., 2015, "The Conceptual Act Theory: A Roadmap," in L. F. Barrett and J. A. Russell (eds.), *The Psychological Construction of Emotion*, New York: Guilford Press, 83–110.

Barton, R. E., 1998, "'Zealous Anger' and the Renegotiation of Aristocratic Relationships in Eleventh-and-Twelfth-Century France," in B. H. Rosenwein (ed.), *Anger's Past*, 153–70.

Beatty, A., 2013, "Current Emotion Research in Anthropology: Reporting the Field," *Emotion Review*, 5/4: 414–22.

Becker, D. V., 2017, "Facial Gender Interferes with Decisions about Facial Expressions of Anger and Happiness," *Journal of Experimental Psychology: General*, 146/4: 457–63.

Bhatt, S., Gregg, T. R. and Siegel, A., 2003, "NK$_1$ Receptors in the Medial Hypothalamus Potentiate Defensive Rage Behavior Elicited from the Midbrain Periaqueductal Gray of the Cat," *Brain Research*, 966/1: 54–64.

Bogart, K. R., Tickle-Degnen, L. and Ambady, N., 2014, "Communicating without the Face: Holistic Perception of Emotions of People with Facial Paralysis," *Basic and Applied Social Psychology* 36/4: 309–20.

Boiger, M. and Mesquita, B., 2012, "The Construction of Emotion in Interactions, Relationships, and Cultures," *Emotion Review*, 4/3: 221–9.

Briggs, J. L., 1970, *Never in Anger: Portrait of an Eskimo Family*, Cambridge: Harvard University Press.

Bunn, G. C., 2012, *The Truth Machine: A Social History of the Lie Detector*, Baltimore: Johns Hopkins.

Camus, R., 2017, *Le Grand Remplacement (Introduction au remplacisme global)*, Plieux: Renaud Camus.

Caruana, F. and Viola, M., 2018, *Come funzionano le emozioni. Da Darwin alle neuroscienze*, Bologna: Il Mulino.

Chemaly, S., 2018, *Rage Becomes Her: The Power of Women's Anger*, New York: Atria.

Cobb, J., 2016, "The Matter of Black Lives: A New Kind of Movement Found its Moment. What Will Its Future Be?" *The New Yorker*. https://bit.ly/2k6Am0a.

Cogley, Z., 2014, "A Study of Virtuous and Vicious Anger," in K. Timpe and C. A. Boyd (eds.), *Virtues and Their Vices*, Oxford: Oxford University Press, 199–224.

Coleman, P., 2011, *Anger, Gratitude, and the Enlightenment Writer*, Oxford: Oxford University Press.

Colombetti, G., 2014, *The Feeling Body: Affective Science Meets the Enactive Mind*, Cambridge: MIT Press.

Cornelius, R. R., 1996, *The Science of Emotions: Research and Tradition in the Psychology of Emotion*, Upper Saddle River: Prentice Hall.

Creasman, A. F., 2012, *Censorship and Civic Order in Reformation Germany, 1517–1648: "Printed Poison & Evil Talk,"* Farnham: Ashgate.

Creasman, A. F., 2017, "Fighting Words: Anger, Insult, and 'Self-Help' in Early Modern German Law," *Journal of Social History*, 51/2: 272–92.

Denson, T. F., Pedersen, W. C., Ronquillo, J. and Nandy, A. S., 2008, "The Angry Brain: Neural Correlates of Anger, Angry Rumination, and Aggressive Personality," *Journal of Cognitive Neuroscience*, 21/4: 734–44.

Dentan, R. K., 1968, *The Semai: A Nonviolent People of Malaya*, New York: Holt.

Dentan, R. K., 2008, "Recent Studies on Violence: What's In and What's Out," *Reviews in Anthropology*, 37: 41–67.

Dentan, R. K., 2012, "'Honey Out of the Lion': Peace Research Emerging from Mid-20th-Century Violence," in A. B. Kehoe and P. L. Doughty (eds.), *Expanding American Anthropology, 1945–1980: A Generation Reflects*, Tuscaloosa: University of Alabama Press, 204–20.

Donini, P., 2008, "Psychology," in R. J. Hankinson (ed.), *The Cambridge Companion to Galen*, Cambridge: Cambridge University Press, 184–209.

Downey, G., 2016, "Being Human in Cities: Phenotypic Bias from Urban Niche Construction," *Current Anthropology*, 57, suppl. 13: S52–S64.

Edwards, H., 2006, "Psychopharmacological Considerations in Anger Management," in E. L. Feindler (ed.), *Anger-Related Disorders*, 189–202.

Ekman, P. and Friesen, W. V., 1971, "Constants across Cultures in the Face and Emotion," *Journal of Personality and Social Psychology*, 17/2: 124–9.

Elzie, J., 2014, "Ferguson Forward," *Ebony*. https://bit.ly/2Vsx5JI.

Enenkel, K. A. E. and Traninger, A., (eds.), 2015, *Discourses of Anger in the Early Modern Period*, Leiden: Brill.

Enenkel, K. A. E., 2015, "Neo-Stoicism as an Antidote to Public Violence before Lipsius's *De constantia*: Johann Weyer's (Wier's) Anger Therapy, *De ira morbo* (1577)," in K. A. E. Enenkel and A. Traninger (eds.), *Discourses of Anger*, 49–96.

Eustace, N., 2008, *Passion Is the Gale: Emotion, Power, and the Coming of the American Revolution*, Williamsburg: University of North Carolina Press.

Feindler, E. L., (ed.), 2006, *Anger-Related Disorders: A Practitioner's Guide to Comparative Treatments*, New York: Springer.

Feleky, A. M., 1914, "The Expression of the Emotions," *Psychological Review* 21/1: 33–41.

Freedman, P., 1998, "Peasant Anger in the Late Middle Ages," in B. H. Rosenwein (ed.), *Anger's Past*, 171–88.

Fridlund, A. J., 1994, *Human Facial Expression: An Evolutionary View*, San Diego: Academic Press.

Gardezi, A., 2017, "America Ferrera at Women's March: We Are All under Attack," *Diverge*. https://bit.ly/2ZC19BN.

Graver, M. R., 2007, *Stoicism and Emotion*, Chicago: University of Chicago Press.

Griffiths, P. E., 1997, *What Emotions Really Are: The Problem of Psychological Categories*, Chicago: University of Chicago Press.

Harré, R., (ed.), 1986, *The Social Construction of Emotions*, Oxford: Basil Blackwell.

Harris, W. V., 2001, *Restraining Rage: The Ideology of Anger Control in Classical Antiquity*, Cambridge: Harvard University Press.

Hatfield, E., Cacioppo, J. T. and Rapson, R. L., 1994, *Emotional Contagion*, Cambridge: Cambridge University Press.

Helmholz, R. H., 1971, "Canonical Defamation in Medieval England," *American Journal of Legal History*, 15: 255–68.

Higgins, K. M., 2012, "Biology and Culture in Musical Emotions," *Emotion Review*, 4/3: 273–82.

Hitchcock, E. and Cairns, V., 1973, "Amygdalotomy," *Postgraduate Medical Journal* 49: 894–904.

Hochschild, A. R., 1983, *The Managed Heart: Commercialization of Human Feeling*, Berkeley: University of California Press.

Hochschild, A. R., 2016, *Strangers in their Own Land: Anger and Mourning on the American Right*, New York: The New Press.

Horowitz, J., 2018, "Italy's Populists Turn Up the Heat as Anti-Migrant Anger Boils," *The New York Times*. https://nyti.ms/2nF8cbM.

James, S., 1997, *Passions and Action: The Emotions in Seventeenth-Century Philosophy*, Oxford: Clarendon Press.

Jensen, U., 2017, *Zornpolitik*, Berlin: Suhrkamp.

Jerryson, M., 2013, "Buddhist Traditions and Violence," in M. Jerryson, M. Juergensmeyer and M. Kitts (eds.), *The Oxford Handbook of Religion and Violence*, Oxford: Oxford University Press.

Jones, T. and Norwood, K. J., 2017, "Aggressive Encounters and White Fragility: Deconstructing the Trope of the Angry Black Woman," *Iowa Law Review*, 102: 2017–69.

Jones, V. E., 2004, "The Angry Black Woman: Tart-Tongued or Driven and No-Nonsense, She Is a Stereotype That Amuses Some and Offends Others," *Boston Globe*. https://bit.ly/2GBAfBp.

Karant-Nunn, S. C., 2004, "'Christians' Mourning and Lament Should Not Be Like the Heathens'': The Suppression of Religious Emotion in the Reformation," in J. M. Headley, H. J. Hillerbrand and A. J. Papalas (eds.), *Confessionalization in Europe, 1555–1700: Essays in Honor and Memory of Bodo Nischan*, Aldershot: Routledge, 107–30.

Kassinove, H. and Tafrate, R. C., 2002, *Anger Management: The Complete Treatment Guidebook for Practitioners*, Atascadero: Impact Publishers.

Kennedy, G., 2000, *Just Anger: Representing Women's Anger in Early Modern England*, Carbondale: Southern Illinois University Press.

Kipnis, L., 2018, "Women are Furious. Now What?" *The Atlantic*. https://bit.ly/2voMufo.

Kövecses, Z., 2010, "Cross-Cultural Experience of Anger: A Psycholinguistic Analysis," in M. Potegal, G. Stemmler and C. D. Spielberger (eds.), *International Handbook of Anger*, 157–74.

Kramer, A. D. I., Guillory, J. E. and Hancock, J. T., 2014, "Experimental Evidence of Massive-Scale Emotional Contagion through Social Networks," *Proceedings of the National Academy of Sciences of the United States*, 111/24: 8788–90.

Krewet, M., 2015, "Descartes' Notion of Anger: Aspects of a Possible History of its Premises," in K. A. E. Enenkel and A. Traninger (eds.), *Discourses of Anger*, 143–71.

Lakoff, G., 1987, *Women, Fire, and Dangerous Things: What Categories Reveal about the Mind*, Chicago: University of Chicago Press.

Leys, R., 2017, *The Ascent of Affect: Genealogy and Critique*, Chicago: University of Chicago Press.

Little, L. K., 1971, "Pride Goes before Avarice: Social Change and the Vices in Latin Christendom," *American Historical Review*, 76: 16–49.

Little, L. K., 1993, *Benedictine Maledictions: Liturgical Cursing in Romanesque France*, Ithaca: Cornell University Press.

Lorde, A., 1981, "The Uses of Anger: Women Responding to Racism," at BlackPast. http://bit.ly/2J7qKwA.

Lutz, C. A., 1988, *Unnatural Emotions: Everyday Sentiments on a Micronesian Atoll and Their Challenge to Western Theory*, Chicago: University of Chicago Press.

Lydon, J. with Perry, A., 2014, *Anger is an Energy: My Life Uncensored*, New York: HarperCollins.

MacIntyre, A., 2007, *After Virtue: A Study in Moral Theory*, 3rd ed., Notre Dame: University of Notre Dame Press.

Mano, L. Y. et al., 2016, "Exploiting IoT Technologies for Enhancing Health Smart Homes through Patient Identification and Emotion Recognition," *Computer Communications*, 89–90: 178–90.

McCarthy, M. C., 2009, "Divine Wrath and Human: Embarrassment Ancient and New," *Theological Studies*, 70: 845–74.

Milhaven, J. G., 1989, *Good Anger*, Kansas City: Sheed & Ward.

Mishra, P., 2017, *Age of Anger: A History of the Present*, New York: Picador.

Nhat Hanh, T., 2001, *Anger: Wisdom for Cooling the Flames*, New York: Riverhead.

Nussbaum, M. C., 2016, *Anger and Forgiveness: Resentment, Generosity, Justice*, Oxford: Oxford University Press.

Olson, G., 1982, *Literature as Recreation in the Later Middle Ages*, Ithaca: Cornell University Press.

Ost, D., 2005, *The Defeat of Solidarity: Anger and Politics in Postcommunist Europe*, Ithaca: Cornell University Press.

Panksepp, J., 2007, "Neurologizing the Psychology of Affects: How Appraisal-Based Constructivism and Basic Emotion Theory Can Coexist," *Perspectives on Psychological Science* 2/3: 281–96.

Panksepp, J. and Zellner, M. R., 2004, 'Towards a Neurobiologically Based Unified Theory of Aggression,' *International Review of Social Psychology/Revue internationale de psychologie sociale*, 17/2: 37–61.

Papillon, F., 1974, "Physiology of the Passions," trans. J. Fitzgerald, *The Popular Science Monthly*, 4: 552–64.

Parks, G. S. and Hughey, M. W., 2010, *12 Angry Men: True Stories of Being a Black Man in America Today*, New York: New Press.

Passamonti, L. et al., 2012, "Effects of Acute Tryptophan Depletion on Prefrontal Amygdala Connectivity While Viewing Facial Signals of Aggression," *Journal of Biological Psychiatry*, 71: 36–43.

Penton-Voak, I. S., Thomas, J., Gage, S. H., McMurran, M., McDonald, S. and Munafò, M. R., 2013, "Increasing Recognition of Happiness in Ambiguous Facial Expressions Reduces Anger and Aggressive Behavior," *Psychological Science* 24/5: 688–97.

Plamper, J., 2012, *The History of Emotions: An Introduction*, trans. K. Tribe, Oxford: Oxford University Press.

Potegal, M. and Stemmler, G., 2010, "Cross-Disciplinary Views of Anger: Consensus and Controversy," in M. Potegal, G. Stemmler and C. D. Spielberger (eds.), *International Handbook of Anger*, 3–8.

Potegal, M., Stemmler, G. and Spielberger, C. D., (eds.), 2010, *International Handbook of Anger: Constituent and Concomitant Biological, Psychological, and Social Processes*, New York: Springer.

Prignano, C., 2018, "A Northeastern Graduate Confronted Jeff Flake in an Elevator," *The Boston Globe*. https://bit.ly/2GGCUv0.

Reddy, W. M., 2001, *The Navigation of Feeling: A Framework for the History of Emotions*, Cambridge: Cambridge University Press.

Reiss, T. J., 1991, "Descartes, the Palatinate, and the Thirty Years War: Political Theory and Political Practice," *Yale French Studies*, 80: 108–45.

Riley-Smith, B., Davies, G. and Allen, N., 2018, "Brett Kavanaugh, Supreme Court Nominee, Gives Evidence—Latest Updates," *The Telegraph*. https://bit.ly/2voMaxc.

Robarchek, C. A., 1977, "Frustration, Aggression, and the Nonviolent Semai," *American Ethnologist*, 4/4: 762–79.

Robarchek, C. A., 1979, "Conflict, Emotion, and Abreaction: Resolution of Conflict among the Semai Senoi," *Ethos*, 7/2: 104–23.

Robarchek, C. A. and Dentan, R. K., 1987, "Blood Drunkenness and the Bloodthirsty Semai: Unmaking Another Anthropological Myth," *American Anthropologist*, new series 89/2: 356–65.

Rogers, K. and Haberman, M., 2018, "Trump's Evolution From Relief to Fury Over the Russia Indictment," *The New York Times*. https://nyti.ms/2C7hgPg.

Rosaldo, R., 1989, *Culture and Truth: The Remaking of Social Analysis*, Boston: Beacon Press.

Rosenwein, B. H., (ed.), 1998, *Anger's Past: The Social Uses of an Emotion in the Middle Ages*, Ithaca: Cornell University Press.

Rosenwein, B. H., 2016, *Generations of Feelings: A History of Emotions, 600–1700*, Cambridge: Cambridge University Press.

Ross, A., 2017, "True West: California Operas by John Adams and Annie Gosfield," *New Yorker*, December 11.

Russell, J. A., 1980, "A Circumplex Model of Affect," *Journal of Personality and Social Psychology*, 39/6: 1161–78.

Russell, J. A., 2017, "Mixed Emotions Viewed from the Psychological Constructionist Perspective," *Emotion Review*, 9/2: 111–17.

Schiefsky, M., 2012, "Galen and the Tripartite Soul," in R. Barney, T. Brennan and C. Brittain (eds.), *Plato and the Divided Self*, Cambridge: Cambridge University Press, 331–49.

Schneewind, J. B., 2003, "Seventeenth- and Eighteenth-Century Ethics," in L. C. Becker and C. B. Becker (eds.), *A History of Western Ethics*, 2nd ed., London: Routledge, 77–91.

Singer, P. N., 2017, "The Essence of Rage: Galen on Emotional Disturbances and their Physical Correlates," in R. Seaford, J. Wilkins and M. Wright (eds.), *Selfhood and the Soul: Essays on Ancient Thought and Literature in Honour of Christopher Gill*, Oxford: Oxford University Press, 161–96.

Sinkewicz, Robert E., 2006, *Evagrius of Pontus: The Greek Ascetic Corpus*, Oxford: Oxford University Press.

Sissa, G., 2017, *Jealousy: A Forbidden Passion*, Cambridge: Polity Press.

Sloterdijk, P., 2010, *Rage and Time: A Psychopolitical Investigation*, trans. M. Wenning, New York: Columbia University Press.

Sorenson, E. R., 1976, *The Edge of the Forest: Land, Childhood and Change in a New Guinea Protoagricultural Society*, Washington: Smithsonian Institution Press.

Sorenson, E. R., 1978, "Cooperation and Freedom among the Fore of New Guinea," in A. Montagu (ed.), *Learning Non-Aggression: The Experience of Non-Literate Societies*, Oxford: Oxford University Press, 12–30.

Staden, H. von, 2011, "The Physiology and Therapy of Anger: Galen on Medicine, the Soul, and Nature," in F. Opwis and D. Reisman (eds.), *Islamic Philosophy, Science, Culture and Religion: Studies in Honor of Dimitri Gutas*, Leiden: Brill, 63–87.

Stauffer, A. M., 2005, *Anger, Revolution, and Romanticism*, Cambridge: Cambridge University Press.

Stearns, C. Z. and Stearns, P. N., 1986, *Anger: The Struggle for Emotional Control in America's History*, Chicago: University of Chicago Press.

Stein, N. L., Hernandez, M. W. and Trabasso, T., 2008, "Advances in Modeling Emotion and Thought: The Importance of Developmental, Online, and Multilevel Analyses," in M. Lewis, J. M. Haviland-Jones and L. Feldman Barrett (eds.), *Handbook of Emotions*, 3rd ed., New York: Guilford Press, 574–86.

Stemmler, G., 2010, "Somatovisceral Activation during Anger," in M. Potegal, G. Stemmler and C. D. Spielberger (eds.), *International Handbook of Anger*, 103–21.

Tafrate, R. C. and Kassinove, H., 2006, "Anger Management for Adults: A Menu-Driven Cognitive-Behavioral Approach to the Treatment of Anger Disorders," in E. L. Feindler (ed.), *Anger-Related Disorders*, 115–37.

Taut, A. and Fisher, M., 2018, "Facebook Fueled Anti-Refugee Attacks in Germany, New Research Suggests," *The New York Times*. https://nyti.ms/2JfNsD4.

Taylor, J., 2018, "NYT: The 'Religion of Whiteness' is a Threat to World Peace," *American Renaissance*. https://bit.ly/2vpiEaw.

Taylor, K.-Y., 2016, *From #Blacklivesmatter to Black Liberation*, Chicago: Haymarket Books.

Tissari, H., 2017, "Current Emotion Research in English Linguistics: Words for Emotions in the History of English," *Emotion Review*, 9/1: 86–94.

Tomkins, S. S., 1962–1992, *Affect, Imagery, Consciousness*, 4 vols., New York: Springer.

Tomkins, S. S. and McCarter, R., 1964, "What and Where are the Primary Affects? Some Evidence for a Theory," *Perceptual and Motor Skills*, 18/1: 119–58.

Traister, R., 2018, "Fury Is a Political Weapon. And Women Need to Wield It," *New York Times. Sunday Review*. https://nyti.ms/2IrmuWF.

Traister, R., 2018, *Good and Mad: The Revolutionary Power of Women's Anger*, New York: Simon & Schuster.

Vagianos, A., 2017, "The 'Me Too' Campaign Was Created by a Black Woman 10 Years Ago," *Huffpost*. https://bit.ly/2gO4j0F.

Wade, F., 2017, *Myanmar's Enemy Within: Buddhist Violence and the Making of a Muslim "Other"*, London: Zed Books.

Wang, Y., Kong, F., Kong, X., Zhao, Y., Lin, D. and Liu, J., 2017, "Unsatisfied Relatedness, Not Competence or Autonomy, Increases Trait Anger through the Right Amygdala," *Cognitive, Affective, and Behavioral Neuroscience*, 17: 932–8.

Warner, C. T., 1986, "Anger and Similar Delusions," in R. Harré (ed.), *The Social Construction of Emotions*, 135–66.

Weber, H., 2004, "Explorations in the Social Construction of Anger," *Motivation and Emotion*, 28/2: 197–219.

Weiner, J., 2018, "The Patriarchy Will Always Have Its Revenge," *New York Times. Sunday Review*. https://nyti.ms/2N0V6iY.

White, S. D., 1998, "The Politics of Anger," in B. H. Rosenwein (ed.), *Anger's Past*, 127–52.

Wierzbicka, A., 2004, "Emotion and Culture: Arguing with Martha Nussbaum," *Ethos*, 31/4: 577–600.

Wingfield, A. H., 2007, "The Modern Mammy and the Angry Black Man: African American Professionals' Experience with Gendered Racism in the Workplace," *Gender and Class*, 14: 196–212.

Woodward, B., 2018, *Fear: Trump in the White House*, New York: Simon & Schuster.

Wortham, J., 2016, "Black Tweets Matter: How the Tumultuous, Hilarious, Wide-Ranging Chat Party on Twitter Changed the Face of Activism in America," *Smithsonian Magazine*. http://bit.ly/2ZN11je.

Wundt, W., 1907, *Outlines of Psychology*, trans. Charles Hubbard Judd, 3rd rev. Engl. ed. from 7th rev. German ed., Leipzig: Wilhelm Engelmann.

# SUGGESTIONS FOR FURTHER READING

Introduction

For an introduction to the history of emotions, see B. H. Rosenwein and R. Cristiani, *What Is the History of Emotions?* (Cambridge: Polity Press, 2018).

Chapter 1: Buddhism

For the background and history of Buddhism, see P. Harvey, *An Introduction to Buddhism: Teachings, History and Practices*, 2nd ed. (Cambridge: Cambridge University Press, 2013). R. A. F. Thurman, *Anger: The Seven Deadly Sins* (New York: Oxford University Press, 2005) maintains the Buddhist position on anger and argues its relevance for the modern world.

Chapter 2: Stoicism

For an in-depth discussion of Stoic philosophy as well as its influence on early Christianity, see R. Sorabji, *Emotion and Peace of Mind: From Stoic Agitation to Christian Temptation* (Oxford: Oxford University Press, 2000). M. C. Nussbaum, *The Therapy of Desire: Theory and Practice in Hellenistic Ethics* (Princeton: Princeton University Press, 1994) discusses Stoicism as part of the ferment of moral philosophies in the classical world.

Chapter 3: Violence and Neostoicism

For the historical background to Neostoicism, see R. S. Dunn, *The Age of Religious Wars, 1559–1715*, 2nd ed. (New York: Norton, 1979). For the explosion of new approaches to the emotions in the period, see S. Gaukroger, *The Soft Underbelly of Reason: The Passions in the Seventeenth Century* (London: Routledge, 1998). Disputing (rightly, in my view) the role of Neostoicism in early Protestant thought and practice is S. C. Karant-Nunn, *The Reformation of Feeling: Shaping the Religious Emotions in Early Modern Germany* (Oxford: Oxford University Press, 2010), which shows how the new confessions fostered some very passionate emotions, including anger.

Chapter 4: Peaceable Kingdoms

For a review of the anthropology of violence and non-violence, see L. E. Sponsel, "The Anthropology of Peace and Nonviolence," *Diogenes* 6 (2017): 30–45. S. Heald, *Controlling Anger: The Anthropology of Gisu Violence* (Oxford: James Currey Ltd., 1998) discusses the relations of anger (*lirima*), masculinity, and human action among the Gisu (a people of Eastern Uganda). For the emotions at Auschwitz from the point of view of a sympathetic official there, see H. Langbein, *People in Auschwitz*, trans. H. Zohn (Chapel Hill: University of North Carolina Press, 2004).

Chapter 5: Angry Words

On the meaning of insults in a historical context, see D. Garrioch, "Verbal Insults in Eighteenth-Century Paris," in *The Social History of Language*, eds. P. Burke and R. Porter (Cambridge: Cambridge University Press, 1987). On sins of the tongue, see M. Veldhuizen, *Sins of the Tongue in the Medieval West: Sinful, Unethical, and Criminal Words in Middle Dutch (1300–1550)* (Turnhout: Brepols, 2017), as well as D. Cressy, *Dangerous Talk: Scandalous, Seditious, and Treasonable Speech in Pre-Modern England* (Oxford: Oxford University Press, 2010). On anger in Early Modern England, see L. A. Pollock, "Anger and the Negotiation of Relationships in Early Modern England," *The Historical Journal* 47/3 (2004): 567–90, an article equally relevant to the subjects treated in Chapter 11.

Chapter 6: Aristotle and His Heirs
On Aristotle's notion of anger and other emotions, see D. Konstan, *The Emotions of the Ancient Greeks: Studies in Aristotle and Classical Literature* (Toronto: University of Toronto Press, 2006). For more on the Thomistic view of anger and other emotions, see R. Miner, *Thomas Aquinas on the Passions. A Study of* Summa Theologiae 1a2ae 22–48 (Cambridge: Cambridge University Press, 2009).

Chapter 7: From Hell to Heaven
The literature on the Christian scheme of virtues and vices is extensive. A classic on the subject is *In the Garden of Evil: The Vices and Culture in the Middle Ages*, ed. R. Newhauser (Toronto: Pontifical Institute of Medieval Studies, 2005), and on anger in particular, R. E. Barton, "Gendering Anger: *Ira, Furor*, and Discourses of Power and Masculinity in the Eleventh and Twelfth Centuries," 371–92. On virtuous anger, see S. A. Throop, "Zeal, Anger and Vengeance: The Emotional Rhetoric of Crusading," in *Vengeance in the Middle Ages: Emotion, Religion and Feud*, eds. S. A. Throop and P. R. Hyams (Aldershot: Ashgate, 2010).

Chapter 8: Moral Sentiments
For the historical context of the moral philosophers, see I. Woloch and G. S. Brown, *Eighteenth-Century Europe: Tradition and Progress, 1715–1789*, 2nd ed. (New York: Norton, 2012). T. Dixon, *From Passions to Emotions: The Creation of a Secular Psychological Category* (Cambridge: Cambridge University Press, 2003), argues that the moral philosophers of the eighteenth century created the category of "emotions" for the many other words—"passions," "affections"—previously used. On emotions in the French Revolution, see W. M. Reddy, "Sentimentalism

and Its Erasure: The Role of Emotions in the Era of the French Revolution," *The Journal of Modern History* 72 (2000): 109–52.

Chapter 9: Early Medical Traditions
For Galen's historical context as well as his thinking on a great variety of topics, see R. J. Hankinson, *The Cambridge Companion to Galen* (Cambridge: Cambridge University Press, 2008), and on the emotions in particular, see P. Donini, "Psychology," 184–209. On the medieval medical view and treatment of the emotions, see N. Cohen-Hanegbi, *Caring for the Living Soul: Emotions, Medicine, and Penance in the Late Medieval Mediterranean* (Leiden: Brill, 2017). Taking the story into the Early Modern period is E. Carrera, "Anger and the Mind-Body Connection in Medieval and Early Modern Medicine," in *Emotions and Health, 1200–1700*, ed. E. Carrera (Leiden: Brill, 2013).

Chapter 10: In the Lab
On emotions in the modern lab, see P. White, "Introduction" to *Focus: The Emotional Economy of Science = Isis* 100 (2009): 792–97. The history of post-War scientific work is taken up in *Science and Emotions after 1945: A Transatlantic Perspective*, eds. F. Biess and D. M. Gross (Chicago: University of Chicago Press, 2014). For the interplay of culture and scientific inquiry, see *History of Science and the Emotions = Osiris* 31 (2016), eds. O. E. Dror, B. Hitzer, A. Laukötter, and Pilar León-Sanz.

Chapter 11: Society's Child
For a survey and critique of the social constructivist view, see Á. Sveinsdóttir, "Social Construction," *Philosophy Compass* 10/12 (2015): 884–92. Exploring the vocabulary of emotions is Z. Kövecses, *Emotion Concepts* (New York: Springer-Verlag, 1990). W. M. Reddy, "Against Constructionism: The Historical Ethnography of Emotions," *Current Anthropology* 38/3 (1997): 327–51 objects to the radical relativism in social constructivism, which tends not to judge social practices.

Chapter 12: Anger Celebrated

On the fable of biological race, see R. W. Sussman, *The Myth of Race: The Troubling Persistence of an Unscientific Idea* (Cambridge: Harvard University Press, 2014). For the history of the American far right movement, see J. Lepore, *The Whites of Their Eyes: The Tea Party's Revolution and the Battle over American History* (Princeton: Princeton University Press, 2010). For its European counterparts, see J.-Y. Camus and N. Lebourg, *Far-Right Politics in Europe*, trans. J. M. Todd (Cambridge: Belknap Press, 2017). Complementing Hochschild's work on the anger of the far right is M. Kimmel, *Angry White Men: American Masculinity at the End of an Era* (rev. ed., New York: Nation Books, 2017). For the role of today's media in political emotions, see Karin Wahl-Jorgensen, *Emotions, Media and Politics* (Cambridge: Polity Press, 2019). On the making of the movie *Network*, see D. Itzkoff, *Mad as Hell: The Making of* Network *and the Fateful Vision of the Angriest Man in Movies* (New York: Henry Holt, 2014).

# SOURCES FOR PLATES

Plate 1   Metropolitan Museum of Art, New York, N.Y.

Plate 2   Napoli, Museo Archeologico Nazionale. © 2018 Foto Scala, Firenze – Su Concessione Ministero Beni e Attività Culturali e del Turismo

Plate 3   MS Stowe 944 f.7 Liber vitae ('The New Minster Liber Vitae') Stowe 944 1031 © The British Library Board – Alinari

Plate 4   Gabinetto dei Disegni e delle Stampe degli Uffizi. © 2018. Foto Scala, Firenze – Su Concessione Ministero Beni e Attività Culturali e del Turismo

Plate 5   Burgerbibliothek Bern, Cod. 264 p. 79 – Prudentius, Carmina (https://www.e-codices.ch/en/list/one/bbb/0264)

Plate 6   Walters Art Museum MS W.72 f.25v – Speculum Virginum

Plate 7   Ghent University Library, BHSL.HS.0092

Plate 8   Bibliothèque nationale de France, département Estampes et photographie, RESERVE QB-370 (45)-FT 4 (https://gallica.bnf.fr/ark:/12148/btv1b6950498b)

Plate 9   Paris, École nationale supérieure des Beaux-Arts (ENSBA). Photo © Beaux-Arts de Paris, Dist. RMN-Grand Palais / Image Beaux-Arts de Paris

Plate 10   https://it.wikipedia.org/wiki/File:Marey_Sphygmograph.jpg

Plate 11   *Psychological Review* 21/1 (1914), photo 32

Plate 12   *Journal of Cognitive Neuroscience* 21/4 (2009), figure 1A, p. 740. © 2008 by the Massachusetts Institute of Technology

Plate 13   Shutterstock

# INDEX